Java™ Database Best Practices

Related titles from O'Reilly

Ant: The Definitive Guide

Building Java™ Enterprise Applications

Database Programming with JDBC and Java™

Developing JavaBeans™

Enterprise JavaBeans™

J2ME in a Nutshell

Java™ 2D Graphics

Java™ and SOAP

Java™ & XML

Java™ and XML Data Binding

Java™ and XSLT

Java™ Cookbook

Java™ Cryptography

Java™ Data Objects

Java™ Distributed Computing

Java™ Enterprise in a Nutshell

Java™ Examples in a Nutshell

Java™ Foundation Classes in a Nutshell

Java™ I/O

Java™ in a Nutshell

Java™ Internationalization

Java™ Message Service

Java™ Network Programming

Java™ NIO

Java™ Performance Tuning

Java™ Programming with Oracle SQLJ

Java™ Security

JavaServer™ Pages

Java™ Servlet Programming

Java™ Swing

Java™ Threads

Java™ Web Services

JXTA in a Nutshell

Learning Java™

Mac OS X for Java™ Geeks

NetBeans: The Definitive Guide

Programming Jakarta Struts

Java™ Database Best Practices

George Reese

O'REILLY®

Beijing · Cambridge · Farnham · Köln · Paris · Sebastopol · Taipei · Tokyo

Java™ Database Best Practices
by George Reese

Copyright © 2003 O'Reilly & Associates, Inc. All rights reserved.
Printed in the United States of America.

Published by O'Reilly & Associates, Inc., 1005 Gravenstein Highway North, Sebastopol, CA 95472.

O'Reilly & Associates books may be purchased for educational, business, or sales promotional use. Online editions are also available for most titles (*safari.oreilly.com*). For more information, contact our corporate/institutional sales department: (800) 998-9938 or *corporate@oreilly.com*.

Editor:	Brett McLaughlin
Production Editor:	Colleen Gorman
Cover Designer:	Emma Colby
Interior Designer:	David Futato

Printing History:

May 2003:	First Edition.

Nutshell Handbook, the Nutshell Handbook logo, and the O'Reilly logo are registered trademarks of O'Reilly & Associates, Inc. Java and all Java-based trademarks and logos are trademarks or registered trademarks of Sun Microsystems, Inc., in the United States and other countries. O'Reilly & Associates, Inc. is independent of Sun Microsystems. The licenses for all the open source tools presented in this book are included with the online examples. Many of the designations used by manufacturers and sellers to distinguish their products are claimed as trademarks. Where those designations appear in this book, and O'Reilly & Associates, Inc. was aware of a trademark claim, the designations have been printed in caps or initial caps. The association between the image of a taguan and the topic of Java database best practices is a trademark of O'Reilly & Associates, Inc.

While every precaution has been taken in the preparation of this book, the publisher and author assume no responsibility for errors or omissions, or for damages resulting from the use of the information contained herein.

ISBN: 0-596-00522-9
[C]

To my beautiful wife, Monique,
and the child she carries.

Table of Contents

Part II. Persistence Models

Part III. Tutorials

Preface

It is never too late to become reasonable and wise; but if the insight comes late, there is always more difficulty in starting the change.
—Immanuel Kant
Prolegomena to Any Future Metaphysics

Java database programming has grown much more complex than it was in 1996 when I wrote the first edition of my book *Database Programming with JDBC and Java* (O'Reilly & Associates). The J2EE platform did not exist. Distributed programming was RMI, JDBC was simple, and transaction management and persistence did not exist in the Java vocabulary. Database programming in 1996 was quite simply JDBC programming.

To place database programming in a real-world context, I spent much of that book introducing ways to build robust persistence models and manage transactions using only the JDBC API. As you can imagine, you had to do a lot of things for yourself that developers now take for granted in the Java platform.

The Java world has certainly changed since then. Not only does Java provide you with a persistence model, it provides you with three different persistence models built right into the core J2EE platform. Outside the J2EE platform is the popular JDO persistence model. In addition, many tools exist to enable you to effectively use third-party and custom persistence models. All of these choices present a problem for database programmers that simply did not exist in 1996: what are the best approaches to database programming with the Java language?

This book seeks to aid the Java developer in appreciating the different approaches Java provides for database programming. It helps you assess what approaches fit which problems, and what the best practices are under each model.

Audience

This book is not an introductory text. It is also not a tutorial on any particular API. It is, instead, a description of the best practices for using a database to drive a variety of Java application architectures. It assumes you have at least a passing familiarity with one or more of the Java enterprise APIs, as well as SQL. You do not, however, need to be an expert in all of them. To help you with any holes in your knowledge of these tools, I provide a few tutorial chapters at the end of the book.

Organization of This Book

This book is divided into three distinct sections. The first two sections are the meat of this book: best practices for Java database architecture and development. The first section focuses on the architecture aspect and the second section on the development aspect.

Part I

Chapter 1 is an overview of the art of database programming. It examines the various tools and skills needed for database programming and covers common database application architectures. The chapter is mostly review material for experienced database programmers.

Chapter 2 tackles one of the more difficult aspects of database programming, especially for the object-oriented programmer: *data architecture*. This chapter begins with relational theory and covers critical topics such as normalization and object-relational modeling. It is a very important chapter for database programmers of all levels of experience.

Though relational architecture is one of the more difficult aspects of database programming, *transaction management* is where database programmers make most of their mistakes. Chapter 3 covers transactions and transaction management.

Part II

The second section begins with an overview of persistence concepts. In short, *persistence* is the practice of saving application state to a data store. Chapter 4 introduces this practice with an eye on using relational databases as your data store for Java applications.

Chapters 5 through 8 go into the best practices for different Java persistence models. Chapter 5 begins with container-managed persistence under the Enterprise Java-Beans component model—for Versions 1 and 2. Chapter 6 tackles the other EJB persistence model, bean-managed persistence. Chapter 7 dives into an evolving, popular persistence model, Java Data Objects. Finally, Chapter 8 looks at alternatives to the standard Java persistence models.

Part III

The third section of the book contains tutorials on the core technologies covered in this book. No reader should need to read all of the tutorial chapters. Instead, I expect that most readers will be familiar with the subject in several, but not all, of the tutorial chapters. The tutorial chapters provide the basic knowledge necessary to understand key concepts used in the first two sections. Don't look to any of the tutorial chapters to make you an expert in its subject matter. I have provided tutorials on the J2EE platform (Chapter 9), SQL (Chapter 10), JDBC (Chapter 11), and JDO (Chapter 12).

I recommend reading the first two sections in order, breaking that order only to refer to a tutorial chapter for a subject on which you lack familiarity.

Conventions Used in This Book

The following typographical conventions are used in this book:

Italic
> Used for filenames and directory names, programs, compilers, tools, utilities, URLs, emphasis, and first use of a technical term.

Constant width
> Used in code examples and to show the contents of files. Also used for tags, attributes, and environment variable names appearing in the text.

Constant width italic
> Used as a placeholder to indicate an item that should be replaced with an actual value in your program.

Constant width bold
> Used to highlight a particular section or change in code, such as a custom tag or a change in a transaction.

Comments and Questions

Please address comments and questions concerning this book to the publisher:

O'Reilly & Associates, Inc.
1005 Gravenstein Highway North
Sebastopol, CA 95472
(800) 998-9938 (in the United States or Canada)
(707) 829-0515 (international/local)
(707) 829-0104 (fax)

There is a web page for this book, which lists errata, examples, or any additional information. You can access this page at:

http://www.oreilly.com/catalog/javadtabp

To comment or ask technical questions about this book, send email to:

bookquestions@oreilly.com

For more information about books, conferences, Resource Centers, and the O'Reilly Network, see the O'Reilly web site at:

http://www.oreilly.com

About the Philosophers

Daniel Dennett (Chapter 1)

Dennett, who teaches at Tufts University, is probably my favorite philosopher. His books are actually well written, which is a rare quality among philosophy texts. His works run the spectrum of philosophy, but his greatest influence lies in the philosophies of mind and science. If you want a fun philosophy book to read that does not require you to be a philosopher, pick up his book *Elbow Room*. If you are looking for something more weighty, but equally accessible, read *Darwin's Dangerous Idea*.

René Descartes (Chapter 2)

Though he lived from 1596 until 1650, Descartes's writings mark the beginning of modern philosophy. He was a French philosopher who emphasized a solipsistic approach to epistemology. He is the author of the famous quote "Cogito, ergo sum," or "I think, therefore I am."

Donald Davidson (Chapter 3)

Donald Davidson is among the most important philosophers of the late 20th century. He is particularly influential in the philosophy of language and action theory. He is currently a professor at the University of California, Berkeley. My senior thesis at Bates College was based on his writings.

Ludwig Wittgenstein (Chapter 4)

Ludwig Wittgenstein was a German philosopher who lived from 1889 until 1951. His primary contributions to philosophy were in the philosophy of language. He once wrote that "philosophy is a battle against the bewitchment of our intelligence by means of language."

Friedrich Nietzsche (Chapter 5)

Nietzsche, who lived in Germany from 1844 until 1900, is likely the most controversial "serious" philosopher. His writings have influenced nearly every kind of philosophy but have had their greatest impact—both positive and negative—in the area of ethics.

Martin Heidegger (Chapter 6)

Heidegger, another 20th-century German philosopher, made popular the movement started by Edmund Husserl known as phenomenology. Phenomenology attempts to understand things as they present themselves rather than to appeal to some sort of essential nature hidden from us. This movement eventually led to the most popularly known philosophical movement, existentialism.

David Kolb (Chapter 7)

David Kolb was my major adviser at Bates College in Lewiston, Maine, where he is a Charles A. Dana Professor of Philosophy. He has written extensively on Hegelian philosophy and nonlinear writing in philosophy.

Immanuel Kant (Preface, Chapter 8)

Immanuel Kant may be the most influential philosopher of the second millennium. He was a German philosopher who lived from 1724 until 1804. He emphasized a rational approach to all philosophical pursuits. This rationalism has had its greatest impact in the area of ethics, where moral principles are, according to Kant, derived entirely from reason.

David Hume (Chapter 9)

David Hume was an 18th-century Scottish philosopher who wrote on a range of philosophical subjects. He is largely responsible for the school of philosophy known as empiricism.

Ruth Garrett Millikan (Chapter 10)

Ruth Garrett Millikan is a professor of philosophy at the University of Connecticut. She is an influential modern philosopher in the philosophy of language and epistemology.

Noam Chomsky (Chapter 11)

Born in 1928, Noam Chomsky is perhaps the most famous living philosopher. While often known for his political activism—especially during the Vietnam era—his greatest contributions to philosophy lie in the philosophy of language.

Jean-Paul Sartre (Chapter 12)

Sartre was a novelist, a philosopher, and a member of the French Resistance during World War II. As a philosopher, he is best known as the force behind the existentialism movement. Existentialism goes beyond phenomenology in its claims about the essential nature of things. While phenomenology claims that we should not appeal to an essential nature of a thing in order to understand it, existentialism says that no such essential nature exists. A thing is exactly as it presents itself.

Acknowledgments

So much work other than that of the author goes into putting together a solid book. First of all, Brett McLaughlin's editing skills and general Java knowledge have been critical to keeping me in line. Also critical to the book was the contribution of Chapter 8 on alternative persistence frameworks by Justen Stepka. I am not much of a fan of leaving the core platform, so this book would have been incomplete without his contribution.

Several people contributed to reviewing this book: Nick Kokotovich, Justen Stepka, and Henri Yandell. In addition, Monique Girgis, Andy Oram, and John Viega have all at times provided a critical eye on this content.

PART I

Data Architecture

Database programming begins with the database. To build effective database applications, you need to fully appreciate the work the database does for those applications. This first section addresses the best practices in data architecture—the design of relational database elements that support database applications.

CHAPTER 1

Elements of Database Applications

If Life is a Tree, it could have arisen from an inexorable, automatic
rebuilding process in which designs would accumulate over time.
—Daniel C. Dennett
Darwin's Dangerous Idea

Once upon a time, database programming on the Java platform was an exercise in native programming; nothing existed within the Java platform to support database programming efforts. The first tool in the database programming arsenal arrived in March 1996 in the form of Java's first proposed enterprise API, JDBC. JDBC enabled application developers to use a single API to access any database from any vendor.

JDBC, however, is the start—not the end—of database programming. JDBC simply enables you to access a database; it does not address all elements of database programming. It does not:

- Ensure your database meets the need of your application
- Automate the mapping of Java classes into relational entities
- Provide a model for structuring your Java components
- Manage application transactions

This book is about database programming; it is not about JDBC. However, because JDBC plays such a critical role in database programming, it will play a critical role in this book. If you need to brush up on your JDBC skills, take a look at the tutorial in Chapter 11 or my earlier book, *Database Programming with JDBC and Java* (O'Reilly). This book addresses all of the elements of database programming and their respective roles in supporting real world database applications.

Database Application Architectures

Database applications require an entire network of software in order to function. Even the most basic of database applications—the command-line SQL tool—is a complex system involving the database engine and a separate client utility. Architecture is the space in which all of the elements of an application operate. Before we look at each of those elements, we should first take a look at the space itself.

Architecture identifies the hardware and software necessary to support an application and specifies how those tools communicate within a network. When referring to architecture, different people tend to have different things in mind. In some cases, architecture refers to the way hardware is placed on a physical network. This kind of architecture is called *network architecture*. Other times, however, architecture refers to the *system architecture*—the way different logical and physical components work together to create a complex network application. The last kind of architecture is *software architecture*, when *architecture* refers to the design of one of the pieces of software that make up the system architecture.

The Network Architecture

The network architecture focuses on hardware issues and how they connect to one another. The quality of your network architecture affects security and bandwidth and limits the ability of your applications to talk with different parts of the system. Figure 1-1 is a simple network architecture diagram.

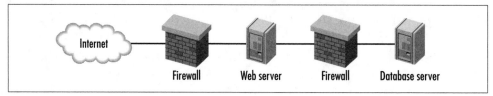

Figure 1-1. A database server in a network architecture diagram

It shows how the network separates the Internet from the network in which the web server runs with a firewall. Similarly, this network diagram places the database server in a separate network segment, again separated by a firewall. In spite of the fact that very little about network architecture is specific to database applications, it can make a significant impact on the performance of those applications. It is therefore helpful to understand those aspects most relevant to database systems.

Network segmentation

Segmentation is the way in which the network is divided for performance and security. Routers, bridges, and firewalls are all tools of network segmentation.

The first rule of segmentation is to divide your network into regions of equal hostility and sensitivity. *Hostility* describes the attitude of people with access to a given network segment. The Internet, for example, is considered an extremely hostile network. Your home network—assuming you have no children—is conversely minimally hostile.

Sensitivity represents the risk profile of the data within a network segment. A high-risk profile means that public exposure or destruction of the data can cause significant harm. A sensitive network segment is therefore one that houses data that must be kept private at all costs. IRS database servers have a very high degree of sensitivity, whereas a Quake server ranks on the low end.

> **BEST PRACTICE** Place your database servers on a high-sensitivity, low-hostility network segment. In other words, you should never place a database server directly on the Internet or a network segment that is even routable to the Internet.

If two software components have very different levels of sensitivity, they should be on different network segments separated by firewalls that limit the interaction between their networks. Because databases serve as primary data storage points, they tend to have higher sensitivity profiles than other software components. As a good general rule of thumb, database servers should be protected in a high-security network segment. In Figure 1-1, for example, a firewall separates the web server from the database server.

> **BEST PRACTICE** Segment your network into regions of equal hostility and sensitivity.

Bandwidth

Databases are the fountain from which data streams to all kinds of applications on the network. It is therefore critical—especially for high-volume database servers—to allocate the necessary bandwidth to database servers. It is not uncommon for database servers to be connected to the network through multiple fiber-based gigabit Ethernet ports.

Proper bandwidth also means paying attention to issues other than the raw size of your pipe. A good network architect also structures the topology of the network to minimize packet collisions and bring the database network as close as possible to the other networks that rely on the databases.

> **BEST PRACTICE** Place your database servers on gigabit or 100-megabit network segments. Never use anything less than 10 megabits.

Hardware

Database engines are among the most resource-intensive applications commonly found in business environments. Solid performance for database applications demands the proper hardware for all parts of the application. If you were to choose only one thing to spend money on, you should spend it on RAM. Running a very close second to RAM in importance, however, is disk access speed.

> **BEST PRACTICE**   When selecting hardware for database servers, spend your money on RAM and high-speed disk access.

Ultimately, a database will run faster if it can cache a lot of data in RAM. Ideally, you have more memory for your database engine than you have data. In reality, however, that much memory is rarely possible. Good database performance therefore needs a solid array of disks. Though SCSI disks are the ideal, a RAID of IDE disks can support a web site's database just fine. The disks should then be divided into at least three sets of responsibilities:

- System data
- Database log files
- Database tables and indexes

It is even better if your database engine enables you to split up tables and indexes on different disks. You want the database tables and indexes on the fastest drives you have available.

> **BEST PRACTICE**   Split your tables and indexes across different physical drives to maximize database performance.

Various System Architectures

The role of the system architect is to look at the overall technology objectives of an organization and establish a system architecture that maximizes the reuse of critical components. A simple web application can work well in any number of different system architectures; it works best, however, when it fits nicely with the other applications in that architecture. For example, you can build an excellent web application using Perl and MySQL. If the organization you are building it for, however, has an established J2EE (Java 2 Enterprise Edition) infrastructure with an Oracle backend, you are introducing new components requiring maintenance that cannot be easily integrated into that organization's existing environment.

The starting point for determining an appropriate system architecture is to understand the basic enterprise platform for the organization. Because I am covering database programming in a J2EE environment, I will assume your basic enterprise platform is J2EE. Alternatives include .NET and general web services. These platforms all come with basic approaches to different kinds of architectural requirements. In this section, I will briefly discuss the different system architectures that fit inside the J2EE platform.

BEST PRACTICE	Develop architectural principles and use them as the basis for all technology decisions for your application.

The client/server architecture

The client/server architecture is one of the oldest distributed computing architectures in use on the J2EE platform. You will sometimes hear people refer to the client/server architecture as a *two-tier* architecture. The term *two-tier* describes the way in which application processing can be divided in a client/server application. A two-tier application ideally provides multiple workstations with a uniform presentation layer that communicates with a centralized database. The presentation layer is generally the client, and the database layer is the server.

Figure 1-2 shows how two-tier systems provide clients with access to centralized data. A client like a Java Swing application talks directly to a database and displays the data in the user interface.

A client/server architecture is definitely appropriate for some applications. Specifically, any application that must deal directly with the database needs to be a client/server application. For example, the command-line tools that enable you to enter arbitrary SQL statements are client/server applications that fit this profile. In fact, just about any database administration tool is a good candidate for a client/server architecture.

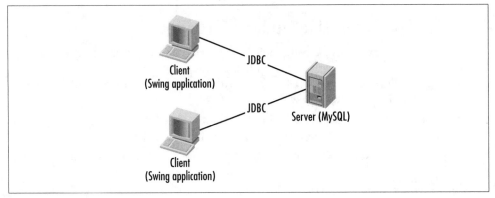

Figure 1-2. The client/server architecture

A client/server architecture falls apart, however, when application logic needs to operate on the data from the database or when application logic needs to be shared among multiple clients. The client/server architecture suffers specifically from the following problems:

The fat client

Perhaps you have seen a client/server application evolve over time to include more and more application logic operating on data from the database. Ideally, the client/server architecture is supposed to let each machine do only the processing relevant to its specialization—graphical presentation of data on the client and the storage and retrieval of data on the server. This breakdown, however, does not clearly provide a place for application logic—also known as *business logic*. As more and more business logic ends up in the client, you end up with a problem known as the fat client. Fat client systems are notorious for their inability to adapt to changing environments and scale with growing user and data volume.

Object reuse

Object reuse[*] is a very vague, yet central concept to object-oriented software engineering. You can reuse code through cutting and pasting or through linking either statically or dynamically to an API, or you can reuse shared object instances. The ideal form of reuse is to reuse shared object instances among applications. Of course, that requires a single point of focus for applications. Only the database is shared under the two-tier model. In order to reuse object instances, you need to embed them in the server—and create a fat server—or move to a different architecture.

As I mentioned before, in spite of its shortcomings, a two-tier architecture does have a place in application development. In addition to applications tied directly to the database, simple applications with immediate deadlines and no maintenance or reuse

---

[*] I am talking specifically about reuse in the development workflows of a project. The most effective reuse occurs in the analysis and design workflows.

requirements are prime candidates. The following checklist provides important questions to ask before committing yourself to a two-tier design. If you can answer "yes" to each of the questions in the checklist, then a two-tier architecture is likely your best solution. Otherwise, you should consider one of the other architectures supported by the J2EE platform.

- Does your application emphasize time-to-market over architecture?
- Does your application use a single database?
- Is your database engine located on a single host?
- Is your database likely to stay approximately the same size over time?
- Is your user base likely to stay approximately the same size over time?
- Is there no web interface to your application?
- Are your requirements fixed with little or no possibility of change?
- Do you expect minimal maintenance after you deliver the application?

The simple web site architecture

Perhaps the simplest—and most familiar—architecture to Internet developers is that of the simple web site. Figure 1-3 shows the simple web site architecture with a page generation technology like JSPs (JavaServer Pages) or servlets talking directly to a database engine. In short, this is the web equivalent to the client/server architecture. Its critical difference is that an intermediate tier is structuring the data for display and providing it to the client.

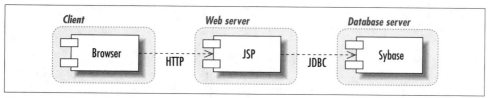

Figure 1-3. The simple web site architecture

In general, all of the faults of the client/server architecture apply to this architecture. It does, however, provide some flexibility on the display side. You can use the web server as the location for your shared object access. Unfortunately, you cannot access the objects directly; you must access them through the display information provided by the web server. The advantage this architecture has over the pure client/server architecture is that you can now provide multiple views of the same object instances. Unfortunately, these views must be browser-based and have roughly the same content.

Peer-to-peer

Peer-to-peer (P2P) is a new name for an old architecture. Every other architecture presented in this book seeks to break processing down into specialized tiers that handle one kind of application processing. The peer-to-peer architecture still has physical divisions among different kinds of logic, but it hides those divisions behind an egalitarian logical façade. Under the P2P architecture, all logical players can perform all tasks.

Figure 1-4 shows how the P2P architecture divides the network into equal nodes. Each node is capable of making direct contact with any other node and requesting services from that node. Similarly, each node is capable of providing services to any other node.

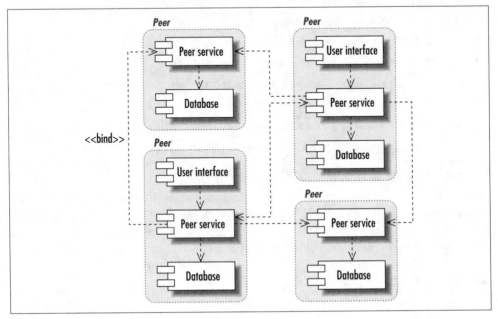

Figure 1-4. The logical view of the P2P architecture

Within a P2P node, the system can be performing any number of tasks. One of the beauties of the P2P architecture is that the details of how a given node is providing its services are completely hidden from the other nodes. You could, for example, implement a P2P auction network in which one node consisted of a database server and a GUI and another node consisted of flat files and a command-line utility.

Another advantage of a P2P architecture is that there's no single point of failure. Assuming the problem domain is appropriate to P2P, the failure of any one node—or even a large group of nodes—doesn't affect the functionality of the system built on top of the architecture. The remaining nodes simply seek services from one another.

In reality, the development of a scalable P2P system is quite a challenge. No one has truly gotten this right yet. Pure P2P networks like Gnutella suffer from serious scalability issues and an inability of many nodes to actually request services from other nodes. Other P2P systems like the infamous Napster compromise on the P2P architecture and thus compromise on its advantages. Napster created a single point of failure for the network and thus ceased to exist in a meaningful sense when that point of failure was shut down.

You should consider a P2P architecture under the following conditions:

- You need massive failover capabilities.
- Replication of services to all nodes is practical.
- The source of services is not important—i.e., no security or trust issues exist.

Distributed architectures

Logic in distributed architectures is divided among any number of specialized tiers for handling that data. The number of tiers runs well beyond the extra tier demanded by client/server for business logic. Distributed architectures include tiers for business logic, content services, and everything else you can imagine.

Like the P2P architecture, distributed architectures are logical in that they provide for a high-level division of labor among the following tiers:

User interface layer
> The user interface (UI) layer is responsible for all direct user interaction. A physical implementation of the UI layer could consist of a web browser or be a combination of browser, command-line, and Swing applications.

Content generation layer
> The content generation layer is responsible for structuring content for display to the UI layer and subsequently routing user input. It is generally a web server or cluster of web servers using static and dynamic content generation tools to pull content from a content management layer.

Content management layer
> The content management layer stores content from structuring and transmission to a UI. It includes content management systems and digital asset management systems.

Web services layer
> Whereas the content generation layer serves content to human users, the web services layer serves it to other applications. It is the integration point for modern applications across a LAN (Local Area Network). It exchanges messages with web services clients using open standards like XML (Extensible Markup Language).

Business logic layer
> Business objects in the business logic layer execute business logic on behalf of web services and users. It serves as a shared point for all business logic within an organization.

Integration services layer
> The integration services layer ties modern applications to their legacy counterparts through tools like enterprise messaging services and proprietary APIs.

Data storage
> This layer is where the database sits. In a real enterprise, the data storage layer consists of many different databases serving up various kinds of data.

Figure 1-5 shows an architecture for distributed applications.

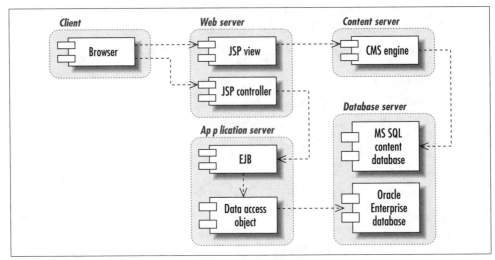

Figure 1-5. An architecture for distributed Internet applications

When you are writing EJB (Enterprise JavaBeans) applications, you're using a distributed architecture. How many of the layers you use depends on the needs of your application. Regardless of how many layers you use, this architecture is definitely the most complex architecture covered in this book. Unlike the P2P architecture, no level of generality hides the physical services behind each layer. The business logic layer seeking data storage services knows what kind of data storage services it seeks.

Though a distributed architecture provides many advantages over other architectures, it is not without its drawbacks. I have already mentioned the complexity it adds to a system. It is also hard to find system architects proficient in all layers of a distributed application architecture. Though the J2EE platform attempts to mitigate these issues, it does not mitigate them completely.

Software Architecture

Software architecture describes the internal design of a software component. It identifies the classes that make up the piece of software and what processes those classes support. Standard software development methodologies provide for two common views of a software architecture: a static view and a behavioral view. Figure 1-6 is a UML (Unified Modeling Language)* class diagram that serves as the static view, and Figure 1-7 is a UML sequence diagram providing the behavioral view.

---

* UML is the standard language in which architects communicate software design decisions.

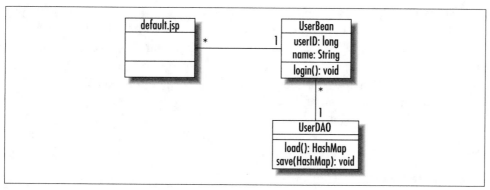

Figure 1-6. A UML class diagram

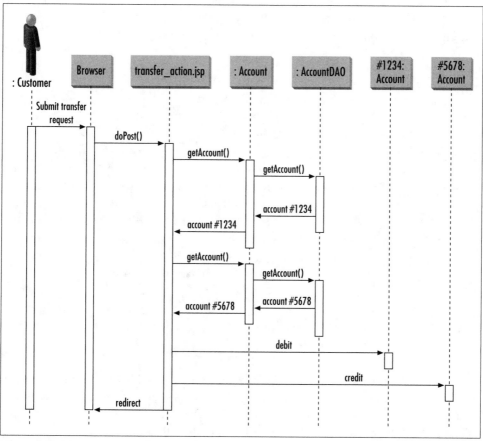

Figure 1-7. A UML sequence diagram

In designing an application, you need to pick out design patterns that will provide a level of reliability to its underlying logic. The first step to identifying the design patterns is identifying problems in generic terms. In database programming, you need design patterns to support persistence and encapsulation of business logic.

Over the course of this book, we will encounter many different design patterns. In this section, my goal is simply to provide an overview of these patterns. If you do not fully understand them after this section, you should not be concerned. I will be talking in more detail about each of them later.

> **BEST PRACTICE**   Leverage design patterns when your problem matches an established pattern.

User interface patterns

The UI provides a view of the system specific to the role of the user in question. Good UI patterns help keep the user interface decoupled from the server. Though to some degree UI patterns depend on the UI technology, there are also some generic patterns like the model-view-controller pattern that serve any form of UI.

The model-view-controller pattern. Java Swing is based entirely on a very important UI pattern called the *model-view-controller pattern* (MVC). In fact, this key design pattern is what makes Java so perfect for distributed enterprise development. The MVC pattern separates a GUI component's visual display (the view) from the thing it is a view of (the model) and the way in which the user interacts with the component (the controller).

In a client/server application that displays the rows from a database table in a Swing display, for example, the database serves as the model. In this application, the columns and rows of the Swing table match the columns and rows of the database table. The Swing table is the view. The controller is a less obvious object that handles user mouse clicks and key presses and determines what the model or view should do in response to those user actions.

Swing actually uses a variant of this pattern called the model-delegate pattern. The *model-delegate pattern* combines the view and the controller into a single object that delegates to its model.

> **BEST PRACTICE**   Use the MVC paradigm or a variation on the MVC paradigm in all applications with user interface needs.

The MVC pattern is not limited to Swing applications. It is also the preferred way of building the HTML (Hypertext Markup Language) pages for web applications. Figure 1-8 illustrates the MVC pattern in a JSP-based web application. In this case, the JSP page is the view, the servlet the controller, and the EJB or JavaBean the model.

The listener pattern. For the Swing example of MVC, it would be nice if the view could be told about any changes to the model. The *listener pattern* provides a mechanism by which interested parties are notified of events in other objects. You have probably seen this pattern in Swing development as well.

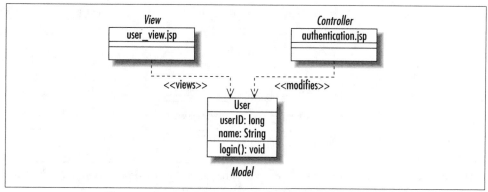

Figure 1-8. The MVC pattern in a JSP application

The listener pattern enables one object to listen to specific events that occur to another object. A common listener in the JavaBeans component model is something called a `PropertyChangeListener`. One object can declare itself a `PropertyChange-Listener` by implementing the `java.beans.PropertyChangeListener` interface. It then tells other objects that it is interested in property changes by calling the `addPropertyChangeListener( )` method in any JavaBean it cares about. The important part of this pattern is that the object being listened to needs to know nothing about its listeners except that those objects want to know when a property has changed. Consequently, you can design objects that live well beyond the uses originally intended for them.

Business patterns

As a general rule, the midtier business logic is likely to use just about every design pattern in common use. The two most common general patterns I have encountered are the *composite* and *factory patterns*. More important to the business logic, however, is the component model.

The component model defines the standards you rely on for encapsulating your application logic. Java has two major component models: JavaBeans and Enterprise JavaBeans. JavaBeans defines a contract between applications and their components that tells applications how to find out what attributes are supported by a component and how to trigger that component's behavior. Enterprise JavaBeans takes the basic contract of JavaBeans into the realm of distributed computing. EJB provides for communication among components across a network, the ability to search for components, and the ability to include components in transactions.

The composite pattern. The composite pattern appears everywhere in the real world. It represents a hierarchy in which some type of object may both be contained by similar objects and contain similar objects. Figure 1-9 shows a UML diagram describing the composite pattern.

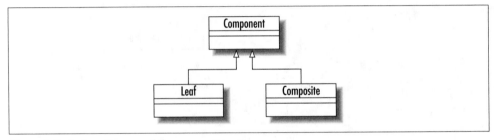

Figure 1-9. A class diagram of the composite pattern

> **BEST PRACTICE**   Look carefully for the composite pattern in the problems you are model-
> ing. It appears everywhere in problem domains.

To put a more concrete face on the composite pattern, think of a virtual reality game
that attempts to model your movements through a maze. In your game, you might
have a Room class that can contain Item objects. Some of those Item objects (like a
bag) can contain other Item objects. Your room is a container, and bags are containers. On the other hand, things like money and stones cannot contain anything. To
complicate matters further, the room cannot be contained by anything greater than
it. The result is the class diagram in Figure 1-10.

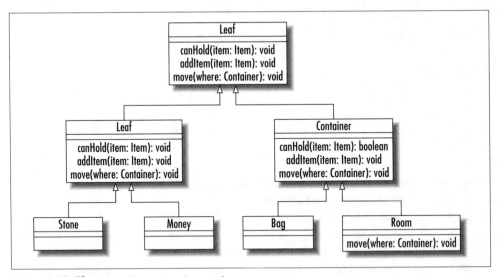

Figure 1-10. The composite pattern in practice

The factory pattern. Another common pattern found in the core Java libraries is the
factory pattern. The pattern encapsulates the creation of objects behind a single
interface. Java internationalization support is peppered with implementations of the
factory design pattern. The java.util.ResourceBundle class, for example, contains

logic that enables you to find a bundle of resources for a specific locale without having to know which subclass of ResourceBundle is the right one to instantiate. A ResourceBundle is an object that might contain translations of error messages, menu item labels, and text labels for your application. By using a ResourceBundle, you can create an application that will appear in French to French users, in German to German users, and in English to English and American users.

Because of the factory pattern, using a ResourceBundle is quite easy. To create a Save button, for example, you might have the following code:

```
ResourceBundle bundle =
    ResourceBundle.getBundle("labels", Locale.getDefault());
Button button = new Button(bundle.getString("SAVE");
```

This code actually shows two factory methods: Locale.getDefault() and ResourceBundle.getBundle(). Locale.getDefault() constructs a Locale instance representing the locale in which the application is running.

The goal of this pattern is to capture the creation logic of certain objects in a single method. The benefit of providing a single location for that logic is that the logic can vary without impacting applications that rely on those classes. Sun Microsystems, for example, could change the getBundle() method to look for XML-based property bundles as well as traditional Java property bundles without any impact to the masses of legacy Java systems.

Persistence patterns

One key to smooth development in a distributed architecture is providing a clear division between data storage code and business logic code. At some point, a business object needs to save itself to a data store. You will chose a persistence model that supports the persistence of your business components. The goal is to make sure that the business object knows nothing about how it is stored in the database—in fact, it should not even know that its persistence form is a database.

The form of your persistence model will determine the underlying pattern you use. Later in the book, we will get into a custom persistence model based on the *data access object pattern*.

The data access object pattern. The data access object pattern—also referred to as the *persistence delegate pattern*—relies on a delegate to make a component persistent. Each business component sees generic methods in its delegate for persistence operations like loading, creating, saving, and deleting the component. Behind those methods are implementations for a specific data storage technology and schema. In our case, the data storage technology is a relational database.

> **BEST PRACTICE**   Use the data access object pattern in your database applications. It is a key aspect of most of the chapters in this book. I describe it in greater detail in Chapter 4.

The memento pattern. In the persistence delegate pattern, how does the persistence delegate know about the state of the object it is persisting? You could pass the object to the persistence methods, but that action requires your delegate to know a lot more about the objects it supports that you probably want. Another design pattern—the *memento pattern*—comes to the rescue here.

A memento is a tool for capturing an object's state and safely passing it around. The advantage of the memento pattern is that it enables you to modify the components and the delegates independently. A change to the component has no effect on the delegate and a change to the delegate has no effect on the component. The persistence handler knows only how to get the data it needs to support the underlying data storage schema from the memento. I provide a concrete implementation of the memento pattern later in the book.

Component Models

We have already touched a bit on component models. A component model defines the various aspects of encapsulating business logic in software. The Java platform provides two major component models:

- The JavaBeans component model
- The Enterprise JavaBeans component model

Enterprise JavaBeans work well only in distributed architectures and the P2P architecture. JavaBeans, on the other hand, work in any architecture. If you use Java-Beans in a distributed architecture, however, you will have to write your own logic to support interprocess communication, security, transaction management, and other functionality that comes free with EJBs.

JavaBeans

The JavaBeans specification defines the way in which you should write your components so they can be used by other components and application elements. When you write JavaBeans, applications that know nothing about those beans can still use them. One example of JavaBeans in action is the development of JSP tag libraries. Your tag handlers are JavaBeans components. A JSP container can access the properties in your tag library because the way in which you write those properties uses standard getter and setter methods defined by the JavaBeans specification.

The beauty of the JavaBeans specification is its simplicity. To conform to it, you need only write your getters and setters using standard getXXX( ) and setXXX( ) method calls. You can optionally implement listener support to enable applications to listen for changes in properties. There is really nothing much more to the component model.

Just as simplicity is JavaBeans advantage, it is also its disadvantage. The JavaBeans specification does not provide for many of the following pieces necessary in distributed architectures:

Transaction support

Transaction support enables your components to put in database transactions without requiring a programmer to worry about when to start and end the transaction. If you want transaction support with JavaBeans, you need to write your own transaction logic.

Distributed access

Distributed access provides direct access to your component through some distributed component model—RMI, CORBA, EJB, DCOM, etc. Because JavaBeans is not a distributed component model, you have to manually combine your JavaBeans with another component model—generally, RMI—for exporting components.

Security

If you make your components available over a network, you need a mechanism for securing them against unauthorized access. If you are using JavaBeans, you will have to write your own code to authenticate clients and authorize their component access.

Persistence management

Persistence management automatically maps your components to a data store. In other words, with a component model that provides persistence management, you never have to write any JDBC code. JavaBeans, however, requires you to become quite familiar with JDBC in order to save the state of the beans to a relational database.

Searching

Searching enables applications to search for the components they need. Again, if you are using JavaBeans, you will have to write your own search methods and leverage JDBC queries to support component searching.

Enterprise JavaBeans

The Enterprise JavaBeans component model is basically a component model for distributed architectures. It provides many of the features lacking in JavaBeans at the cost of JavaBeans simplicity. Because the EJB component model handles all of these aspects of distributed component management, you can literally pick and choose the best-designed business components from different vendors and make them work and play well with one another in the same environment. EJB is now the standard component model for capturing distributed components on the Java platform. It hides from you the details you would have had to worry about with JavaBeans.

One of the benefits of the EJB approach is that it separates different application development roles into distinct parts so that the outputs of one role are usable in different environments by the players of the other roles. You can use your EJB container, for example, to house components written by third-party vendors or custom written by your team. Similarly, a JDBC service provider can deploy their JDBC drivers in any EJB container without impacting transaction management.

Figure 1-11 illustrates what it takes to code a single component under the EJB component model. You have the actual bean, the home interface, and a remote interface. When you deploy a bean in a container, the container creates implementations of your home and remote interfaces. Contrast all of this work with the simplicity of the JavaBeans component model. Not only do you write just one class, but what you see is what you get—nothing fancy happens out of your view.

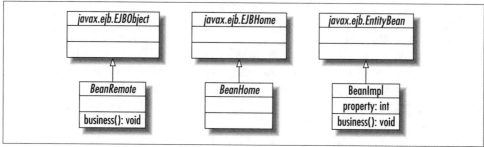

Figure 1-11. The EJB component model

Persistence Models

A persistence model dictates how your components persist themselves to a data store. The EJB component model, for example, comes with a built-in persistence model in the form of container-managed persistence. When you use the container-managed persistence model with Enterprise JavaBeans, you do not have to write a line of database access code. Instead, you specify a database mapping when you deploy the application through deployment configuration files. The EJB container manages the rest.

Other persistence models may perform all or part of the work necessary to implement component persistence. Over the course of this book, we will examine the most popular persistence models for both the JavaBeans and EJB component models.

EJB Persistence

Until recently, container-managed persistence in EJB has proven to be insufficient for most application development. Most EJB developers write their own persistence logic for their beans—a practice called bean-managed persistence. Bean-managed

EJB programmers use some other persistence model when constructing their components. The full gamut of EJB-specific persistence models include:

EJB 1.x CMP
This model is container-managed persistence (CMP) under the EJB 1.x specification. As I noted earlier, few people actually use this persistence model. It has difficulties with such basic persistence operations as searching and primary key management. It also does not provide a solid mapping of many-to-many relationships.

BMP
Bean-managed persistence (BMP) is not itself a persistence model. It instead means that you are using some non-EJB persistence model for storage of your EJB components.

EJB 2.x CMP
Because of the massive shortcomings of EJB 1.x CMP, EJB 2.0 introduced a new container-managed persistence model. Though it is not yet widely supported, it does promise to address the shortcomings of EJB 1.x CMP. To meet this challenge, however, it introduces a new query language. Because many alternative persistence models have evolved, it is unclear if EJB 2.x CMP will be accepted.

Other Persistence Models

Many persistence models have evolved both to address shortcomings in EJB persistence models and to support the persistence of non-EJB systems. If you have read my book *Database Programming with JDBC and Java*, then you have seen one such alternative persistence model. Among today's most popular alternatives is Java Data Objects (JDO). We will examine JDO and my custom persistence model as well as several others over the course of this book.

CHAPTER 2

Relational Data Architecture

*Good sense is the most evenly shared thing in the world, for each of us
thinks that he is so well endowed with it that even those who are the
hardest to please in all other respects are not in the habit of wanting more
than they have. It is unlikely that everyone is mistaken in this. It indicates
rather that the capacity to judge correctly and to distinguish true from
false, which is properly what one calls common sense or reason, is
naturally equal in all men, and consequently the diversity in our opinions
does not spring from some of us being more able to reason than others, but
only from our conducting our thoughts along different lines and not
examining the same things.*
—René Descartes
Discourse on the Method

Database programming begins with the database. A well-performing, scalable database application depends heavily on proper database design. Just about every time I have encountered a problematic database application, a large part of the problem sat in the underlying data model. Before you worry too much about writing Java code, it is important to lay the proper foundation for that Java code in the database.

Relational data architecture is the discipline of structuring databases to serve application needs while remaining scalable to future demands and usage patterns. It is a complex discipline well beyond the scope of any single chapter. We will focus instead on the core data architecture needs of Java applications—from basic data normalization to object-relational mapping.

Though knowledge of SQL (Structured Query Language) is not a requirement for this chapter, I use it to illustrate some concepts. I provide a SQL tutorial in the tutorial section of the book should you want to dive into SQL now. You will definitely need it as we get further into database programming.

Relational Concepts

Before we approach the details of relational data architecture, it helps to establish a base understanding of relational concepts. If you are an experienced database programmer, you will probably want to move on to the next section on normalization. In this section, we will review the key concepts behind relational databases critical to an in-depth understanding of relational data architecture.

Databases and Database Engines

Developers new to database programming often run into problems understanding just what a *database* is. In some contexts, it represents a collection of data like the music library. In other contexts, however, it may refer to the software that supports that collection, a process instance of the software, or even the server machine on which the process is running.

Technically speaking, a database is really the collection of related data and the relationships supporting the data. The database software—a.k.a the database management system (DBMS)—is the software, such as Oracle, Sybase, MySQL, and DB2, that is used to store that data. A database engine, in turn, is a process instance of the software accessing your database. Finally, the database server is the computer on which the database engine is running.

In the industry, this distinction is often understood from context. I will therefore continue to use the term "database" interchangeably to refer to any of these definitions. It is important, however, to database programming to understand this breakdown.

The Relational Model

A database is any collection of related data. The files on your hard drive and the piles of paper on your desk all count as databases. What distinguishes a relational database from other kinds of databases is the mechanism by which the database is organized—the way the data is modeled. A relational database is a collection of data organized *in accordance with the relational model* to suit a specific purpose.

Relational principles are based on the mathematical concepts developed by Dr. E. F. Codd that dictate how data can be structured to define data relationships in an efficient manner. The focus of the relational model is thus the data relationships. In short, by organizing your data according to the relational model as opposed to the hierarchical principles of your filesystem or the random mess of your desktop, you can find your data at a later date much easier than you would have had you stored it some other way.

A relationship in relational parlance is a table with columns and rows.* A row in the database represents an instance of the relation. Conceptually, you can picture a table as a spreadsheet. Rows in the spreadsheet are analogous to rows in a table, and the spreadsheet columns are analogous to table attributes. The job of the relational data architect is to fit the data for a specific problem domain into this relational model.

Other Data Models

The relational model is not the only data model. Prior to the widespread acceptance of the relational model, two other models ruled data storage:

- The hierarchical model
- The network model

Though systems still exist based on these models, they are not nearly as common as they once were. A directory service like ActiveDirectory or OpenLDAP is where you are most likely to engage in new hierarchical development.

Another model—the object model—is slowly coming into favor for limited problem domains. As its name implies, it is a data model based on object-oriented concepts. Because Java is an object-oriented programming language, it actually maps best to the object model. However, it is not as widespread as the relational model and is definitely not proven to support systems on the scale of the relational model.

Entities

The relational model is one of many ways of modeling data from the real world. The modeling process starts with the identification of the things in the real world that you are modeling. These real world things are called *entities*. If you were creating a database to catalog your music library, the entities would be things like compact disc, song, band, record label, and so on. Entities do not need to be tangible things; they can also be conceptual things like a genre or a concert.

> **BEST PRACTICE**   Capture the "things" in your problem domain as relational entities.

An entity is described by its *attributes*. Back to the example of a music library, a compact disc has attributes like its title and the year in which it was made. The individual values behind each attribute are what the database engine stores. Each row describes a distinct *instance* of the entity. A given instance can have only a single value for each attribute.

---

* You will sometimes see a row referred to as a *tuple*—especially in more theoretical discussions of relational theory. Columns are often referred to as attributes or fields.

Table 2-1 describes the attributes for a CD entity and lists instances of that entity.

Table 2-1. A list of compact discs in a music library

Artist	Title	Category	Year
The Cure	Pornography	Alternative	1983
Garbage	Garbage	Grunge	1995
Hole	Live Through This	Grunge	1994
The Mighty Lemon Drops	World Without End	Alternative	1988
Nine Inch Nails	The Downward Spiral	Industrial	1994
Public Image Limited	Compact Disc	Alternative	1986
Ramones	Mania	Punk	1988
The Sex Pistols	Never Mind the Bollocks, Here's the Sex Pistols	Punk	1977
Skinny Puppy	Last Rights	Industrial	1992
Wire	A Bell Is a Cup Until It Is Struck	Alternative	1989

You could, of course, store this entire list in a spreadsheet. If you wanted to find data based on complex criteria, however, the spreadsheet would present problems. If, for example, you were having a "Johnny Rotten Night" party featuring music from the punk rocker, how would you create this list? You would probably go through each row in the spreadsheet and highlight the compact discs from Johnny Rotten's bands.

Using the data in Table 2-1, you would have to hope that you had in mind an accurate recollection of which bands he belonged to. To avoid taxing your memory, you could create another spreadsheet listing bands and their members. Of course, you would then have to meticulously check each band in the CD spreadsheet against its member information in the spreadsheet of musicians.

Constraints

What constitutes identity for a compact disc? In other words, when you look at a list of compact discs, how do you know that two items in the list are actually the same compact disc? On the face of it, the disc title seems as if it might be a good candidate. Unfortunately, different bands can have albums with the same title. In fact, you probably use a combination of the artist name and disc title to distinguish among different discs.

The artist and title in our CD entity are considered identifying attributes because they identify individual CD instances. In creating the table to support the CD entity, you tell the database about the identifying attributes by placing a *constraint* on the database in the form of a unique index or primary key. Constraints are limitations you place on your data that are enforced by the DBMS. In the case of unique indexes (primary keys are a special kind of unique index), the DBMS will prevent the insertion of two rows with the same values for the entity's identifying attributes. The DBMS would prevent, for example, the insertion of another row with values of 'Ramones' and 'Mania' for the artist and title values in a CD table having artist and title as a unique index. It won't matter if the values for all of the other columns differ.

> **BEST PRACTICE** Use constraints to help enforce the data integrity of your system.

Constraints like unique indexes help the DBMS help you maintain the overall data integrity of your database. Another kind of constraint is formally known as an *attribute domain*. You probably know the domain as its data type. Choosing data types and indexes along with the process of normalization are the most critical design decisions in relational data architecture.

Indexes

An *index* is a constraint that tells the DBMS about how you wish to search for instances of an entity. The relational model provides for three main kinds of indexes:

Index
> An index in the generic sense is a simple tool that tells the DBMS what kind of searches you intend to perform. With this information, the DBMS can organize information to make the searches go quickly. A very crude way to think of an index is as a Java HashMap in which the key is your index attribute and the values are arrays of matching rows.

Unique index
> A unique index is an index whose values are guaranteed to be unique. In other words, instead of an array of matching rows, this index is like a HashMap that returns a single value for its key. The index created earlier for the artist and title columns in the CD table is an example of a unique index.

Primary key
> A primary key is a special unique index that acts as the main identifier for the row. A table can have any number of unique indexes, but it can have only one primary key.

We can examine the impact of indexes by creating the CD entity as a table in a MySQL database and using a special SQL command called the EXPLAIN command. The SQL to create the CD table looks like this:

```
CREATE TABLE CD (
    artist      VARCHAR(50)   NOT NULL,
    title       VARCHAR(100)  NOT NULL,
    category    VARCHAR(20),
    year        INT
);
```

The EXPLAIN command tells you what the database will do when trying to run a query. In this case, we want to look at what happens when we are looking for a specific compact disc:

```
mysql> EXPLAIN SELECT * FROM CD
    -> WHERE artist = 'The Cure' AND title = 'Pornography';
+-------+------+---------------+------+---------+------+------+------------+
| table | type | possible_keys | key  | key_len | ref  | rows | Extra      |
+-------+------+---------------+------+---------+------+------+------------+
| CD    | ALL  | NULL          | NULL |    NULL | NULL |   10 | where used |
+-------+------+---------------+------+---------+------+------+------------+
1 row in set (0.00 sec)
```

The important information in this output for now is to look at the number of rows. Given the data in Table 2-1, we have 10 rows in the table. The results of this command tell us that MySQL will have to examine all 10 rows in the table to complete this query. If we add a unique index, however, things look much better:

```
mysql> ALTER TABLE CD ADD UNIQUE INDEX ( artist, title );
Query OK, 10 rows affected (0.20 sec)
Records: 10  Duplicates: 0  Warnings: 0
mysql> EXPLAIN SELECT * FROM CD
    -> WHERE artist = 'The Cure' AND title = 'Pornography';
+-------+-------+---------------+--------+---------+-------------+------+
| table | type  | possible_keys | key    | key_len | ref         | rows |
+-------+-------+---------------+--------+---------+-------------+------+
| CD    | const | artist        | artist |     150 | const,const |    1 |
+-------+-------+---------------+--------+---------+-------------+------+
1 row in set (0.00 sec)
mysql>
```

The same query can now be executed simply by examining a single row.

> **BEST PRACTICE**   Make indexes for attributes you intend to search against.

Unfortunately, the artist and title probably make a poor unique index. First of all, there is no guarantee that a band will actually choose distinct names for its albums. Worse, in some circumstances, bands have chosen to have the same album carry different names. Public Image Limited's *Compact Disc* is an example of such an album. The cassette version of the album is called *Cassette*.

Even if artist and title were solid identifying attributes, they still make for a poor primary key. A primary key must meet the following requirements:

- It can never be NULL.
- It must be unique across all entity instances.
- The primary key value must be known when the instance is created.

In addition to these requirements, good primary keys have the following characteristics:

- The primary key should never change value.
- The primary key attributes should have no meaning except to uniquely identify the entity instance.

It is very common for people to find attributes inherent in an entity and chose one or more of those identifying attributes as a primary key. Perhaps the best example of this practice is the use of an email address as a primary key. Email addresses, however, can and do change. A change to a primary key attribute can cause an instance to become inaccessible to anyone with old information about the instance. In plain English, it can break your application.

Another example of a common primary key with meaning is a U.S. Social Security number. It is supposed to be unique. It is never supposed to change. You, however, have no control over its uniqueness or whether it changes. As it turns out, sometimes the uniqueness of Social Security numbers is violated. In addition, they do sometimes change. Furthermore, in many cases, the law restricts your ability to share this information. It is therefore best to choose a primary key with no external meaning; you will control exactly how it is used and have the full power to enforce its uniqueness and immutability.

> **BEST PRACTICE**   Never use meaningful attributes or attributes whose values can change as
> primary keys.

The solution is to create a new attribute to serve as the primary identifier for instances of an entity. For the CD table, we will call this new attribute the cdID. The SQL to create the table then looks like this:

```
CREATE TABLE CD (
    cdID          INT            NOT NULL,
    artist        VARCHAR(50)    NOT NULL,
    title         VARCHAR(100)   NOT NULL,
    category      VARCHAR(20),
    year          INT,
    PRIMARY KEY ( cdID ),
    INDEX ( artist, title ),
    INDEX ( category ),
    INDEX ( year )
);
```

 You may have noted that my naming style does not redundantly name columns like title cdTitle. Yet I chose to name the primary key for the CD table cdID instead of id. This choice basically makes the use of data modeling tools a lot simpler. In short, data modeling tools look for natural joins—joins between two tables when the common columns share the same name, data type, and value. I discuss natural joins in more detail in Chapter 10.

Ideally, you always search on unique indexes. In the real world, however, you will select on attributes like the year or genre that are not unique. You can still help the database organize the underlying data storage by creating plain indexes. In general, you want any attribute you commonly search on to be indexed. An index does, however, come with some downsides:

- Indexes are stored apart from the table data. Every index thus adds to the disk space requirements of the database.
- Every change to the table requires every index to be updated to reflect the changes.

In other words, if you have a table on which you perform a significant number of write operations, you want to minimize your indexes to those attributes that appear frequently in queries.

Finally, as you have already seen, you can have indexes—including primary keys—that are formed out of any number of identifying columns so long as those columns together sufficiently identify a single entity instance. It is always a good idea, however, to build primary keys out of the minimal number of columns possible.

Domains

The proper choice of data type is another critical aspect of relational data architecture. It constrains the kind of data that can be stored for a given attribute. By creating an email attribute as a text value, you prevent people from storing numbers in the field. A time-oriented domain like a SQL DATE enables you to perform time arithmetic on date values.

The domains that exist in a relational database depend on the DBMS of choice. Those that support the SQL specification generally support a core set of data types. Just about every database engine comes with its own, proprietary data types. When modeling a system, you should use SQL-standard data types.

Primary keys deserve special consideration when you are putting domain constraints on an entity. Because they are the primary mechanism for getting access to an entity instance, it is important that the database is able to do quick matches against primary key values. In general, numeric types form the best primary keys. I recommend the use of 64-bit, sequentially generated integers for primary key columns. The only exception is for lookup tables.

A lookup table is a small table with a known, finite set of data like a table containing a list of states or, with respect to the music library example, a set of genres. In the case of lookup tables, they more often than not have codes against which you will do most lookups. For example, you will almost always retrieve the state of Maine from a State table by its abbreviation ME. It therefore makes more sense to use fixed character data types like SQL's CHAR for primary keys in lookup tables. The length of these fixed character values should be no more than a few characters.

> **BEST PRACTICE**   Use fixed character data types like CHAR for primary keys in lookup tables.

The data types for other kinds of attributes vary with the diversity in the kinds of data you will want to store in your databases. These days, many databases even support the creation of user-defined data types. These pseudo-object data types prove particularly useful in the development of Java database applications.

Relationships

The creation of relationships among the entities in the database lies at its heart. These relationships enable you to easily answer the question, "On what compact discs in my library did Johnny Rotten play?" Unlike other models, the relational model does not create hard links between two entities. In the hierarchical model, a hard relationship exists between a parent entity and its child entities. The relational model, on the other hand, creates relationships by matching a primary key attribute in one entity to a *foreign key* attribute in another entity.

The relational model supports three kinds of entity relationships:

- One-to-one
- One-to-many
- Many-to-many

With any of these relationships, one side of the relationship may be optional. An optional relationship allows the foreign key to contain NULL values to indicate the relationship does not exist for that row.

One-to-one relationships

The one-to-one relationship is the most rare relationship in the relational model. A one-to-one relationship says that for every instance of entity A, there is a corresponding instance of entity B. It is so rare that its appearance in a data model should be met with skepticism as it generally indicates a design flaw. You indicate a one-to-one relationship in the same way you indicate a one-to-many relationship.

> **BEST PRACTICE**   Recheck your design whenever you encounter one-to-one relationships, as they are often indicators of problematic design choices.

One-to-many relationships

A one-to-many relationship means that for every instance of entity A, there can be multiple instances of entity B. As Figure 2-1 shows, the "many" side of the relationship houses the foreign key that points to the primary key of the "one" side of the relationship.

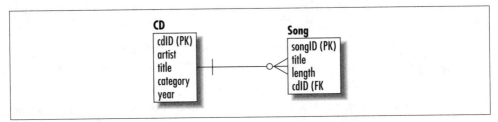

Figure 2-1. A One-to-Many Relationship

Table 2-2 lists data from a Song table whose rows are dependent on rows in the CD table.

Table 2-2. The Song entity with a foreign key from the CD entity

Attribute	Domain	Notes	NULL?
songID	INT	PRIMARY KEY	No
cdID	INT	FOREIGN KEY	No
title	VARCHAR(100)		No
length	INT		No

Under this design, one compact disc is associated with many songs. The placement of cdID into the Song table as a foreign key indicates the dependency on a row of the CD table. In databases that manage foreign key constraints, this dependency will prevent the insertion of songs into the Song table that do not already have a corresponding CD. Similarly, the deletion of a disc will cause the deletion of its associated songs. You should note, however, that not all database engines support foreign key constraints. Of those that do support them, you often have the option of turning them on or off.

 Why would you want foreign key constraints off? Many application environments—particularly multitier distributed object systems—prefer to manage dependencies in the object layer instead of the database. It is generally a trade-off between a combination of speed with object purity and guaranteed data integrity. When foreign key constraints are not checked in the database, updates occur more quickly. Furthermore, you do not end up with a situation in which objects exist in the middle tier that have been automatically deleted by the database. On the other hand, if your middle-tier logic is not sound, your application can damage the data integrity without proper foreign key constraints.

You now have a proper relationship between compact discs and their songs. To ask which songs are on a particular compact disc, you need to ask the Song table which songs have the disc's cdID. Assuming you are looking for all songs from the disc *Garbage* (cdID 2), the SQL to find the songs looks like this:

```
SELECT songID, title FROM Song WHERE cdID = 2;
```

More powerfully, however, you can ask for all songs from a compact disc by the disc title:

```
SELECT Song.songID, Song.title
FROM Song, CD
WHERE CD.title = 'Last Rights'
AND CD.cdID = Song.cdID;
```

The last part of the query where the cdID was compared in both tables is called a *join*. A join is where the implicit relationship between two tables becomes explicit.

Many-to-many relationships

A many-to-many relationship allows an instance of entity A to be associated with multiple instances of entity B and an instance of entity B to be associated with multiple instances of entity A. These relationships require the creation of a special table to manage the relationship. You may hear these tables referred to by any number of names: composite entities, join tables, cross-reference tables, and so forth. This extra table creates the relationship by having the primary keys of each table in the relationship as foreign keys. It then uses the combination of foreign keys as its own compound primary key. If, for example, we had an Artist table in our music library, we indicate a many-to-many relationship between an Artist and a CD through an ArtistCD join table. Table 2-3 shows this special table.

Table 2-3. The ArtistCD table creates a many-to-many relationship between Artist and CD

Attribute	Domain	Notes	NULL?
cdID	INT	FOREIGN KEY, PRIMARY KEY	No
artistID	INT	FOREIGN KEY, PRIMARY KEY	No

You can now ask for all of the compact discs by Garbage:

```
SELECT CD.cdID, CD.title
FROM CD, ArtistCD, Artist
WHERE ArtistCD.cdID = CD.cdID
AND ArtistCD.artistID = Artist.artistID
AND Artist.name = 'Garbage';
```

> **BEST PRACTICE**   Use join tables to model many-to-many relationships.

Another useful aspect of join tables is that you can use them to contain information about a relationship. If, for example, you wanted to track guest artists on albums, where would you store that information? It really is not an attribute of an artist or a compact disc. It is instead an attribute of the relationship between the two entities. To capture this information, you would therefore add a column to `ArtistCD` called guest. Finding which compact discs on which Sting appeared as a guest artist would then be as simple as:

```
SELECT CD.cdID, CD.title
FROM CD, ArtistCD, Artist
WHERE ArtistCD.cdID = CD.cdID
AND ArtistCD.artistID = Artist.artistID
AND Artist.name = 'Sting'
AND ArtistCD.guest = 'Y';
```

NULL

NULL is a special value in relational databases that indicates the absence of a value. If you have a pet store site that gathers information on your users, for example, you may track the number of pets your users have. Without the concept of NULL, you have no proper way to indicate that you do not know how many pets a user has. Applications commonly resort to nonsense values (like -1) or unlikely values (like 9999) as a substitute for NULL.

BEST PRACTICE   Use NULL to represent unknown or missing values.

Though the basic concept of NULL is pretty straightforward, beginning database programmers often have trouble figuring out how NULL works in database operations. A basic example would come about by adding a new column to our Song table that is a rating. It can be NULL since it is unlikely anyone wants to rate every single song in their library. The following SQL may not do what you think:

```
SELECT songID, title FROM Song WHERE rating = NULL;
```

No matter what data is in your database, this query will always return zero rows. Relational logic is not Boolean; it is three-value logic: true, false, and unknown. Most NULL comparisons therefore result in NULL since a NULL comparison is indeterminate under three-value logic. SQL provides special mechanisms to test for NULL in the form of IS NULL and IS NOT NULL so that it is possible to ask for the unrated songs:

```
SELECT songID, title FROM Song WHERE rating IS NULL;
```

Modeling

Throughout this book, I will be using industry-standard diagrams to illustrate designs. A critical part of relational data architecture is understanding a special kind of diagram called an entity relationship diagram, or ERD. An ERD graphically captures the entities in your problem domain and illustrates the relationships among them. Figure 2-2 is the ERD of the music library database.

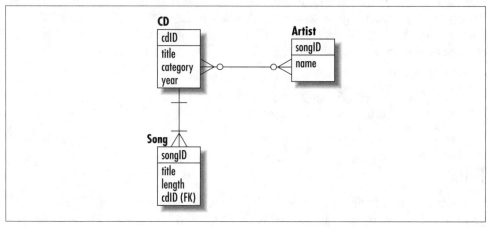

Figure 2-2. The ERD for the music library

There are in fact several forms of ERDs. In the style I use in this book, each entity is indicated by a box with the name of the entity at the top. A line separates the name of the entity from its attributes inside the box. Primary key attributes have "PK" after them, and foreign key attributes have "FK" after them.

The lines between entities indicate a relationship. At each end of the relationship are symbols that indicate what type of relationship it is and whether it is optional or mandatory. Table 2-4 describes these symbols.

Table 2-4. Symbols for an ERD

Symbol	Description
	The many side of a mandatory one-to-many or many-to-many relationship
	The one side of a mandatory one-to-one or one-to-many relationship
	The many side of an optional one-to-many or many-to-many relationship
	The one side of an optional one-to-one or one-to-many relationship

Our ERD therefore says the following things:

- One compact disc contains one or more songs.
- One song appears on exactly one compact disc.
- One compact disc features one or more artists.
- One artist is featured on one or more compact discs.
- An artist can optionally be part of one or more artists (bands).

This ERD is a *logical* representation of the music library. The entities in a logical model are not tables. First of all, you probably noticed there is no composite entity handling the relationship between an artist and a compact disc—I have drawn the relation directly as a many-to-many relationship. Furthermore, all of the entity names and attributes are in plain English. Finally, no foreign keys are shown.

> **BEST PRACTICE**   Develop an ERD to model your problem before you create the database.

The physical data model transforms the logical data model into the tables that will be created in the working database. A data architect works with the logical data model while DBAs (database administrators) and developers work with the physical data model. You translate the logical data model into a physical one by adding join tables, turning domains into database-specific data types, and using table and column names appropriate to your DBMS. Figure 2-3 shows the physical data model for the music library as it would be created in MySQL.

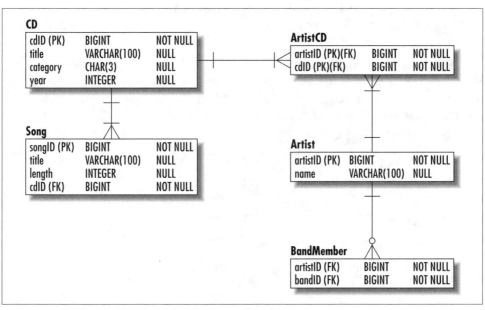

Figure 2-3. The physical data model for the music library

Normalization

When beginning the development of a data architecture for a project, you first want to capture all the entities in your problem domain and the attributes associated with those entities. Depending on your software engineering processes, these entities may be driven by your object model or your object model may be driven by the logical ERD. Either way, you should not initially concern yourself in any way with issues like performance, scalability, or flexibility—the task is to model the problem domain properly.

Unlike other areas of software architecture, relational data architecture provides a very formal process for optimizing your model for efficient resource usage, scalability, and flexibility. This formal process is known as *normalization*. Normalization seeks to achieve the following goals:

Remove redundant data

A fully normalized database repeats nothing other than foreign keys. Removal of redundant data guarantees that you are storing the minimum data necessary to model your domain and protects the integrity of your data by requiring just a single point of maintenance for any piece of information.

Protect the relational model

The process of normalization forces you to examine all aspects of your data model to make certain that you are not violating any of the basic principles of the relational model (e.g., all attributes must be single-valued; only the table name, column name, and primary key value should be needed to identify a row; etc.).

Improve scalability and flexibility

A normalized database guarantees the ability of the data model to evolve with even the most drastic of changes in the problem domain with a minimal impact on the applications it supports.

As I noted earlier, normalization is a formal process. It defines very specific criteria for your data model that it breaks out into *normal forms*. The normal forms establish a stringent and objective set of rules to which a data model must adhere. Each one builds on requirements of the previous, as is shown in Figure 2-4, and improves upon the overall design of the model.

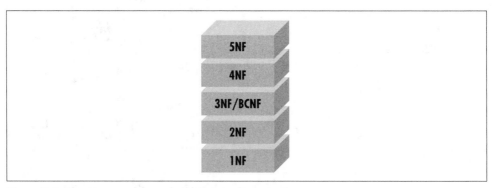

Figure 2-4. The six normal forms build on top of one another

Before a data model can be said to be in a certain normal form, it must meet all of the requirements of that normal form and any lesser normal forms. The second normal form, for example, necessitates that a data model meet the requirements for both the first and second normal forms.

No matter what your problem domain, you will want to normalize your data model at least to the third normal form. For most simple problem domains, the third normal form is good enough. Deeper normal forms represent specific data modeling issues that do not apply to most data models. Most data models in the third normal form are therefore already in the fifth normal form. If you have a very complex system, you should go ahead and verify that it is in at least the fourth normal form. Formally normalizing your data model to the fifth normal form should be left for very specific problem domains. I will dive into the details of each of these normal forms later in the chapter.

> **BEST PRACTICE** Very complex systems should be normalized to the fourth normal form.

In addition to the six normal forms noted here, a seventh normal form called the domain/key normal form (DKNF) exists. The rule for DKNF is that every logical restriction on attribute values results from the definition of keys and domains. In theory, a table in DKNF cannot contain anomalies. If nothing about DKNF makes any sense to you, don't worry about it—no process exists to prove a table is in DKNF and therefore it is not used in real world modeling.

Before Normalization

Before you begin the process of normalization, you should already have a logical ERD describing your problem domain. This logical ERD should describe all of the entities that make up the problem domain, their major attributes, and their relationships. For the purposes of this section, I will be referring to a data model to support a web site for film fans. It specifically stores information about films and enables people to browse the films in the database based on that information. Figure 2-5 shows the data model before normalization.

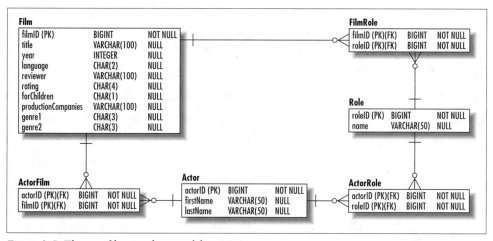

Figure 2-5. The raw film site data model

Because we want this web site to be accessible to all North American visitors, it has translations into Spanish and French. These translations are supported through a duplication of the logical data model into three separate physical databases.

Basic Normalization

Basic normalization addresses the design demands common to any relational database. As a data architect, you will always want to carry your design through to the third normal form.

First normal form

A table is in the first normal form (1NF) when all attributes are single-valued. This requirement is not simply a good design requirement; it is a fundamental requirement of the relational model. At its simplest, it means that only a single value may exist at the intersection of a column and a row.

The film database has three different violations of 1NF:

- The `productionCompanies` attribute in the `Film` table is multivalued.
- The genre1 and genre2 columns in effect represent a multivalued attribute.
- The duplication of the database for multilingual content also represents turning all values into multivalue attributes.

The problem with the first violation is that it makes the database very inflexible. For one thing, searching for films by a specific production company is difficult. You cannot use a simple equality check like:

```
SELECT filmID, title
FROM Film
WHERE productionCompanies = 'Imaginary Productions';
```

That column, after all, contains a comma-separated list of companies. Instead, you need a much less efficient query like:

```
SELECT filmID, title
FROM Film
WHERE productionCompanies LIKE '%Imaginary Productions%';
```

The solution to the problem of multivalued attributes is to create a new entity to support that attribute. In the case of the film database, we should create a `ProductionCompany` table with foreign key references to the primary key in the `Film` table. We now have a one-to-many relationship between films and their production companies.

Another, less obvious multivalue attribute is the genre support for films. Because of a need to support the classification of films like *Blazing Saddles* that fall into two genres, we have in our data model two genre columns. This approach has several problems associated with it.

The problems are:

- It limits the assignment of genres to films to two genres.
- Searching for a film by genre becomes a complex operation.
- Space is wasted for any film with a single genre.

The solution, again, is the creation of a new entity to support the multiple values. In this case, we will create a lookup table for genres and a many-to-many relationship between Film and Genre.

The final problem with the raw data model is the fact that the entire database is duplicated for every language we want to support. In order to add a new language, we need to create a new duplicate of that database and replace its text values with translations for the target language. The application then needs to be configured to use that database as a data source for the new language.

For this problem, we need to create translation entities for each of the text attributes in the database. Adding support for a new language means nothing more than adding new rows to each translation table.

Figure 2-6 contains the film database in 1NF.

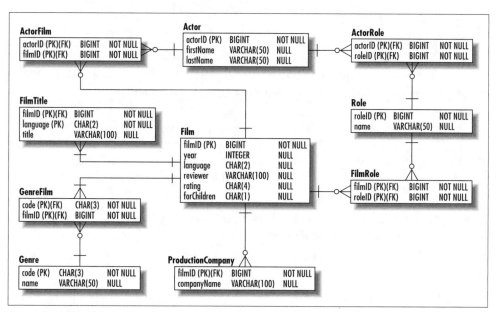

Figure 2-6. The film database in 1NF

Second normal form

A table is in the second normal form (2NF) when it is in 1NF and all non-key attributes are *functionally dependent* on the table's entire primary key. Functional dependency means that an attribute is determined by another attribute. In the case of `filmID` and `title`, the `title` is functionally dependent on the `filmID` because which film the row represents determines what its title is. On the other hand, the title of the film does not necessarily indicate which film you are dealing with.

When an attribute is not dependent on the entire primary key of the table it is in, it has likely been placed in the wrong table. Our data model has this problem in the `reviewer` attribute of the `Film` entity. The purpose of this attribute is to capture the name of the person who initially reviewed the film for the site. The `reviewer` attribute, however, does not depend on the `filmID`—the reviewer exists independent of the film.

The existence of attributes that violate 2NF causes database anomalies. A database anomaly is an error or inconsistency that occurs when some event takes place. Specifically, there are:

Insertion anomalies
> An insertion anomaly occurs when you are forced to know information about an entity instance that may not yet be knowable in order to create an instance of another entity. In the case of reviewer, a person cannot be a reviewer until he has reviewed a film. More to the point, we cannot capture any information about our reviewers until they have reviewed a film.

Deletion anomalies
> A deletion anomaly occurs when a delete causes data that is not related to the instance being deleted to be removed from the database. In our existing model, removing a film may remove the reviewer from the database.

Update anomalies
> An update anomaly occurs when the same data must be changed in more than one location to preserve database integrity. If a reviewer has a name change, our data model requires the change be made to each film reviewed and every other place in the database with that reviewer's name.

Again, the solution to this normalization problem is the creation of a new entity to remove the nondependent attribute. This entity, `Reviewer`, contains the name of the reviewer and is related to many films.

Figure 2-7 shows our data model in 2NF.

Third normal form

A table is in the third normal form (3NF) when it is in 2NF and no *transitive dependencies* exist. A transitive dependency occurs when a functional dependency is inherited through some other identifying attribute. In our data model, the `forChildren` attribute depends on the `rating` attribute, which in turn depends on the `filmID`. Because the `forChildren` attribute has no direct dependency on the `filmID`, it is thus transitively dependent on the `filmID`.

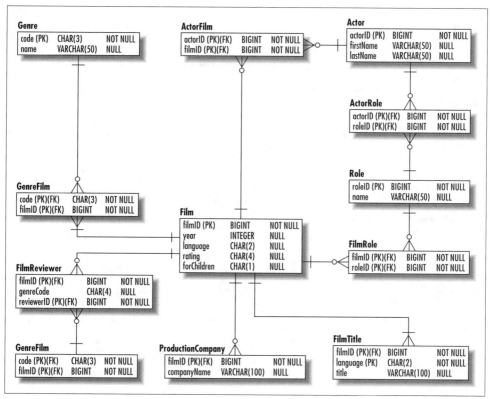

Figure 2-7. The film database in 2NF

Violation of 3NF causes database anomalies. First of all, if the MPAA changes which ratings are suitable for children, you will need to update every instance of the `Film` entity to reflect that change. An insertion anomaly also exists in that any new ratings for children will not be reflected in existing films. Of course, the insertion anomaly is not a huge problem for this database since films rarely change ratings. Finally, deletion of the only row with a rating associated with being for children causes us to lose all information about it being for children.

> **BEST PRACTICE**   Normalize your data model minimally to the third normal form.

To fix this problem, you need to move the transitively dependent value into a table that provides functional dependency. In other words, move the `forChildren` attribute into the `Rating` table as shown in Figure 2-8.

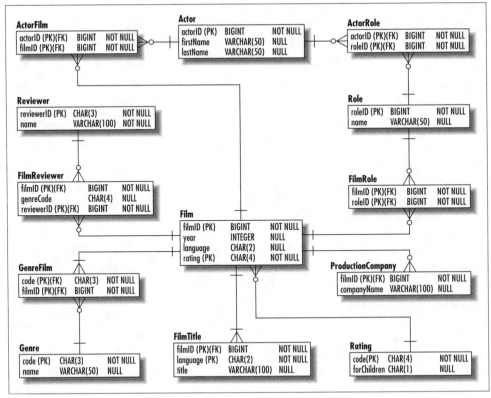

Figure 2-8. The film database in 3NF

Specialized Normalization

Having your database in 3NF is generally good enough to guarantee your system is free of the most common anomalies. The other forms of normalization handle special situations. In fact, if your database is not subject to the special considerations of Boyce-Codd normal form or fourth normal form, your database is automatically in 4NF. The fifth normal form is impossible to verify without computer-aided modeling tools and is rarely worth seeking.

Boyce-Codd normal form

A table is in Boyce-Codd normal form (BCNF) when every determinant is a candidate key. A *candidate key* is a set of attributes that could potentially serve as a primary key. BCNF is essentially a more generalized form of 3NF. It specifically addresses issues that arise in tables with one or more of the following characteristics:

- Multiple candidate keys
- Composite candidate keys
- Overlapping candidate keys

Our data model contains no relations to which BCNF applies. To illustrate BCNF, consider a table that contains three or more columns with a couple of the combinations capable of uniquely identifying a row. An example might be a Showing table that represents when a real estate agent shows a house to a client. The table has the structure shown in Table 2-5.

Table 2-5. The structure of a table meeting BCNF

Attribute	Domain	Notes	NULL?
propertyID	BIGINT	PRIMARY KEY, FOREIGN KEY	No
agentID	BIGINT	PRIMARY KEY, FOREIGN KEY	No
timeslot	INT	PRIMARY KEY, FOREIGN KEY	No
buyerID	BIGINT	FOREIGN KEY	No
notes	VARCHAR(255)		

For the sake of this example, assume that a buyer gets only one chance to view a property. Furthermore, only one agent can show a property to one buyer in a given time slot. In that case, it is possible for notes to be determined by either of the following combinations:

- propertyID, agentID, timeslot
- propertyID, agentID, buyerID

You could choose either of the two combinations. BCNF simply states that as long as every column that determines notes is a candidate key, the table is in BCNF.

Fourth normal form

A table is in the fourth normal form when it is in BCNF and all multivalued dependencies are also functional dependencies. The problem here with the current model is the FilmReviewer table. It ties film reviewers with the films and genres they review. Table 2-6 shows some sample data from the table.

Table 2-6. Data in FilmReviewer

filmID	reviewerID	genreCode
101	1	ACT
101	1	SCI
102	2	DRA
102	2	COM
103	1	ACT
103	1	SCI

The full set of columns forms the primary key for this table. It is thus normalized to BCNF. Unfortunately, it still contains redundant data. The redundancy is caused by multivalued dependencies. Specifically, `reviewerID` determines the values of `filmID` and `genreCode` independently. In the relations we have seen so far, the determinant establishes the full set of values that together form the instance.

We can fix this problem by splitting `genreCode`'s dependence into one table and `reviewerID`'s dependence into another. For example, we can create a `ReviewGenre` table that captures the genres the reviewer specializes in. We can similarly create a `ReviewerFilm` table that contains the film reviews. Figure 2-9 shows the resulting data model.

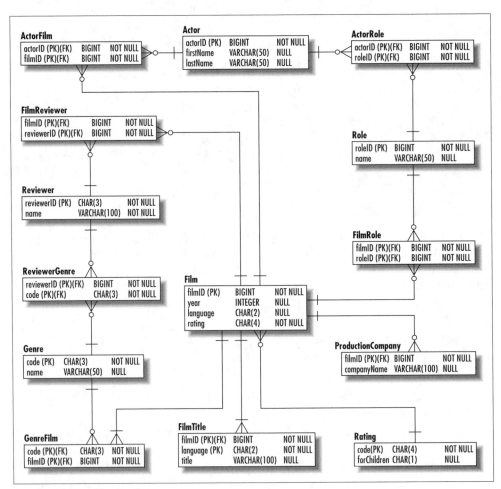

Figure 2-9. The film database in 4NF

Spending time normalizing to the fourth normal form is useful only for data models that have a lot of complex join tables. If you have just a few such tables, you are probably already in 4NF anyway. If you are not, the anomaly is almost certainly of no consequence to your system.

Fifth normal form

A table is in the fifth normal form (5NF) if it is in 4NF and cannot have lossless decomposition into any number of smaller tables. It is actually very hard to tell when a table is truly in 5NF—just about any table in 4NF is also in 5NF. It can occur in situations in which you have a many-to-many-to-many relationship as exists with Film, Actor, and Role. Given certain data, the database can end up making claims that simply are not true.

For simplicity's sake, assume that the database has a single actor in it who has appeared in two separate films playing two separate roles. The joined information from these tables looks like the data in Table 2-7.

Table 2-7. Joining actor, film, and role

actorID	filmID	roleName	Description
1	101	The president	Stanley Anderson (1) played the president in *Armageddon* (101).
1	102	Edwin Sneller	Stanley Anderson (1) played Edwin Sneller in *The Pelican Brief* (102).

So far, this structure should seem quite normal to you. The three entities have three corresponding join tables ActorFilm, FilmRole, and ActorRole to help manage the relationships. The problem arises when you insert particular data, such as adding Robert Culp who also played the president, but in the movie *The Pelican Brief*. In short, we add one row to Actor, one row to ActorFilm, one row to ActorRow, and one row to FilmRole. No rows are added to Role or Film. The join suddenly ends up with both true claims and some utterly false ones as Table 2-8 shows.

Table 2-8. The false claims (in italic) of a database not in 5NF

actorID	filmID	roleName	Description
1	101	The president	Stanley Anderson (1) played the president in *Armageddon* (101).
1	102	Edwin Sneller	Stanley Anderson (1) played Edwin Sneller in *The Pelican Brief* (102).
2	102	The president	Robert Culp (2) played the president in *The Pelican Brief* (102).
1	*102*	*The president*	*Stanley Anderson (1) played the president in The Pelican Brief (102).*
2	*101*	*The president*	*Robert Culp (2) played the president in Armageddon (101).*

The important thing to note about the database is that there is nothing wrong with the data in the tables. The only thing wrong is what the relationships among the tables imply given a very specific data set.

By now, you have probably guessed that the solution is to create another entity to manage this trinary relationship. The Appearance table in the fully normalized Figure 2-10 manages this solution.

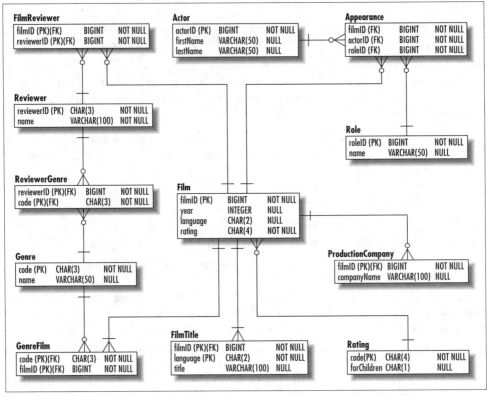

Figure 2-10. The film database in 5NF

Denormalization

Denormalization is the process of consciously removing entities created through the normalization process. An unnormalized database is *not* a denormalized database. A database can be denormalized only after it has been sufficiently normalized, and solid justifications need to exist to support every act of denormalization.

Nevertheless, fully normalized databases can require complex programming and generally require more joins than their unnormalized or denormalized counterparts. Joins are resource-intensive operations; thus, the more joins, the more time a query will take.

To deal with queries that take too long or are too complex to be maintainable, a database architect denormalizes the database. As we have seen from the process of normalization, each lower normal form introduces database anomalies that can compromise the integrity, maintainability, and extensibility of the database. Denormalization is thus a reasoned trade-off between query complexity/performance and system integrity, maintenance, and extensibility.

The Perils of Denormalization

Denormalization must be approached with caution. In general, a table should have proven it requires denormalization in testing or even in production before you actually denormalize it. Data architects very commonly denormalize based on hunches about performance or experience with similar applications in the past—a practice that leads down the path to a poorly designed database.

Denormalization can in some circumstances incur performance penalties. More important, however, most of the time you do not see the kinds of performance improvements from denormalization that actually make a difference. When you denormalize without concrete performance benchmarks backing the denormalization, you end up:

* Denormalizing tables without appreciable performance improvement
* Denormalizing again later, after you have done performance testing

The result is a database that looks more unnormalized than denormalized. The best rule of thumb is to prove the database needs denormalization and document that need for the people who will be maintaining the database. Subsequently, you should prove that your denormalization actually improves performance and back out the changes if they fail to address the performance concerns.

In most cases, you can deal with complexity simply by creating views that hide the complexity. Performance is thus the general driver of denormalization. To determine whether denormalization makes sense, I recommend Craig Mullins's simple guidelines posted in an online article for *The Data Administration Newsletter* in an article called "Denormalization Guidelines" (*http://www.tdan.com/i001fe02.htm*):

* Can you achieve performance goals without denormalization?
* Will the system still fail to achieve performance goals with denormalization?
* Will the system be less reliable as a result of denormalization?

If you answer "yes" to any of these questions, you should not use denormalization as your performance tuning tool.

> **BEST PRACTICE** Denormalize only when you have concrete proof that denormalization will boost performance.

The most common temptation to denormalize comes from queries that require joins to retrieve a single value. Any query pulling a film's suitability for children along with the film from the database would fall into this category. For example:

```
SELECT Film.title, Film.language, Film.year, Rating.forChildren
FROM Film, Rating
WHERE Film.filmID = 2
AND Film.rating = Rating.code;
```

Denormalization would move the rating code and suitability for children back into the Film table. Wouldn't the query perform much better without that join? Actually, it probably would *not* perform *noticeably* better—the join is done using a unique index (Rating.code). Denormalization, however, would incur all of the anomalies that led us to normalize the table in the first place.

A better candidate for normalization might be pulling a state name into an Address table along with the state code used in the join. If most queries actually want the state name and the query would definitely benefit from avoiding the join to the State table, it can make sense to add an extra column to Address for stateName. You do not, however, remove the State table. This denormalization works—assuming real performance benefits are achieved for the application—because the state name is a candidate key for the State table. Though stateName would technically be a transitive depencency in the Address table (and thus violate 3NF), its status as a candidate key for State makes it almost a functional depencency and consequently almost acceptable to put into the Address table.

A common situation in which performance does truly become a problem is reporting. For reporting, database normalization is just one of many factors that lead to performance degradation. Because complex reports generally eat server resources regardless of normalization issues, it is generally a bad idea to empower users to execute complex reports against live tables. Instead, you can denormalize by replicating the data into special tables designed to support reporting needs. To create a table for reporting on westerns, we might create a WesternReport table that looks like the table in Table 2-9.

Table 2-9. A table for reporting on westerns

Attribute	Domain	Notes	NULL?
filmID	BIGINT	PRIMARY KEY	No
title	VARCHAR(100)		No
rating	CHAR(5)		Yes
forChildren	CHAR(1)	DEFAULT 'N'	No
otherGenres	VARCHAR(255)		Yes
directors	VARCHAR(255)		Yes
actors	VARCHAR(255)		Yes
ranking	INT		No
year	INT		No

Reporting on all of the westerns from 1992 would look like this:

```
SELECT * FROM WesternReport
WHERE year = 1992;
```

The alternative is to have users constantly executing the following query against the tables that actually maintain your data:

```
SELECT Film.filmID, Film.title, Film.rating,
    IFNULL(Rating.forChildren, 'N'), Film.ranking, Film.year
```

```
FROM Film, FilmGenre
LEFT OUTER JOIN Rating ON Film.rating = Rating.code

WHERE FilmGenre.code = 'WES'
AND year = 1992
AND Film.filmID = FilmGenre.filmID;
```

Use follow-up queries to get other genres, directors, and actors associated with the film.

Object-Relational Mapping

You now have your data structured for optimal performance and extensibility in your database. To make use of that data, you need to pull it into applications—in our case, Java applications—that manipulate the data. Java is an object-oriented programming language. In other words, it models its problem domain using object-oriented principles. In general, object-oriented principles can be summed up as:

Encapsulation
> Encapsulation is the hiding of the data and behavior of a thing behind a limited and well-described interface. In Java terms, the limited and well-described interface is the set of your public methods and attributes.

Abstraction
> Abstraction is the modeling of only the essential characteristics of a thing and ignoring or hiding the details of its nonessential characteristics. A Java interface is an example of an abstraction.

Polymorphism
> Polymorphism means that a single interface can be used for a generic class of actions rather than a single specific action. The equals( ) method in Object is an example of a polymorphic interface because it means different specific things in different classes even though it generally means testing for equality.

Inheritance
> Inheritance is the ability for one thing to take on the behavior and characteristics of another. Java supports inheritances through extending classes.

Though a relational database is a model of a problem domain, it is a different kind of model. Your Java application models behavior and uses data to support that behavior. The database, however, models the data in your problem domain and its relationships. Java application logic is inefficient at determining what actors who have played the president during their career have appeared in films together. Similarly, a database is a poor tool for determining pricing rules for a set of products.

When a Java application needs to save its state to some sort of data storage, it is said to require persistence. Often, complex Java applications persist against a relational database. The use of a relational database for persistence has several advantages:

- Relational databases are efficient at storing data for later retrieval using complex criteria. You cannot search on your stored objects nearly as efficiently if they are serialized to a filesystem or stored somewhere in XML.

- Java's JDBC API is simple to learn. Other persistence mechanisms tend to be much harder. Java's file access APIs, for example, are painful to write cross-platform code with.

- Most people have easy access to a relational database. MySQL and PostgresSQL are freely available to those with limited budgets, and most organizations already have a huge investment in enterprise database engines like Oracle and DB2.

When you attempt to persist your Java objects to a relational database, however, you run into the problem of the object-relational mismatch. The most basic question facing the object-oriented developer using a relational database is how to map relational data into objects. Your immediate thought might be to simply map object attributes to entity attributes. Though this approach creates a solid starting point, it does not create the perfect mapping for two reasons:

- Unlike relational attributes, object attributes are multivalued. An object stores within itself attributes with multiple simple values as well as direct references to groups of complex objects.

- The relational model has no natural way of modeling inheritance relationships.

> **BEST PRACTICE**   Normalize data models based on object-relational mapping just as you would normalized any other data model: to 3NF or 4NF.

Figure 2-11 contains a sample class diagram for a system that should persist against a relational database. In the class diagram, you are modeling a person who can play many roles—including the roles of employee and customer. Each employee has many addresses and phone numbers.

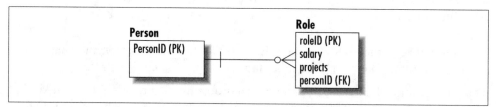

Figure 2-11. A simple class diagram for a persistent system

Inheritance Mapping

The biggest difficulty in object-relational mapping arises in inheritance mapping—the mapping of class inheritance hierarchies into a relational database. In our class diagram, this problem appears in the structure related to roles. Do you need separate entities for Role, Employee, and Customer? Or does it make more sense to have Employee and Customer entities? Or perhaps just a Role entity will sufffice?

Depending on the nature of your class diagram, all three solutions can work. Figure 2-12 shows three possible data models for supporting the class diagram from Figure 2-11.

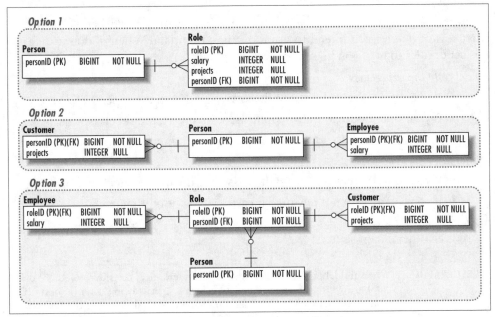

Figure 2-12. Three possible data models for roles

As you can see from all three data models, the relational model's inability to support abstraction does some serious damage to the application. While the class diagram enables the addition of new roles to the system without impacting the Person class, you cannot accomplish the same flexibility in the data model. All three data models demand some understanding of all possible roles available.

The simplest data model—the one with only a Role entity—must contain all data associated with all possible roles. This approach to object-relational inheritance mapping when the implementation classes contain mostly the same data and the differences among the roles from a data perspective can be summarized through a role type.

On the other hand, if the commonalities in the different roles are not interesting from a data perspective, you can solve the problem with the second data model. In other words, model each role with its own entity and ignore the entire Role abstraction in the database. This approach fails if you need to ask questions like "What roles does this person have?" without necessarily knowing what possible roles can exist.

The third approach is a sometimes unwieldy compromise between the first and second approaches. When you need to deal with the roles both abstractly and concretely, you have to create a relationally artificial structure to model those nuances. In this data model, the entities for the concrete classes—Employee and Customer—

borrow their primary keys from the Role entity. Only the Role entity contains the foreign key of Person with whom the role is associated. You can now deal with the roles in an abstract sense by joining with the Role entity, or you can get specific information about individual roles through a complex join.

In short, the proper way of modeling an inheritance relationship depends heavily on what sort of queries you intend to use to retrieve that data. When in doubt, refer to this set of rules to help you in inheritance mapping:

Model only the superclass
- If your queries rely heavily on data associated with the superclass and
- If your queries do not rely on data associated with the subclasses and
- If the subclasses do not contain a significant number of distinct attributes

Model only the subclasses
- If your queries rely heavily on data associated with the subclasses and
- If your queries do not rely on data associated with the superclass

Model the superclass and its subclasses
For all other circumstances.

> **BEST PRACTICE** When modeling OO (object-oriented) inheritance, consider whether your database will be used by non-OO systems. If it is being used by non-OO systems, focus more on the data model and less on mapping the OO concepts to the relational world.

Multivalued Attributes

Collections such as arrays, HashMaps, and ArrayLists present another problem to object-relational mapping. In relational terms, these kinds of object attributes represent multivalued attributes. The solution to this problem starts with the same solution for multivalued attributes in your relational model: create entities to support the multivalued attributes.

That approach is simple enough for collections of objects like the Phone and Address classes in our class diagram. You create a Phone entity with a foreign key of personID and a primary key of personID and type and you are done. The mapping becomes tricky with attributes like int arrays or String collections.

> **BEST PRACTICE** If your database engine supports SQL3 data types, map multivalued attributes to the SQL ARRAY type.

In our class diagram, we store a list of favorite colors as a String[ ]. The solution again is to handle this mapping in the same way you would handle the normalization of an entity with multivalued attributes: create a new entity. In this case, we would create a FavoriteColor table with personID and color as a primary key.

CHAPTER 3

Transaction Management

> *Substances owe their special importance in the enterprise of identification*
> *to the fact that they survive through time. But the idea of survival is*
> *inseparable from the idea of surviving certain sorts of change—of position,*
> *size, shape, colour, and so forth. As we might expect, events often play an*
> *essential role in identifying a substance... Neither the category of*
> *substance nor the category of change is conceivable apart from the other.*
>
> —Donald Davidson
> *The Individuation of Events*

This quote from Donald Davidson comes from a paper he wrote in the field of event theory. Event theory is an entire subdiscipline of philosophy focused on the question of what it means to be an event. As a software architect for a database application, your job is to be an event theorist. Specifically, you identify what changes will occur in your database and how they combine into indivisible sequences that will not leave the database in an inconsistent state.

This is the practice of event management. You then package those indivisible events into a database operation called a *transaction*. A transaction is a group of database events that must execute without interference from other transactions; and they must execute together or not at all. The transaction helps you guarantee the integrity of the data in your database.

The classic example of a database transaction is the transfer of money from one bank account to another. When executing a transfer, a banking application needs to make sure that both the debit from the source account and the credit to the target account execute. If one should fail, the system should return to the state it was in before the debit. Without the ability to abort the transaction, a successful debit followed by a failed credit (perhaps the server crashed between the two operations) will result in missing money.

Transactions

A transaction is an event or sequence of events that takes a database from one consistent state to the next. If any of the events fails or the sequence fails to complete, the system is returned to its initial state. Once it completes, it is guaranteed to be in the new consistent state until it is acted upon to completion by another transaction.

ACID Requirements

Formally, a transaction is a group of database operations that together have a shared set of guaranteed properties—commonly known as ACID properties. ACID is an acronym that stands for Atomicity, Consistency, Isolation, and Durability.

Atomicity

> The atomicity of a transaction means that it represents an indivisible unit of work. Any attempt to break the transaction into smaller parts breaks the transaction. Atomicity is what guarantees that all of the operations that make up a transaction succeed or none of them succeeds.

Consistency

> The consistency of a transaction means that all of the operations that make up a transaction operate on a consistent set of data and leave the database in a consistent state once it has completed. In other words, the transaction is ignorant of any changes made to the database by other transactions. Data is considered consistent when all of its constraints such as unique indexes and foreign indexes are intact.

Isolation

> A transaction should be ignorant of the existence of any other transactions. In other words, from the point of view of a given transaction, it is the only thing operating on the database.

Durability

> When a transaction commits, its changes are permanent—even in the event of a system failure.

In other words, if you have an account transfer, it meets ACID requirements in the following ways:

- The transfer is atomic if and only if the sum of the two bank accounts is the same before and after the transfer. The debit to the savings account cannot occur without the credit to the checking account following.

- The transfer is consistent as long as nothing else happens to either account while the transfer is in process. For example, the checking account cannot be deleted from the database while the debit to the savings is occurring.

- The transfer is isolated as long as another transaction is incapable of seeing the debited savings account before the transfer has completed.

- The transfer is durable as long as the transfer can survive a catastrophic event such as a server crash or other kind of system failure.

Your database engine is largely responsible for guaranteeing the ACIDity of your transactions. You, the software architect, are nevertheless responsible for identifying what events make up a transaction and how the application should package those transactions for the database.

BEST PRACTICE   Choose technologies that will guarantee the ACIDity of your application's transactions.

Transaction Design

The key to identifying transactions is determining what stages in your use cases represent consistent database states. If we examine the transfer example, we see two distinct events that make up the transfer:

1. Debit the savings account.
2. Credit the checking account.

After the debit of the savings account, the database is said to be in an inconsistent state because important information about the system would be lost should the transfer fail to complete. In this case, the important information is someone's money!

Inconsistency can also mean having orphaned data in the database. Consider, for example, the deletion of a person from a database with the following steps:

1. Delete the person from the Person table.
2. Delete all addresses for the person from the Address table.
3. Delete all phone numbers for the person from the Phone table.

If something goes wrong after the first step, you could end up with a database full of unreferenced addresses and phone numbers unless the transaction returns the system to its initial state. The database is therefore in an inconsistent state until all addresses and phone numbers are deleted.

Though you want your transactions to be large enough to prevent the database from entering inconsistent states, you also want them as small as possible. As you will see later in this chapter, transactions make huge demands on a database. The larger the transaction, the more resources it eats and the worse the performance of your application.

> **BEST PRACTICE** Define your transactions to have the minimum number of steps necessary while leaving the data store in a consistent state.

To illustrate this problem in action, consider an e-commerce application that needs to create a customer before the customer can place an order. To make the application as easy to use for the customer as possible, you may let her enter her customer information along with her first order. The use case thus looks something like this:

1. Add the customer information to the Customer table.

2. Add address information to the Address table.

3. Add phone information to the Phone table.

4. Create an order in the Order table.

5. Add a line item in the LineItem table.

6. Decrease the inventory count in the Product table.

It is the combined job of the business analyst and information architect to craft this use case as the best way for a new customer to buy something. It is your job as the software architect to figure out its implications on the database. In many situations, there will be a one-to-one correspondence between use cases and transactions. In this case, however, we have two separate transactions because the database can be in a consistent state with the customer information and no order information. In other words, steps 1–3 make up the first transaction and steps 4–6 make up the second. Figure 3-1 contrasts the use case from the client's perspective with the sequence from the architect's perspective.

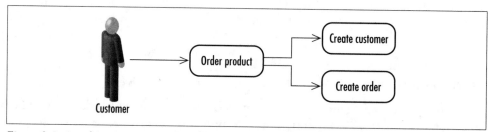

Figure 3-1. A multitransaction use case from the perspectives of a client application and an architect

By breaking this one use case into two transactions, you will not sacrifice database consistency but you will gain performance. The division enhances performance because you enable other transactions that may be waiting on resources blocked only by the first three steps to execute prior to the completion of the entire use case. If you encapsulated the use case in a single transaction, then those other transactions would have to wait until the completion of the use case. Figure 3-2 shows how breaking the use case into two transactions can reduce blocking.

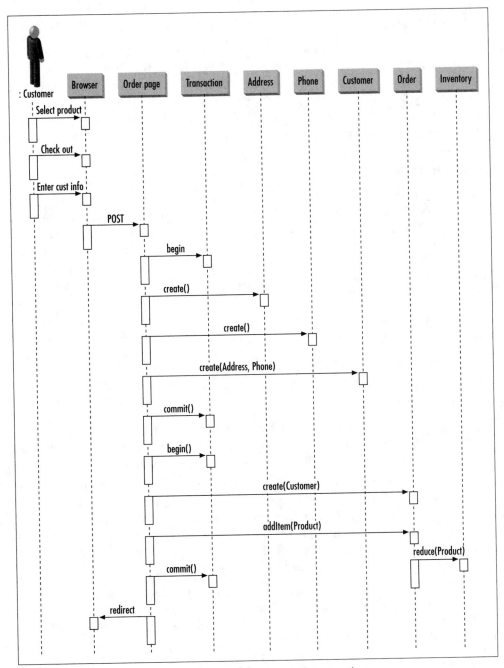

Figure 3-2. Reduced blocking by dividing work between two transactions

Concurrency

Transaction management is a big enough problem worrying only about consistency, atomicity, and durability. Perhaps one of the biggest issues is isolation—how do you manage the concurrent access to database resources by many different users? The mechanism your database uses is generally hidden from the software architect and database programmer. A data architect, however, should be familiar with how their database of choice manages isolation.

Isolation Levels

Before talking about the various mechanisms to support transaction isolation, it is useful to examine the concept in more detail. As I mentioned earlier, isolation is the *I* in ACID. When a second transaction attempts to read the data being modified by a first transaction, that second transaction will not see any changes the first transaction has made. For example, if my wife read a joint savings account balance at the same time I was transferring money from savings to checking, the following events might occur:

1. I see a savings account balance of $1,000.
2. I initiate a transfer of $500 from savings to checking.
3. The system debits my savings account.
4. My wife requests the balance for the savings account and sees $1000.
5. The system credits my checking account.

My wife should see $1,000 as the balance in the savings account *even though the system has already debited the savings account*. She reads the old value because the transfer transaction is in an inconsistent state at the time of her request.

So far in this chapter, we have looked at transaction isolation only in the context of full transaction isolation—where a transaction can act on the database as if it were the only thread operating on that database. In the real world, databases must support concurrent access by multiple transactions. Business applications in particular have significant concurrency demands. Because of the performance penalty of full transaction isolation, it is rarely practical for most systems.

ANSI SQL identifies four distinct transaction isolation levels that enable you to balance performance needs with data integrity needs. In order to understand the different transaction isolation levels, however, you should first understand a few terms relating to the interaction of concurrent transactions:

Dirty read
> A dirty read occurs when one transaction views the uncommitted changes of another transaction. If the original transaction rolls back its changes, the one that read its changes is said to have "dirty" data.

Nonrepeatable read

A nonrepeatable read occurs when one transaction reads different data from the same query when it is issued multiple times and other transactions have changed the rows between reads by the first transaction. In other words, a transaction that mandates repeatable reads will not see the committed changes made by other transactions. An application needs to start a new transaction to see those changes.

Phantom read

A phantom read deals with changes occurring in other transactions that would result in new rows matching your transaction's WHERE clause. For example, if you had a transaction that reads all accounts with a balance of less than $100 and your transaction performs two reads of that data, a phantom read allows for new rows to appear in the second read based on changes made by other transactions. This situation can occur if someone withdrew money between your reads. The new rows are called phantom rows.

The four ANSI SQL transaction isolation levels are:

Read uncommittted transactions

The transaction allows dirty reads, nonrepeatable reads, and phantom reads.

Read committed transactions

Only data committed to the database may be read. The transaction can, however, perform nonrepeatable and phantom reads.

Repeatable read transactions

Committed, repeatable reads as well as phantom reads are allowed. Nonrepeatable reads are not allowed.

Serializable transactions

Only committed, repeatable reads are allowed. Phantom reads are specifically disallowed at this level.

Assuming your database engine supports these levels of transaction isolation, a Java database application can control its transaction isolation level through the JDBC Connection interface using the setTransactionIsolation( ) method:

```
Connection conn = dataSource.getConnection( );

conn.setTransactionIsolation(
    Connection.TRANSACTION_READ_COMMITTED);
// perform your transaction
```

To find out what transaction isolation levels your database engine and driver support, use the supportsTransactionIsolationLevel( ) method in DatabaseMetaData. Table 3-1 shows the transaction isolation constants in java.sql.Connection. You may also want to check whether the database supports transactions at all (mSQL, for example, does not support them). The method supportsTransactions( ) answers this question.

Table 3-1. Constants for managing JDBC transaction isolation levels

Constant	Meaning
TRANSACTION_NONE	Transactions are not supported by the database engine. You never set the transaction isolation level with this value. It is simply a return value from drivers when transactions are not supported.
TRANSACTION_READ_UNCOMMITTED	Reads are read uncommitted. This level represents the least-restrictive form in databases in which transactions are supported.
TRANSACTION_READ_COMMITTED	Reads pull only committed data from the database.
TRANSACTION_REPEATABLE_READ	Reads are repeatable, but phantom reads are allowed.
TRANSACTION_SERIALIZABLE	Phantom reads are not allowed.

As an application architect, your job is to balance database integrity with application performance. You therefore want to select the lowest level of transaction isolation that will protect the integrity of the data as you have it structured in your data model.

> **BEST PRACTICE**   Use the lowest transaction isolation level that will still maintain the integrity of your database.

Locking

The way in which your database engine manages concurrency is specific to your database engine. As long as it maintains ACIDity, it does not matter from a standards perspective how it does it. Nevertheless, database engines all use some form of locking.

Conceptually, concurrency at the database level can be understood using Java as an example. Java, of course, uses locks on objects to manage concurrent access to synchronized blocks of Java code. Consider the following three methods:

```java
public class MyClass {
    public synchronized void first( ) {
        // do something
    }

    public void second( ) {
        synchronized( this ) {
            // do something else
        }
    }

    public void third( ) {
        synchronized( otherObject ) {
            // do yet a third thing
        }
    }
}
```

If two threads call first( ) at the same time, one will be allowed to execute the method to completion before the other can start. This sequencing occurs because the synchronized keyword indicates that you are locking against a monitor. In the default case, the monitor is always this. Thus the monitor in first( ) and second( ) is this and the monitor for third( ) is otherObject. Only one thread at a time can execute code monitored by a common object. In this example, first( ) and the synchronized section of second( ) cannot be executed concurrently by multiple threads. However, first( ) and third( ) can be concurrently executed by two separate threads since they are guarded by different monitors.

Databases use a different concurrency mechanism, but the Java concepts are relevant. A database allows for locks to be taken on different scopes of data. A database can lock a table at any of the following levels:

Table
Page
Row

Depending on your database engine, your lock level can also be modified as read, update, exclusive, shared, or any other number of attributes. SQL Server, for example, supports the following kinds of locks:

Intent
Shared
Update
Exclusive
Schema
Bulk update

You need a nice spreadsheet and an understanding of your database of choice to appreciate how two kinds of locks interact. For example, many different threads can acquire a shared lock. These shared locks may—depending on the database engine—prevent another thread from acquiring an update lock until the shared locks are released. Because interaction varies by database, a discussion is beyond the scope of this book.

The easiest lock level to understand is a table-level lock. In this case, only one thread can touch the locked table during the lifetime of the lock. This approach is much like using MyClass.class as the monitor for access to all methods in your MyClass class. In other words, no two threads would be able to access any MyClass instance concurrently. As you can imagine, such a trick would not perform well in a Java application. Similarly, table-level locking performs horribly for databases. Page-level locking has no Java analogy. In short, it prevents concurrent access to all of the rows in a single page of memory. If, for example, you have rows 1–3 in one page of memory and 4–6 in another, access to data from rows 1–3 with page-level locking prevents other threads from accessing any of those three rows. A concurrent thread can, however, access the data in rows 4–6.

Row-level locking is like making every nonstatic method in a Java class synchronized. It prevents concurrent access by two threads to the same row in the database. Two threads may, however, access two different rows concurrently.

On one hand, locking is necessary to guarantee proper transaction isolation in a concurrent environment. On the other, locking slows down database applications. Any transaction that has a long duration and a large number of resources associated with it is going to drag down any application. Later in the chapter, I introduce some approaches to concurrency that enable you to strike a balance between isolation and performance.

JDBC Transaction Management

No matter what style of database programming you select or what persistence model you follow, transactions will always be the most fundamental element in database programming. Consequently, we will be returning to transaction management repeatedly over the course of this book. For now, it is time to lay the foundation for that database programming by showing the basics of transaction management in Java code.

Basic Transaction Management

In any programming language, basic transaction management is indicating the start and end of a transaction as well as handling any errors that come up during the transaction. In JDBC, a transaction begins implicitly whenever you create a statement of any kind. It ends when you call commit( ) in the Connection instance. Finally, you abort the transaction and return the database to its initial state by calling rollback( ) in the Connection instance.

The Connection governs all of this transaction management. You therefore cannot use statements from different Connection instances in the same transaction. You also have to tell the connection that your application is managing transactions; otherwise, it will commit every statement after you send it to the database. The following code executes two updates in a single transaction and rolls back on any errors:

```java
public void transfer(Account targ, float amt) {
    Connection conn = null;

    try {
        PreparedStatement stmt;

        conn = dataSource.getConnection( );
        conn.setAutoCommit(false);
        stmt = conn.prepareStatement("UPDATE Account SET balance = ? " +
                                     "WHERE id = ?");
        stmt.setFloat(1, balance-amt);
        stmt.setInt(2, id);
        stmt.executeUpdate( );

        stmt.setFloat(1, targ.balance + amt);
        stmt.setInt(2, targ.id);
        stmt.executeUpdate( );
        balance -= amt;
        targ.balance += amt;
        conn.commit( );
    }
```

```
        catch( SQLException e ) {
            try { conn.rollback(); }
            catch( SQLException e ) { }
        }
        finally {
            if( conn != null ) {
                try { conn.close(); }
                catch( SQLException e ) { }
            }
        }
    }
```

Optimistic Concurrency

In the days of client/server programming, applications often started a transaction by reading data from a database and ended the transaction by modifying that data. In other words, you locked the data you read so that someone else didn't overwrite any changes you made. For example, if you and I read a customer record from the database with my goal to change the phone number and your goal to change the last name, one of us runs the risk of overwriting the other's changes if neither of us has a read lock. If I saved my changes first, your client application will likely overwrite my phone number change with the old phone number since applications tend to send all fields with their updates. Figure 3-3 illustrates what can go wrong in this example.

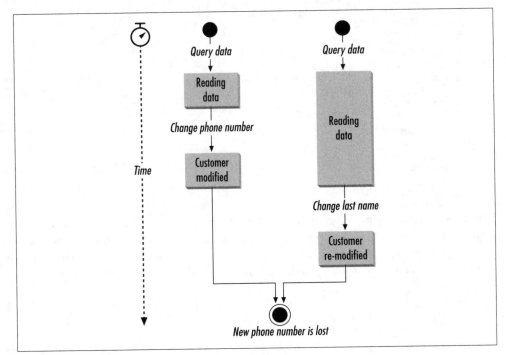

Figure 3-3. Updates overwriting each other

I can prevent you from overwriting my changes by starting a transaction when I read the data. That way you cannot even read the customer record until my change is saved. This technique is called *pessimistic concurrency*, and it is a terrible bottleneck. If I manage to walk away from my desk while entering the phone number, your client will be waiting a long time to read that data. In web-based applications, this kind of pessimistic concurrency is completely untenable.

You can make pessimistic concurrency a little more acceptable by performing a SELECT FOR UPDATE just prior to actually sending changes to the database using the values returned from the first query. If the rows no longer match the original select, then you will receive no rows and lock no resources in the database. Though this form of pessimistic concurrency locks resources for a much shorter time than the original, it is still a relatively long-lived transaction. It also requires placing columns that are probably not indexed in a SELECT statement. The following example illustrates this flow:

```
SELECT firstName, lastName, phone, birthDay
FROM Customer
WHERE id = ?;

// on the client, make changes here
// this could take a long, long time
// minutes, even tens of minutes

SELECT firstName, lastName, phone, birthDay
FROM Customer
WHERE id = ?
AND firstName = ?
AND lastName = ?
AND phone = ?
AND birthDay = ?
FOR UPDATE

UPDATE Customer
SET firstName = ?,
lastName = ?,
phone = ?,
birthDay = ?
WHERE id = ?
```

The alternative is optimistic concurrency. Where pessimistic concurrency pessimistically assumes that some other transaction will attempt to make changes to your data behind your back, optimistic concurrency happily hopes that such a situation will not occur. As a backup, it uses values from the original row in the WHERE clause:

```
SELECT firstName, lastName, phone, birthDay
FROM Customer
WHERE id = ?

// again, make changes here... this could take a long time
```

```
UPDATE Customer
SET firstName = ?,
lastName = ?,
phone = ?,
birthDay = ?
WHERE id = ?
AND firstName = ?
AND lastName = ?
AND phone = ?
AND birthDay = ?
```

Under optimistic concurrency, you acquire a lock only when you are actually performing your changes. You still avoid overwriting the changes of another because
you match your update against the values you read. If someone else changes the
lastName field, then your WHERE clause will not match and the update will fail. Unfortunately, you are still very likely matching against unindexed columns.

The approach I use in nearly every database application I write is to create a special
column or two to store a value unique to each update. For example, you could use
the natural primary key of the table along with a last update timestamp. Each time
you modify the database, you modify the last update timestamp and use the old one
in your WHERE clause:

```
Connection conn = null;

try {
    PreparedStatement stmt;
    long ts;

    conn = ds.getConnection();
    stmt = conn.prepareStatement("UPDATE Customer " +
                        "SET firstName = ?, lastName = ?, phone = ?, " +
                        "birthDay = ?, lastUpdateTS = ? " +
                        "WHERE id = ? AND lastUpdateTS = ?");
    stmt.setString(1, firstName);
    stmt.setString(2, lastName);
    stmt.setString(3, phone);
    stmt.setDate(4, birthDate);
    stmt.setLong(5, ts = System.currentTimeMillis());
    stmt.setInt(6, id);
    stmt.setLong(7, lastUpdateTS);
    stmt.executeUpdate();
    lastUpdateTS = ts;
}
catch( SQLException e ) {
    e.printStackTrace();
}
finally {
    if( conn != null ) {
        try { conn.close(); }
        catch( SQLException e ) { }
    }
}
```

Figure 3-4 contrasts how optimistic concurrency prevents this mishap, in contrast to Figure 3-3.

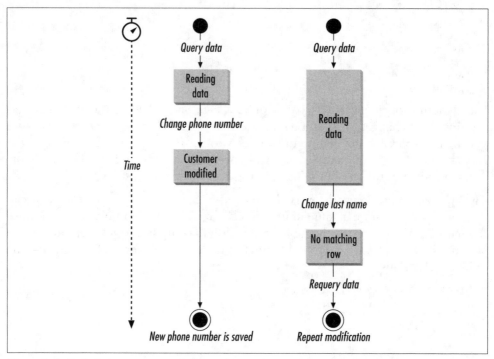

Figure 3-4. Optimistic concurrency prevents dirty writes

This approach has the advantage of preserving database integrity just like pessimistic concurrency while at the same time minimizing the lifetime of the transaction and guaranteeing that only indexed values are in the WHERE clause. The only true downside is that you are also updating an indexed column, and updates to indexes have their own performance impact.

> **BEST PRACTICE**   Use optimistic concurrency along with timestamps to help maintain data integrity while still getting solid performance.

Batch Transactions

We have been dealing with transactions in an interactive context—where a user is initiating the transaction through some action in a user interface. Complex business systems have not only interactive transactions, but also *batch transactions*. Batch transactions are sets of transactions that occur on the server independent of user interaction. For example, the monthly process that calculates interest for a savings account is a batch transaction.

Until JDBC 2.0, Java was a miserable language for the execution of major batch transactions. Sometimes, people would have processes that needed to execute nightly but took two days to run. The overhead, of course, was partly due to the interpreted nature of Java and the lack of HotSpot VMs (virtual machines) at that time. It was also due to the fact that batch JDBC programming required a lot of back-and-forth between the batch application and the database as well as unnecessary string processing.

JDBC 2.0 introduced a batch processing mechanism that addressed the non-VM issues (HotSpot addressed the VM issues). Specifically, JDBC enables you to store multiple statements on the client to be sent over to the database as a group—as a batch. When running that monthly interest process, you previously could send the update for each account to the database only one at a time. Now you can choose to send the updates for all accounts at once, or you can group a bunch of the updates together and send them in waves.

As a general rule, the more updates you hold on the client, the faster the batch processing occurs. However, you are limited in the number you can hold by several factors:

RAM

You have to store those updates in memory. Thus, the more updates you hold for batch execution, the more RAM you are eating. If you eat up so much RAM that you start swapping, you will destroy the performance benefits of batch processing.

The database transaction log

If you have auto-commit turned off, then the whole batch sent to the database is executed as a single transaction. If you send too many updates over, you risk filling up the database's transaction log.

Recovery processing

If you have auto-commit on and you are batching numerous transactions, recovery processing is much more involved because you have to figure out what the last successful update was in your batch and then recover from there. The more updates, the more complex the recovery process can potentially be.

The trick is to batch up a reasonable number of updates together. Unfortunately, a reasonable number depends on the amount of RAM available to the application, the size of your database transaction log, the amount of RAM on the database server, and the complexity of any recovery processing. In some situations, it makes sense to batch up 10 updates, while in others 100 or more makes sense. The following code illustrates batching together 10 statements at a time for updating account balances:

```
PreparedStatement stmt;

conn.setAutoCommit(false);
stmt = conn.prepareStatemment("UPDATE account " +
                        "SET balance = ? " +
                        "WHERE id = ?");
for(int i=0; i<accts.length; i++) {
    int[ ] rows;
```

```
    while( (i%10 != 9) && (i<accts.length) ) {
        accts[i].calculateIntterest( );
        stmt.setDouble(1, accts[i].getBalance( ));
        stmt.setInt(2, accts[i].getId( ));
        stmt.addBatch( );
        i++;
    }
    rows = stmt.executeBatch( );
}
```

For a more complete discussion of the way JDBC manages batch processing, see the tutorial in Chapter 11.

Savepoints

While JDBC 2.0 added batch processing to the transaction arsenal of the JDBC programmer, JDBC 3.0 added something called *savepoints*. Without the benefit of savepoints, JDBC allows for only two possible consistent states in a transaction: the beginning state and the end state. Some transactions, however, may have more than two possible consistent database states. For example, you may have a transaction in which an error condition during processing is itself meaningful to the transaction and thus should cause an alternate flow with an alternate consistent end state.

BEST PRACTICE	Use savepoints to support transactions with multiple possible consistent end states.

I honestly have never encountered a situation in business programming in which I felt I needed savepoints. One possible example, however, would be a flexible tool for managing the addition of new users to a web site. On your web site, you probably want to empower users to identify themselves by unique names but you want them to be able to change those names. Because they can change, they make poor candidates for a primary key. Instead, you automatically generate an otherwise meaningless primary key and let them pick meaningful names that are used as a unique index.

Of course, it is possible that whatever name a user chooses is already in use. To make the process as simple for the user as possible, you would have the following events in your transaction:

1. Generate a unique primary key from a Sequence table (requires an update).
2. Save the user contact information to the Contact table.
3. Add the username and timestamp to a new user log.
4. Insert the user profile information (including username) into the Profile table.
5. If the chosen username is a duplicate, insert the profile information into the Profile table using the primary key as a temporary username. After that, log the new user ID and timestamp to the new user log.

In this example, you could set a savepoint after step 2 and roll back the transaction to that point in the event the chosen username is a duplicate. Using a savepoint, you can guarantee that the user will appear in the new user log under the proper username.

Of course, you can avoid the need for savepoints by restructuring this contrived transaction. Nevertheless, it does illustrate the conditional processing inherent in savepoint transactions. The following code shows how it works in practice:

```
Connection conn = null;

try {
    // the sequencer generates unique user ID's for us
    Sequencer seq = Sequencer.getInstance("userID");
    PreparedStatement stmt;
    Savepoint sp;
    long id;

    conn = ds.getConnection( );
    conn.setAutoCommit(false);
    id = seq.next(conn);
    stmt = conn.prepareStatement("INSERT INTO Contact ( userID, email ) " +
                                 "VALUES ( ? , ? )");
    stmt.setLong(1, id);
    stmt.setString(2, email);
    stmt.executeUpdate( );
    sp = conn.setSavepoint("contact");
    stmt = conn.prepareStatement("INSERT INTO NewUser ( userName, when ) " +
                                 "VALUES ( ?, ? )");
    stmt.setString(1, userName);
    stmt.setLong(2, System.currentTimeMillis( ));
    stmt.executeUpdate( );
    stmt = conn.prepareStatement("INSERT INTO Profile ( userID, userName, pass ) "+
                                 "VALUES ( ?, ?, ? )");
    stmt.setLong(1, id);
    stmt.setString(2, userName);
    stmt.setString(3, password);
    try {
        stmt.executeUpdate( );
    }
    catch( SQLException e ) {
        conn.rollback(sp);
        userName = "" + userID;
        stmt = conn.prepareStatement("INSERT INTO NewUser ( userName, when ) " +
                                     "VALUES ( ?, ? )");
        stmt.setString(1, userName);
        stmt.setLong(2, System.currentTimeMillis( ));
        stmt.executeUpdate( );
        stmt = conn.prepareStatement("INSERT INTO Profile ( userID, userName, " +
                                     "pass ) VALUES ( ?, ?, ? )");
        stmt.setLong(1, id);
        stmt.setString(2, userName);
        stmt.setString(3, password);
        stmt.executeUpdate( );
```

```
        }
    }
    catch( SQLException e ) {
        try { conn.rollback( ); }
        catch( SQLException e ) { }
    }
    finally {
        if( conn != null ) {
            try { conn.close( ); }
            catch( SQLException e ) { }
        }
    }
```

Transaction Management Paradigms

By this point, you should understand the role of transactions in database programming and the tools that Java provides through JDBC to enable you to manage transactions. The final step is to understand how they fit into the bigger picture, into the
overall architecture of a transactional system.

There is no "one size fits all" paradigm for transactional systems. Different programming tasks require different design patterns to help you support your database transactions. The most common paradigms are:

Auto-commit transactions

> This pattern is the simplest transaction management pattern. You simply let the
> database commit every statement you send by leaving the connection in auto-
> commit mode. Unfortunately, there are few real world problems for which you
> can use auto-commit mode.

JDBC transactions

> This paradigm is the one you see in most JDBC texts. You turn off auto-commit
> and manage the transactions yourself. You are responsible for commits, roll-
> backs, and recovery in your Java code.

Stored procedure transactions

> Using stored procedures, you can capture the complexity of any transaction and
> leave your Java code as simple as auto-commit mode programming. The stored
> procedure begins the transaction and contains commits and rollbacks. This
> approach would be the ideal if stored procedures did not require writing in some
> proprietary stored procedure language.

EJB transactions

> In an EJB environment, you can have the EJB container manage your transac-
> tions for you. If you are unfamiliar with the term "container," we will cover that
> and other details of the J2EE platform in Chapter 9. For now, using EJB transac-
> tions means you do not have to have to do any transaction handling in your Java
> code. A third-party product manages the transactions for you.

Distributed transactions

Any one of the preceding transactions can also be a distributed transaction. A distributed transaction is one that spans multiple databases. You will generally be using distributed transactions in an EJB environment. Consequently, your Java code does not do any transaction management—distributed transactions are also managed by the container.

Throughout the rest of the book I will build on these transaction patterns and show different persistence metaphors that rely on these transaction management patterns.

PART II

Persistence Models

In the object-oriented world of Java development, Java objects are said to *persist* against a data store. In other words, the objects that make up your Java application save their data to a relational database so that data may be referenced at a later time. The approach you take to mapping your Java objects to the data store is called a *persistence model*.

These days, Java programmers have many persistence models from which to choose. In this section, we look at many of the most popular persistence models, including:

- EJB, both container-managed and bean-managed
- Java Data Objects
- Third-party tools such as Hibernate and Castor
- Custom persistence models

CHAPTER 4

Persistence Fundamentals

Objects contain the possibility of all situations.
—Ludwig Wittgenstein
Tractatus Logico Philosphicus

Persistence grants immortality to your business applications. Without it, you lose all of your application data every time the server shuts down. Database programming is the development of persistence mechanisms to save an application's state to a relational database. In this book, I will cover a variety of persistence mechanisms, but this chapter introduces the basics through a custom guest book JSP application.

Patterns of Persistence

The excellent book *Design Patterns* by Erich Gamma, Richard Helm, Ralph Johnson, and John Vlissides (Addison-Wesley) has popularized the concept of design patterns. They are recurring forms in software development that you can capture at a low level and reuse across dissimilar applications. Within any application scope are problems you have encountered; patterns are the result of recognizing common problems and leveraging a common solution.

People have been writing database applications for nearly three decades. Over that time, many best practices have evolved into design patterns. As we explore different modes of persistence in this book, we will see many of these patterns over and over again.

Division of Labor

Perhaps the most essential element of good persistence design is a clear separation of application logic into the following areas:

View logic
> The view logic is responsible for displaying the user interface. It is the user's window into the control and business logic.

Control logic

> The control logic handles user actions and decides what should happen based on those actions. It handles data validation and triggers the appropriate business logic on behalf of the user.

Business logic

> Business logic* encapsulates the basic business concepts behind your application. They provide the view with getter methods to access business data and provide the interface for creating, searching, modifying, and deleting the business objects they support.

Data access logic

> Data access logic maps business objects to the data storage layer. They are the heart of persistence.

Data storage logic

> The database engine provides you with this type of logic, which simply ensures your data is not lost at application shutdown.

Separation of logic with dependencies based on simple interfaces is a core principle of object-oriented software engineering. When you capture the essence of a business concept in a business object without burdening it with other logic, you enable it to be reused in other environments. For example, a bank account object that does not contain display or data access logic can be reused with JSP, Swing, and other kinds of frontends. It can also persist against different database engines.

> **BEST PRACTICE**   Divide application functionality into different logical components to facilitate component reuse.

This same principle extends beyond the business object layer. It also makes it easier to divide the work of building software among developers with different skills. With a good tag library, the view developer needs to know only XHTML and your tag library to write the view. The more difficult work of JDBC programming can be easily handed off to an experienced JDBC programmer without having to hand the entire application to a JDBC programmer.

> **BEST PRACTICE**   Divide application logic into multiple tiers to match the complexity of your application.

---

* You do not need to be writing a business application to have business logic. Business logic is a generic term that refers to any of the basic concepts in your problem domain. If you are building a first-person shooter game, your "business objects" are monsters, weapons, hazards, and the like.

Sequence Generation

In almost any database application, you need to generate unique identifiers to serve as primary keys in your database. Most databases have some sort of proprietary mechanism to help you generate sequences. Unfortunately, you cannot port a database application that relies on these proprietary schemes to other databases without changing the code that relies on those schemes.

I always recommend the use of a database-independent approach to sequence generation. Later in this chapter, I develop a sequence generator that will work for most database applications. It stores sequence seeds in the database. When an application needs a new unique number, it requests the unique number from the sequence generator. If the sequence generator has the seed in memory, it uses the following formula to create a new unique number:

```
unique = (seed * 1000000) + last;
last++;
```

If the seed is not in memory, it is loaded from the database, incremented, and the incremented value is stored back in the database. When the seed runs out of unique values—when `last` reaches 1000000*—it loads a new seed from the database, increments that new seed, and saves the incremented seed back to the database.

This approach has several important features:

- It generates unique values in a distributed environment. Multiple application servers can save business objects to multiple databases and still have the guarantee that the sequences being generated are unique across the entire system.

- You do not need to go to the database every single time you generate a sequence. You go to the database only every million sequences.

- The sequences are not tied to a specific table. You can create a sequence that is shared among several tables or even across the entire database. Similarly, you can have multiple values in the same table rely on different sequences.

BEST PRACTICE   Use database-independent sequence generation.

Mementos

In the division of labor discussed earlier, the data access object needs to know about the state of the object it is persisting. You could pass the business object to the data access object, but doing so would require the data access object to know the intimate

---

* The value 1,000,000 depends on the system. You will want lower numbers for systems with short uptimes and larger numbers for systems with long uptimes.

details of how the business object is implemented. The memento design pattern from the *Design Patterns* book comes to the rescue here.

A memento enables one object to share its state with another without either object needing to know anything about the other. Consider a common situation in which you have one class (class A) that references the values of another (class B). If you delete an attribute in class B, class A will no longer compile if it has direct references to the deleted attribute of class B. In general, this behavior is exactly what you want.

Sometimes—especially in mapping objects to a database—you want a looser coupling between two classes. The memento pattern creates this independence. It specifically enables you to make code changes to the business objects and data access objects independently of each other. A change to the business object will not require any changes to the data access object unless you are adding new data elements or removing obsolete ones. The data access object knows that the only changes it will care about come in the form of changes in the data contained in the memento. Similarly, any change to the underlying tables in the database is hidden from the business object. It always passes its state to the data access object and lets the data access object worry about persistence issues.

> **BEST PRACTICE**   Use mementos to pass component state between application tiers.

Object Caching

A database application must use the database as a persistent store—not as a memory store. In other words, you need to pull data from the database and hold it in memory in business objects. If you go to the database every time you want to display some data about a business object, your database application will perform terribly and fail to scale at all.

On the other hand, you don't want to load the entire database in memory and keep it there. If you have a large amount of data, you will quickly run out of memory. It is therefore important to develop an object caching mechanism that strikes a solid balance between memory usage and database access.

In architectures like the EJB architecture, the application server automatically manages caching for you. The Guest Book later in this chapter, however, does not use EJBs. It therefore needs something else to manage caching. It leverages a Cache class that uses a SoftReference to cache objects loaded from the database.

> **BEST PRACTICE**   If you are building your own persistence system, implement an efficient caching scheme to prevent exhausting system resources.

A `SoftReference` is a special kind of object in `java.lang.ref` that creates a *soft reference* to the object it stores. In Java, references between objects are generally *strong references*. For example:

```
StringBuffer buffer = new StringBuffer();
```

The reference to `buffer` is a strong reference. The strong reference is in force as long as the reference is in scope. If the references fall out of scope, then the object is said to be no longer strongly reachable. It is thus potentially available for garbage collection.

A soft reference is a reference via a `SoftReference` object. By storing an object indirectly through a `SoftReference` instead of directly, you make the object available for potential garbage collection while still maintaining the ability to access the object until it is garbage collected.

The `Cache` class implements the Java `Collection` interface. Internally, it even uses a `HashMap` internally to store data. When an application loads an object from the database, it can put it in the cache using the `cache()` method:

```
public void cache(Object key, Object val) {
    cache.put(key, new SoftReference(val));
}
```

This method creates a soft reference around the business object and then stores the soft reference in the internal `HashMap`. As time goes by and the business object is no longer in use, the soft reference will expire and the memory the business object occupies will be freed. The code that checks for the existence of a specific business object in the cache thus needs to verify that the soft reference has not expired:

```
public boolean contains(Object ob) {
    Iterator it = cache.values().iterator();

    while( it.hasNext() ) {
        SoftReference ref = (SoftReference)it.next();
        Object item = ref.get();

        if( item != null && ob.equals(item) ) {
            return true;
        }
    }
    return false;
}
```

The get() method has to perform similar checks:

```
public Object get(Object key) {
    SoftReference ref = (SoftReference)cache.get(key);
    Object ob;

    if( ref == null ) {
        return null;
    }
    ob = ref.get();
```

```
        if( ob == null ) {
            release(key);
        }
        return ob;
    }
```

A Guest Book Application

To illustrate these most fundamental persistence concepts, I will use a simple Guest Book JSP application from my web site. You can see this example in action at *http://george.reese.name/guestbook.jsp*. The Guest Book enables visitors to a web site to leave comments and view the comments left by others. To prevent abuse, the application also includes an administrative approval mechanism. The full code for the Guest Book can be found on O'Reilly's FTP site.

In accordance with the common persistence design patterns described earlier in the chapter, this application divides into view, control, business, data access, and data storage logic. Figure 4-1 is a UML class diagram illustrating this division.

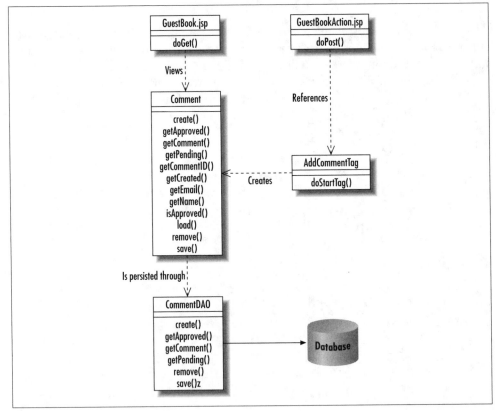

Figure 4-1. A UML class diagram for the Guest Book application

The view and control logic exist in two separate JSP pages. These JSP pages reference a Comment object containing the business logic. They are blissfully ignorant of any persistence logic—or of the existence of persistence at all. The Comment object, however, knows only that its data is persisted, but not *how* that data is persisted, because it delegates its data access through a CommentDAO data access object.

I have chosen here to break down the data access even further, into individual objects supporting specific database operations. Without this trick, the data access object fills up with a jumble of SQL and JDBC that becomes difficult to manage.

The View

The view is a JSP page that displays a form and then lists all approved comments. Example 4-1 contains the code for this JSP.

Example 4-1. A JSP view that lists comments and accepts new ones

```jsp
<%@ page info="Guest Book Form" %>

<%@ page import="java.util.ArrayList" %>
<%@ page import="org.dasein.gb.Comment" %>

<%@ taglib uri="/WEB-INF/tlds/dasein.tld" prefix="dasein" %>

<jsp:useBean id="user" scope="session" class="org.dasein.security.User"/>

<% pageContext.setAttribute("user", user); %>

<% String d = request.getParameter("done"); %>
<% boolean done = ((d==null) ? false : d.trim().equalsIgnoreCase("true")); %>
<% String email, name, comment; %>

<% email = request.getParameter(Comment.EMAIL); %>
<% name = request.getParameter(Comment.NAME); %>
<% comment = request.getParameter(Comment.COMMENT); %>
<% if( user != null ) { %>
  <% String fn = user.getFirstName( ); %>
  <% String ln = user.getLastName( ); %>

  <% name = ((fn == null) ? "" : (fn + " ")) + ((ln == null) ? "" : ln); %>
  <% email = user.getEmail( ); %>
<% } %>
<% if( email == null ) { %>
  <% email = ""; %>
<% } else { %>
  <% email = email.trim( ); %>
<% } %>
<% if( name == null ) { %>
  <% name = ""; %>
<% } else { %>
  <% name = name.trim( ); %>
```

Example 4-1. A JSP view that lists comments and accepts new ones (continued)

```
<% } %>
<% if( comment == null ) { %>
  <% comment = ""; %>
<% } else { %>
  <% comment = comment.trim( ); %>
<% } %>

<% String err = request.getParameter("errorID"); %>
<% if( err != null ) { %>
  <% err = err.trim( ); %>
  <% if( err.length( ) < 1 ) { %>
    <% err = null; %>
  <% } %>
<% } %>
<% if( err != null ) { %>
  <dasein:printError/>
<% } else if( done ) { %>
  <p class="text">
    Thank you for your comment! I will review the comment. Assuming
    you did nothing offensive, it will appear below after I review it.
  </p>
<% } %>
<% if( !done ) { %>
  <p class="text">
    <form method="POST" action="guestbook-action.jsp">
      <label class="text" for="<%=Comment.NAME%>">Name:</label>
      <input id="<%=Comment.NAME%>" type="text" name="<%=Comment.NAME%>"
          value="<%=name%>" size="25"/>
      <br/><br/>
      <label class="text" for="<%=Comment.EMAIL%>">Email:</label>
      <input id="<%=Comment.EMAIL%>" type="text" name="<%=Comment.EMAIL%>"
          value="<%=email%>" size="25"/>
      <br/><br/>
      <label class="text" for="<%=Comment.COMMENT%>">Comments:</label>
      <br/>
      <textarea id="<%=Comment.COMMENT%>" name="<%=Comment.COMMENT%>"
            wrap="virtual" rows="10"
            cols="60"/><dasein:clean><%=comment%></dasein:clean></textarea>
      <br/>
      <input type="submit" value="Submit"/>
    </form>
  </p>
<% } %>
<h3 class="section">Comments</h3>
<dl class="guestbook">
  <% ArrayList cmts = Comment.getApproved( ); %>
  <% pageContext.setAttribute("cmts", cmts); %>
  <dasein:foreach id="cmt" source="cmts" className="org.dasein.gb.Comment">
    <dt>On <%= cmt.getCreated( ) %>, <%=cmt.getName( )%> wrote:</dt>
    <dd><%=cmt.getComment( )%></dd>
  </dasein:foreach>
</dl>
```

The first part of this example pulls CGI (Common Gateway Interface) parameters into Java variables. It is specifically looking for all of the form fields as well as a done parameter and an errorID parameter. As we will see in the controller, whenever an error occurs, it sets the errorID parameter and redisplays the view. If any field values are passed in, it uses those values as default values for the form. On success, it will redisplay the list of comments—minus the form.

After the initial parameter parsing logic, it displays a form unless the done parameter was set. Finally, the page uses a tag library containing a looping construct in the form of the dasein:foreach tag. For each comment it pulls from the Comment.getApproved( ) call, it displays the data from the comment.

The Controller

The form from the view posts to the controller page. Example 4-2 shows this simple code.

Example 4-2. The Guest Book controller that handles new comments

```
<%@ page info="Guest Book Action" %>

<%@ taglib uri="/WEB-INF/tlds/dasein.tld" prefix="dasein" %>
<%@ taglib uri="/WEB-INF/tlds/guestbook.tld" prefix="guestbook" %>

<%@ page import="org.dasein.jsp.Log" %>

<guestbook:addComment error="error">
  <% response.sendRedirect("guestbook-form.jsp?done=true"); %>
</guestbook:addComment>

<dasein:isNull name="error">
  <dasein:when state="false">
    <jsp:include page="guestbook-form.jsp">
      <jsp:param name="errorID" value="<%=Log.storeException(error)%>"/>
    </jsp:include>
  </dasein:when>
</dasein:isNull>
```

The complexity of this action controller is hidden inside a couple of tag libraries. The first is the guestbook:addComment tag. It triggers the action of adding a new comment to the database. On success, the body of the comment is executed. In this case, the body of the comment redirects to the view page with the done parameter set.

> **BEST PRACTICE**   Delegate controller logic in JavaServer Pages through custom tags.

The special tag dasein:isNull will execute the body of the tag if the specified value—in this case, error—is a null value. In this page, error will be null only if an error occurred while attempting to add a comment. It therefore stores the error message for later retrieval and displays the view page again so that the user may correct the error.

As you can see from this simple page, a controller does not do much in and of itself. It simply acts as a traffic cop, determining what should actually happen in response to a user action. In this case, it triggers an event in the business object through a tag library. The code in the tag library is shown in Example 4-3.

Example 4-3. A custom tag to trigger business logic

```
public int doStartTag( ) throws JspException {
    try {
        ServletRequest request = pageContext.getRequest( );
        String name = request.getParameter(Comment.NAME);
        String email = request.getParameter(Comment.EMAIL);
        String comment = request.getParameter(Comment.COMMENT);
        HashMap data = new HashMap( );
        Comment cmt;

        if( name != null ) {
            name = name.trim( );
            if( name.length( ) < 1 ) {
                name = null;
            }
        }
        if( name == null ) {
            if( error != null ) {
                pageContext.setAttribute(error, NO_NAME);
                error = null;
                return SKIP_BODY;
            }
            else {
                throw new JspException(NO_NAME);
            }
        }
        data.put(Comment.NAME, name);
        if( email != null ) {
            email = email.trim( );
            if( email.length( ) < 1 ) {
                email = null;
            }
        }
        data.put(Comment.EMAIL, email);
        if( comment != null ) {
            comment = comment.trim( );
            if( comment.length( ) < 1 ) {
                comment = null;
            }
        }
        if( comment == null ) {
            if( error != null ) {
                pageContext.setAttribute(error, NO_COMMENT);
                error = null;
```

Example 4-3. A custom tag to trigger business logic (continued)

```
                return SKIP_BODY;
            }
            else {
                throw new JspException(NO_COMMENT);
            }
        }
        data.put(Comment.COMMENT, comment);
        cmt = Comment.create(data);
        pageContext.setAttribute(error, null);
        return EVAL_BODY_TAG;
    }
    catch( PersistenceException e ) {
        if( error != null ) {
            pageContext.setAttribute(error, "<p class=\"error\">" +
                                     e.getMessage() +"</p>");

            error = null;
            return SKIP_BODY;
        }
        else {
            throw new JspException(e.getMessage());
        }
    }
}
```

This tag library reads all of the form parameters and validates them. If they are not valid values, it sets an error value and ignores its body. Valid values are stuck in a HashMap that acts as a memento. This memento is then passed to the Comment.create( ) method to create a·new comment in the database.

The Business Object (Model)

Business objects form the heart of any major application. They model the underlying concepts of the application's problem domain. In the case of the Guest Book, the underlying concepts are users and the comments they leave behind. For simplicity's sake, we are not capturing users as objects in this system. In a more complex system, we probably would.

The only business object being modeled here, then, is the Comment object. The *guestbook-form.jsp* view is, in short, a view of Comment objects. The Comment business object encapsulates everything there is about being a comment. It stores comment data captured in the comment forms and manages the creation, deletion, approval, and retrieval of comments. These operations have two elements:

* Metaoperations such as creation and retrieval of comments via static methods
* Object-specific operations via instance methods

Example 4-4 contains the meta-operations.

Example 4-4. The metaoperations of the Comment business object

```java
package org.dasein.gb;

import java.util.ArrayList;
import java.util.Date;
import java.util.HashMap;
import java.util.Iterator;

import org.dasein.gb.persist.CommentDAO;
import org.dasein.persist.PersistenceException;
import org.dasein.persist.Sequencer;
import org.dasein.util.Cache;

public class Comment {
    static private final Cache cache = new Cache();

    static public final String APPROVED   = "approved";
    static public final String COMMENT    = "comment";
    static public final String COMMENT_ID = "commentID";
    static public final String CREATED    = "created";
    static public final String EMAIL      = "email";
    static public final String NAME       = "name";

    static public Comment create(HashMap data) throws PersistenceException {
        Sequencer seq = Sequencer.getInstance(Comment.COMMENT_ID);
        Comment cmt;
        Long id;

        id = new Long(seq.next());
        data.put(Comment.COMMENT_ID, id);
        CommentDAO.create(data);
        cmt = new Comment(id, data);
        synchronized( cache ) {
            cache.cache(id, cmt);
        }
        return cmt;
    }

    static public ArrayList getApproved() throws PersistenceException {
        Iterator results = CommentDAO.getApproved().iterator();
        ArrayList cmts = new ArrayList();

        while( results.hasNext() ) {
            Long id = (Long)results.next();

            cmts.add(Comment.getComment(id.longValue()));
        }
        return cmts;
    }
```

```
    static public Comment getComment(long cid) throws PersistenceException {
        Long id = new Long(cid);

        synchronized( cache ) {
            Comment cmt = (Comment)cache.get(id);

            if( cmt == null ) {
                HashMap data = CommentDAO.getComment(cid);

                data.put(Comment.COMMENT_ID, id);
                cmt = new Comment(id, data);
                cache.cache(id, cmt);
            }
            return cmt;
        }
    }

    static public ArrayList getPending( ) throws PersistenceException {
        Iterator results = CommentDAO.getPending( ).iterator( );
        ArrayList cmts = new ArrayList( );

        while( results.hasNext( ) ) {
            Long id = (Long)results.next( );

            cmts.add(Comment.getComment(id.longValue( )));
        }
        return cmts;
    }
}
```

In addition to representing a comment, the Comment class acts as a factory that contains four meta-operations:

create( )
> Creates new comment objects

getApproved( )
> Retrieves all approved comments

getComment( )
> Retrieves a specific comment by its comment ID

getPending( )
> Retrieves all comments awaiting approval

The central data element for these operations is the comment cache stored in the static cache attribute. This cache uses the Cache class described earlier in the chapter. Whenever a comment is sought externally, this cache is checked first to see if the desired Comment instance has already been loaded. If not, the class will go to the data access object to load a new instance from the database. Otherwise, we can avoid a costly trip to the database and pull the object straight from the cache.

You probably also notice the constants defined at the top of the class. We saw them referenced earlier in the view page. It is simply a solid coding practice never to use literals in code. Instead, you should use constants like these to help avoid application bugs caused by spelling errors.

```java
private Boolean approved  = null;
private String  comment   = null;
private Long    commentID = null;
private Date    created   = null;
private String  email     = null;
private String  name      = null;

private Comment(Long cid, HashMap data) {
    super();
    commentID = cid;
    load(data);
}

public String getComment() {
    return comment;
}

public long getCommentID() {
    return commentID.longValue();
}

public Date getCreated() {
    return created;
}

public String getEmail() {
    return email;
}

public String getName() {
    return name;
}

public boolean isApproved() {
    return approved.booleanValue();
}

private void load(HashMap data) {
    approved = (Boolean)data.get(Comment.APPROVED);
    comment = (String)data.get(Comment.COMMENT);
    commentID = (Long)data.get(Comment.COMMENT_ID);
    created = (Date)data.get(Comment.CREATED);
    email = (String)data.get(Comment.EMAIL);
```

```
        name = (String)data.get(Comment.NAME);
    }

    public void remove( ) throws PersistenceException {
        HashMap data = new HashMap( );

        data.put(Comment.COMMENT_ID, commentID);
        CommentDAO.remove(data);
        synchronized( cache ) {
            cache.release(commentID);
        }
    }

    public void save(HashMap data) throws PersistenceException {
        data.put(Comment.COMMENT_ID, commentID);
        CommentDAO.save(data);
        load(data);
    }
}
```

The instance operations are largely simple getter methods. The exceptions are the following:

load( )
:   The load method pulls data from our HashMap memento and assigns that data to instance variables.

remove( )
:   The remove( ) method deletes the object and removes it from the cache.

save( )
:   The save( ) method tells the data access object to save changes to the comment.

The most critical thing to notice about the business object is that it hides all knowledge about persistence from the view and the controller. The view and controller simply do not need to know if the object persists or how it persists. In fact, the business object knows only that it persists—it knows nothing about how it persists. That knowledge is saved for the data access objects.

The Data Access Objects

The data access object, CommentDAO, provides a simple interface to the business object for persisting comments to the database. In short, it has methods to load, delete, update, and create comments. When the methods require data from the comment, the data is passed via a memento. They throw generic persistence exceptions. The data access object thus needs to know nothing about the internal structure of comments, and comments need to know nothing about the persistence details of the data access object. Example 4-5 contains the code for the CommentDAO class.

Example 4-5. The CommentDAO data access object

```java
package org.dasein.gb.persist;

import java.util.ArrayList;
import java.util.HashMap;

import org.dasein.gb.Comment;
import org.dasein.persist.Execution;
import org.dasein.persist.PersistenceException;

public abstract class CommentDAO {
    static public void create(HashMap data) throws PersistenceException {
        CreateComment.getInstance().execute(data);
    }

    static public ArrayList getApproved() throws PersistenceException {
        HashMap data = new HashMap();

        data.put(Comment.APPROVED, new Boolean(true));
        data = ListComments.getInstance().execute(data);
        return (ArrayList)data.get(ListComments.COMMENTS);
    }

    static public HashMap getComment(long cid) throws PersistenceException {
        HashMap data = new HashMap();

        data.put(Comment.COMMENT_ID, new Long(cid));
        data = LoadComment.getInstance().execute(data);
        return data;
    }

    static public ArrayList getPending() throws PersistenceException {
        HashMap data = new HashMap();

        data.put(Comment.APPROVED, new Boolean(false));
        data = ListComments.getInstance().execute(data);
        return (ArrayList)data.get(ListComments.COMMENTS);
    }

    static public void save(HashMap data) throws PersistenceException {
        SaveComment.getInstance().execute(data);
    }

    static public void remove(HashMap data) throws PersistenceException {
        RemoveComment.getInstance().execute(data);
    }
}
```

This data access object further delegates to operation-specific objects to avoid clutter in this class.

Loading comments

These delegates use the framework I described earlier in the chapter. Example 4-6 shows the LoadComment delegate that performs the SQL to load a comment from the database.

Example 4-6. Loading a comment through a special delegate

```
package org.dasein.gb.persist;

import java.sql.SQLException;
import java.util.HashMap;

import org.dasein.gb.Comment;
import org.dasein.persist.Execution;
import org.dasein.persist.PersistenceException;

public class LoadComment extends Execution {
    static public LoadComment getInstance( ) {
        return (LoadComment)Execution.getInstance(LoadComment.class);
    }

    static private final String LOAD =
        "SELECT approved, email, name, comment, created " +
        "FROM Comment " +
        "WHERE Comment.commentID = ?";

    static private final int COMMENT_ID = 1;

    static private final int APPROVED  = 1;
    static private final int EMAIL     = 2;
    static private final int NAME      = 3;
    static private final int COMMENT   = 4;
    static private final int CREATED   = 5;

    public HashMap run( ) throws PersistenceException, SQLException {
        long id = ((Long)data.get(Comment.COMMENT_ID)).longValue( );
        HashMap res = new HashMap( );
        String tmp;

        statement.setLong(COMMENT_ID, id);
        results = statement.executeQuery( );
        if( !results.next( ) ) {
            throw new PersistenceException("No such comment: " + id);
        }
        tmp = results.getString(APPROVED);
        res.put(Comment.APPROVED,
                new Boolean(tmp.trim( ).equalsIgnoreCase("Y")));
        tmp = results.getString(EMAIL);
        if( results.wasNull( ) ) {
            res.put(Comment.EMAIL, null);
```

Example 4-6. Loading a comment through a special delegate (continued)

```
            }
            else {
                res.put(Comment.EMAIL, tmp.trim());
            }
            res.put(Comment.NAME, results.getString(NAME));
            res.put(Comment.COMMENT, results.getString(COMMENT));
            res.put(Comment.CREATED, results.getDate(CREATED));
            return res;
        }

        public String getDataSource() {
            return "jdbc/george";
        }

        public String getStatement() {
            return LOAD;
        }
    }
}
```

You should notice here again the liberal use of constants instead of literals through-out the code. This practice is very important in JDBC programming since the most efficient way to access columns in a result set is by column number.

> **BEST PRACTICE**   Access JDBC columns by number and use constants to keep those column values readable and maintainable.

The code executes a SQL SELECT and places the result into a memento. That memento goes back to the calling business object, which then sends it through the business object's load() method. If a JDBC error or some other exception occurs, the exception will be wrapped up in a PersistenceException and sent back to the calling business object.

Sequence generation

Throughout this book, I reference the best practice of relying on your own, database-independent primary key generation mechanism. No discussion of the data access tier would be complete without a discussion of primary key generation.

Every database engine provides a feature that enables applications to automatically generate values for identity columns. MySQL, for example, has the concept of AUTO_INCREMENT columns:

```
CREATE TABLE Person (
    personID    BIGINT UNSIGNED NOT NULL PRIMARY KEY AUTO_INCREMENT,
    lastName    VARCHAR(30)     NOT NULL,
    firstName   VARCHAR(25)     NOT NULL
);
```

When you insert a new person into this table, you omit the primary key columns:

```
INSERT INTO Person ( lastName, firstName)
VALUES ( 'Wittgenstein', 'Ludwig' );
```

MySQL will automatically generate the value for the personID column based on the highest current value. If one row exists in the database with a personID of 1, Ludwig Wittgenstein's personID will be 2. Some other databases have similar ways to generate primary keys; others provide wildly different tools.

Reliance on your database engine's primary key generation tools has the following drawbacks:

- Every database engine handles key generation differently. It is thus difficult to build a truly portable JDBC application that uses proprietary key generation schemes.

- Until JDBC 3.0, a Java application had no clear way of finding out what keys were generated on an insert.

- In many databases, you can autogenerate only a single unique value per table.

- In many databases, you cannot use the primary key generation mechanism to generate values unique across multiple tables.

I recommend the development of a database-independent primary key generation API that stores potential primary key values in the database. If you take this approach, you need to take care not to make too many trips to the database. You can avoid this pitfall by generating keys in memory and storing seed values in the database.

The heart of this database-independent scheme is the following table:

```
CREATE TABLE Sequencer (
    name        VARCHAR(20)     NOT NULL,
    seed        BIGINT UNSIGNED NOT NULL,
    lastUpdate  BIGINT UNSIGNED NOT NULL,
    PRIMARY KEY ( name, lastUpdate )
);
```

The first time your application generates a key, it grabs the next seed from this table, increments the seed, and then uses that seed to generate keys until the seed is exhausted. Examples 4-7 through 4-9 contain some of the code for a database-independent utility that handles unique number generation. It enables your application to simply use the following calls to create primary keys:

```
Sequencer seq = Sequencer.getInstance("personID");

personID = seq.next( );
```

The tool guarantees that you will receive a value that is unique across all personID values. Example 4-7 contains the static elements that implement the singleton design pattern to hand out shared sequencers.

Example 4-7. The code to serve up sequencers

```
public class Sequencer {
    static private final long     MAX_KEYS  = 1000000L;
    static private final HashMap sequencers = new HashMap( );

    static public final Sequencer getInstance(String name) {
        synchronized( sequencers ) {
            if( !sequencers.containsKey(name) ) {
                Sequencer seq = new Sequencer(name);

                sequencers.put(name, seq);
                return seq;
            }
            else {
                return (Sequencer)sequencers.get(name);
            }
        }
    }

    ...
}
```

The code provides two critical guarantees for sequence generation:

- All code that needs to create new numbers for the same sequence (like personID) will share the same sequencer object.

- Because of the synchronized block, two attempts to get a previously unreferenced sequence at the same instant will not cause two different sequencers to be generated.

The attribute declarations and initialization for a sequencer define two attributes that correspond to values in the Sequencer table as well as a third attribute, sequence, to track the values handed out for the current seed, as shown in Example 4-8.

Example 4-8. Setting up the sequencer

```
private String name      = null;
private long   seed      = -1L;
private long   sequence = 0L;

private Sequencer(String nom) {
    super( );
    name = nom;
}
```

The core element of the sequencer—its public API—is the next( ) method. It contains the algorithm for generating unique numbers. The algorithm has the following process:

- Check to see if the seed is valid. The seed is invalid if this is a newly generated sequencer or if the seed is exhausted. A seed is exhausted if the next sequence has a value greater than MAX_KEYS.

- If the seed is not valid, get a new seed from the database.

- Increment the sequence.

- Multiply the seed by MAX_KEYS and add that value to the incremented sequence. This is the unique key.

Example 4-9 contains the algorithm.

Example 4-9. Generating a sequence ID

```
public synchronized long next( ) throws PersistenceException {
    Connection conn = null;

    // when seed is -1 or the keys for this seed are exhausted,
    // get a new seed from the database
    if( (seed == -1L) || ((sequence + 1) >= MAX_KEYS) ) {
        try {
            String dsn = System.getProperty(DSN_PROP, DEFAULT_DSN);
            InitialContext ctx = new InitialContext( );
            DataSource ds = (DataSource)ctx.lookup(dsn);

            conn = ds.getConnection( );
            reseed(conn);
        }
        catch( SQLException e ) {
            throw new PersistenceException(e);
        }
        catch( NamingException e ) {
            throw new PersistenceException(e);
        }
        finally {
            if( conn != null ) {
                try { conn.close( ); }
                catch( SQLException e ) { }
            }
        }
    }
    // up the sequence value for the next key
    sequence++;
    // the next key for this sequencer
    return ((seed * MAX_KEYS) + sequence);
}
```

The rest of the code is the database access that creates, retrieves, and updates seeds in the database. The next( ) method triggers a database call via the reseed( ) method when the seed ceases to be valid.

The logic for reseeding the sequencer is fairly straightforward:

- Fetch the current values for the sequence in question from the database.

- If the sequence does not yet exist in the database, create it.

- Increment the seed from the database.

- Update the database
- Set the new seed and reset the sequence attribute to −1 (this makes the first number generated 0).

You can find the full code for the Sequencer class on O'Reilly's FTP site in the directory for this book.

CHAPTER 5

EJB CMP

Blessed are the sleepy ones:
for they shall soon doze off.
—Friedrich Nietzsche
Also Sprach Zarathustra

Container-managed persistence (CMP) is a persistence model in which the EJB container worries about persistence issues while you worry about business logic management. Under the CMP model, you leave most of the EJB persistence methods—ejbFindXXX( ), ejbLoad( ), ejbStore( ), and ejbRemove( )—empty. Based on a mapping you define in the application's deployment descriptor, the container implements those methods and crafts the SQL to map your beans to the database.

EJB 2.0 CMP is a drastic departure from—and improvement upon—EJB 1.0 CMP. Nevertheless, the majority of systems in production these days are still in EJB 1.x environments. This chapter takes a look at both CMP models and describes how to use them in a production environment. As with any automated persistence mechanism, there is not a lot that EJB CMP requires you as the developer to do. The focus for this chapter is specifically on the aspects of the EJB 1.0 and EJB 2.0 CMP models that most impact persistence issues. Once you understand these concepts, you will find that you are left with almost no persistence coding to do under EJB CMP—all your work lies in setting up the database and writing deployment descriptors.

This chapter assumes you have a basic understanding of Enterprise JavaBeans. It specifically assumes that you know the difference between entity and session beans and are familiar with home interfaces, remote interfaces, and implementation objects. If you do not have this background, you should review the Enterprise JavaBeans section of Chapter 9. I also strongly recommend the book *Enterprise JavaBeans* (O'Reilly) by Richard Monson-Haefel if you intend to do serious programming in an EJB environment.

Which CMP Model to Use?

While container-managed persistence sounds great, the initial EJB implementations of CMP through EJB 1.1 have had some serious drawbacks:

- Most EJB servers will provide automated persistence only against JDBC-supported database engines. If you are using some other data storage product like an object-oriented database or a specialized digital asset management data store, you will have to do the work yourself.

- Container-managed persistence demands that your persistent attributes have public visibility. Public attributes violate a key element of good OO design: encapsulation. Consequently, container-managed beans make it very easy for people to make poor design choices that rely on the public nature of those attributes.

- Container-managed persistence makes it difficult to tweak your data model for maximum performance. For example, if you want to perform lazy-loading of certain attributes, you must use bean-managed persistence.

- Container-managed persistence is incapable of supporting the complex class relationships common to enterprise systems. For example, container-managed persistence cannot support some one-to-many or many-to-many relationships. If your analysis models require those kinds of relationships, your architecture must use an alternative persistence model.

 Lazy-loading is a technique through which certain attributes in an object are not restored from the database immediately but are instead restored in a background thread or when the system asks for that data. A Country object, for example, may be associated with quite a few cities—likely more cities than you want to load into memory when most clients are looking only for the name and ISO code for the country. Using lazy-loading, you can put off loading all associated cities until a later time.

In spite of its drawbacks, EJB 1.x CMP does have some redeeming qualities. Specifically, it is a great tool if you are writing a simple application but you do not want to worry about the database at all. By *simple application*, I mean an application that has no complex dependencies among entity beans and whose attributes are primitives or serializable objects. The minute the slightest complexity enters the picture or you need to control the data model, EJB 1.x CMP falls apart.

> **BEST PRACTICE**   Use CMP—especially EJB 2.0 CMP—whenever possible, but be prepared to use BMP if EJB 2.0 CMP is not an option.

The EJB 1.0 CMP Model

EJB 1.x CMP generates the code to map persistent entity bean fields to columns in a relational database. Under this model, you can map only Java primitives and serializable fields. You cannot, for the most part, map entity beans or any other nonserializable Java object. Table 5-1 shows the attributes of two analysis-level business objects: an Author class and a Book class.

Table 5-1. The attributes of two business objects and EJB 1.x CMP's ability to manage them

Class	Attribute	Type	Manageable by EJB 1.x CMP?
Author	authorID	long	Yes
	firstName	String	Yes
	lastName	String	Yes
Book	bookID	long	Yes
	author	Author	No
	title	String	Yes

EJB 1.1 introduced the ability to map entity bean references to the database. The actual implementation of this support, unfortunately, varies from container to container. As a general rule, you should store the primary keys of any entity bean references and let the request object map it to the entity reference. The Book bean in Table 5-1, for example, could have an authorID field instead of an author field. Example 5-1 shows this approach.

Example 5-1. A container-managed Book bean that references an Author bean

```
package book;

import javax.ejb.EntityBean;
import javax.ejb.EntityContext;

public class BookEntity implements EntityBean {
    public Long          authorID;

    public Long          bookID;
    public EntityContext context;
    public String        title;

    public void ejbActivate() {
    }

    public Long ejbCreate(Long bid, Long aid, String ttl) {
        bookID = bid;
        authorID = aid;
        title= ttl;
```

```java
        return null;
    }

    public void ejbLoad( ) {
    }

    public void ejbPassivate( ) {
    }

    public void ejbPostCreate(Long bid, Long aid, String ttl) {
    }

    public void ejbRemove( ) {
    }

    public void ejbStore( ) {
    }

    public Long getAuthorID( ) {
        return authorID;
    }
    public Long getBookID( ) {
        return bookID;
    }

    public String getTitle( ) {
        return title;
    }

    public void setEntityContext(EntityContext ctx) {
        context = ctx;
    }

    public void unsetEntityContext( ) {
        context = null;
    }
}
```

I will discuss the details of this class later. If I have code that needs the author of the book, I can get the `authorID` and then request the `Author` by its primary key:

```java
public Author getBookAuthor(Book book) throws Exception {
    Context ctx = new InitialContext();
    Object ref = ctx.lookup("java:comp/env/Author");
    AuthorHome home =
     (AuthorHome)PortableRemoteObject.narrow(ref, AuthorHome.class);

    return home.findByPrimaryKey(book.getAuthorID( ));
}
```

This approach has two virtues. First, it avoids the lack of ability in EJB 1.x CMP to map between entities. Second, it creates the same effect as lazy-loading by loading the Author only when a client actually needs access to it.

Field Mapping

One of the weaknesses in the EJB 1.x CMP model lies in how it maps attributes to the database. Each container provides its own mechanism for defining the mapping between an entity bean and a table. In most cases, you can use a GUI tool that enables you to relate a bean attribute to a relational column. If you do not care at all about the underlying data model, you can simply write up an XML deployment descriptor that enumerates the entity attributes to be mapped. Example 5-2 shows a sample deployment descriptor.

Example 5-2. A sample EJB deployment descriptor

```
<?xml version="1.0"?>
<!DOCTYPE ejb-jar
    PUBLIC "-//Sun Microsystems, Inc.//DTD Enterprise JavaBeans 1.2//EN"
    "http://java.sun.com/j2ee/dtds/ejb-jar_1_2.dtd">

<ejb-jar>
  <description>
  </description>
  <enterprise-beans>
    <entity>
      <description>
      </description>
      <ejb-name>BookBean</ejb-name>
      <home>book.BookHome</home>
      <remote>book.Book</remote>
      <ejb-class>book.BookEntity</ejb-class>
      <primkey-class>java.lang.Long</primkey-class>
      <reentrant>False</reentrant>
      <persistence-type>Container</persistence-type>
      <cmp-field><field-name>bookID</field-name></cmp-field>
      <cmp-field><field-name>title</field-name></cmp-field>
      <cmp-field><field-name>authorID</field-name></cmp-field>
      <primkey-field>bookID</primkey-field>
    </entity>
    <entity>
      <description>
      </description>
      <ejb-name>AuthorBean</ejb-name>
      <home>book.AuthorHome</home>
      <remote>book.Author</remote>
      <ejb-class>book.AuthorEntity</ejb-class>
      <primkey-class>java.lang.Long</primkey-class>
```

Example 5-2. A sample EJB deployment descriptor (continued)

```
        <reentrant>False</reentrant>
        <persistence-type>Container</persistence-type>
        <cmp-field><field-name>authorID</field-name></cmp-field>
        <cmp-field><field-name>firstName</field-name></cmp-field>
        <cmp-field><field-name>lastName</field-name></cmp-field>
        <primkey-field>authorID</primkey-field>
      </entity>
    </enterprise-beans>
    <assembly-descriptor>
      <container-transaction>
        <method>
          <ejb-name>BookBean</ejb-name>
          <method-name>*</method-name>
        </method>
        <trans-attribute>NotSupported</trans-attribute>
      </container-transaction>
      <container-transaction>
        <method>
          <ejb-name>AuthorBean</ejb-name>
          <method-name>*</method-name>
        </method>
        <trans-attribute>NotSupported</trans-attribute>
      </container-transaction>
    </assembly-descriptor>
</ejb-jar>
```

This deployment descriptor tells your container that you have created an entity bean with the specified home, remote, and implementation classes. The fields in the `<cmp-field>` tags identify which `BookEntity` attributes should persist to your database.

If you deploy this simplistic application on an Orion Server, it will create a `BookBean` table in your database and set up `bookID`, `title`, and `authorID` columns for you with `bookID` established as the primary key. You do not have to write any JDBC code. You do not have to write any SQL. You do not have to create any tables.

If you have a data model constructed already, you will need to use the proprietary tools that come with your J2EE container to map the bean to the data model. In the case of Orion Server, for example, you can create an *orion-ejb-jar.xml* file to handle custom mappings. Most application servers provide a GUI to help identify the mappings.

Persistence Methods

If you look back to Example 5-1, you will notice that most of the methods required for an EJB entity bean are empty. They are empty because the container is handling the persistence operations for you. The persistence operations that generally contain code under a CMP model are the `ejbCreate( )` and `ejbPostCreate( )` methods.

The container passes both methods the values specified by the client. It calls ejbCreate( ) before persisting the bean to the database and ejbPostCreate( ) afterward. Assuming you have no business logic associated with object creation, the responsibility of ejbCreate( ) is to assign the initial values to the bean:

```
public Long ejbCreate(Long bid, Long aid, String ttl) {
    bookID = bid;
    authorID = aid;
    title= ttl;
    return null;
}
```

The return value has no meaning under CMP. You should therefore return null as I did in the BookEntity class.

You must make sure you assign the primary key value in all ejbCreate( ) methods. You consequently cannot rely on any underlying database tools, such as the MySQL AUTO_INCREMENT feature, to generate primary keys. At the end of Chapter 4, I introduced a database-independent approach to generating unique values. This approach uses a Sequencer object to generate unique long values. The AuthorEntity class takes advantage of the Sequencer:

```
public Long ejbCreate(String fn, String ln) throws CreateException {
    try {
        Sequencer seq = Sequencer.getInstance(AUTHOR_ID);

        authorID = new Long(seq.next( ));
    }
    catch( PersistenceException e ) {
        throw new CreateException(e.getMessage( ));
    }
    firstName = fn;
    lastName = ln;
    return null;
}
```

Instead of requiring the client to worry about primary key generation, the burden has been placed where it belongs—inside the creation logic for the bean.

BEST PRACTICE   Perform primary key generation in your CMP EJB instead of the client.

The container calls ejbPostCreate( ) once the bean is established as a persistent entity to enable you to perform any extra initialization. The state differs at the time of ejbCreate( ) in two significant ways:

- A record is inserted into the database or other persistent store between the two calls.

- The association between the bean and the EJB object is established between the two calls.

Searches

One of the great weaknesses of EJB 1.x CMP is its poor support for searching on anything but the primary key. To search for a book with a specific title, for example, you would add a finder method to your home interface:

```
Collection findByTitle(String ttl)
throws RemoteException, FinderException;
```

The good news is that you do not have to code anything other than the basic search signature in the home interface. The bad news is that there is no container-neutral method for telling an EJB container exactly what findByTitle( ) is supposed to do. Is it supposed to look for exact matches? Is the ttl value being passed a regular expression? The only thing a container knows from a finder method signature is whether that method is expected to find a unique value or multiple hits. The EJB 1.x specifications say nothing about how a container is supposed to identify what you mean to search for. As a result, you must rely on proprietary deployment tools to assist the container in defining your EJB finder methods.

Transactions

Without being flip, I believe it is safe to say that if you need complex transactions you probably should not be using EJB 1.x CMP—you should instead be using 2.x CMP or BMP. You describe the level of transaction support your beans need in the EJB deployment descriptor. The deployment descriptor in Example 5-2 had no transaction support. Indeed, this simple application needed no transaction support.

EJB lets you specify the transaction characteristics of beans on a method-by-method basis as part of the deployment descriptor. The deployment descriptor approach is called *declarative transaction management*. Declarative transaction management is a huge advantage of all EJB persistence models. Whereas most other models require the programmer to manage transaction semantics in code—the hardest part of database programming—EJB does not require the programmer to understand anything about transaction semantics. Only the deployer needs to worry about such things, and the deployer can tweak the transactional attributes of the system without modifying and recompiling code.

 If you are unfamiliar with the basic concepts of transaction management, now is an excellent time to go back and read Chapter 3.

When you deploy a bean—entity or session—you assign it a transactional attribute in the deployment descriptor. The transactional attribute tells the container how to handle transactions for that bean. You can even assign different transactional attributes to different methods within the bean if you desire that level of control. The transactional attributes are:

NotSupported

> No transaction scope is propagated to the method. In other words, if this method is called in the middle of another transaction, that transaction is suspended to allow this method to execute. No transactional context exists for any calls made within this method. Once this method completes, the original transaction resumes.

Supports

> This attribute says that the method in question will act with whatever transaction scope it is executed in. If not called in an existing transactional scope, it will not attempt to create one.

Required

> A method with a Required attribute must be executed in a transactional context. If not called in an existing transactional context, it will initiate a new one.

RequiresNew

> No matter what context in which the method in question is called, this method will create a new transaction context. It will suspend any existing transactional context until it completes.

Mandatory

> The method in question can never initiate its own transactional context—it must always occur inside a caller's transactional context. If it is called without any transactional context, the container will throw an exception.

Never

> The opposite of Mandatory, Never means that the method in question can never be called inside a transactional context. If it is, the container will throw an exception.

The transactional attributes in Example 5-2 were specified in the following lines:

```
<container-transaction>
  <method>
    <ejb-name>BookBean</ejb-name>
    <method-name>*</method-name>
  </method>
  <trans-attribute>NotSupported</trans-attribute>
</container-transaction>
<container-transaction>
  <method>
    <ejb-name>AuthorBean</ejb-name>
    <method-name>*</method-name>
  </method>
  <trans-attribute>NotSupported</trans-attribute>
</container-transaction>
```

This descriptor states that transactions for all methods in both beans are not supported. If for some reason a client calls them within a transactional context, that context will be suspended until the methods in these beans complete.

The `<container-transaction>` tag associates a method with a transactional attribute. Inside the `<method>` tag, I use * for the method name to indicate that the attribute applies to all methods in the specified bean. The `<trans-attribute>` tag is the tag that identifies which transactional attribute to assign. You can override a * value by naming a specific method in a later `<container-transaction>` tag.

I have just touched on the basics of transaction management in the EJB 1.x CMP persistence model. Much of the detail, however, applies both to the BMP and EJB 2.x CMP persistence models, which are covered in the next section and later in this chapter.

The EJB 2.0 CMP Model

EJB 2.0 is a significant, revolutionary improvement over the original EJB specification—especially when it comes to component persistence. Persistence changes include a more solid CMP architecture and a specialized EJB query language (EJBQL) for performing bean searches. Beyond persistence, EJB 2.0 provides for exciting features such as message-driven beans.

Container-Managed Relationships

Under EJB 1.x, container-managed persistence meant the container managed keeping all bean attributes in sync with the data store. This job became problematic for any attributes representing relationships to other beans. The general solution was to store a primary key for the relationship and let clients worry about referencing the other bean.

EJB 2.0 introduces a concept called *container-managed relationships*, or CMR. A CMR field is a bean attribute that is a relationship to another bean. CMR relationships can take any of the following forms:

    One-to-one
    One-to-many
    Many-to-many

In addition, each relationship can be *unidirectional* or *bidirectional*. If, for example, the relationship between Author and Book is unidirectional, I can ask for all books by a specific author but I cannot ask for the author of a specific book. In other words, the Author bean has a reference to its Book instances but the Book bean has no reference to its author. Of course, it would be more appropriate for this particular relationship to be bidirectional, meaning that I can navigate from Author to Book and Book to Author.

> **BEST PRACTICE**   Try to make relationships unidirectional unless absolutely necessary.

CMR basics

You identify CMR relationships in your deployment descriptor inside the <relationships> tag. For each relationship, you specify an ejb-relation element:

```
<ejb-jar>
  ...
  <enterprise-beans>
    <entity>
      <ejb-name>BookEJB</ejb-name>
      <local-home>com.imaginary.ora.BookHome</local-home>
      <local>com.imaginary.ora.Book</local>
      <cmp-version>2.x</cmp-version>
      ...
    </entity>
    <entity>
      <ejb-name>AuthorEJB</ejb-name>
      <local-home>com.imaginary.ora.AuthorHome</local-home>
      <local>com.imaginary.ora.Author</local>
      <cmp-version>2.x</cmp-version>
      ...
    </entity>
  </enterprise-beans>
  <relationships>
    <ejb-relation>
      <ejb-relation-name>Book-Author</ejb-relation-name>
      <ejb-relationship-role>
        <ejb-relationship-role-name>
          A Book has an Author
        </ejb-relationship-role-name>
        <multiplicity>Many</multiplicity>
        <cascade-delete/>
        <relationship-role-source>
          <ejb-name>BookEJB</ejb-name>
        </relationship-role-source>
        <cmr-field>
          <cmr-field-name>author</cmr-field-name>
        </cmr-field>
      </ejb-relationship-role>
      <ejb-relationship-role>
        <ejb-relationship-role-name>
          An Author has many Books
        </ejb-relationship-role-name>
        <multiplicity>One</multiplicity>
        <relationship-role-source>
```

```
      <ejb-name>AuthorEJB</ejb-name>
     </relationship-role-source>
     <cmr-field>
       <cmr-field-name>books</cmr-field-name>
     </cmr-field>
    </ejb-relationship-role>
   </ejb-relation>
  </relationships>
  ...
 </ejb-jar>
```

Though for our purposes the bean declarations themselves are not relevant to persistence, I included part of their declarations to show that the relationships section references by the names you declare in the <ejb-name> tags under the enterprise-beans element.

This deployment descriptor says that an author has many books and a book has one author. The Author bean tracks its books via the CMR field books. Similarly, the Book bean tracks its author by the author CMR field.

You must define a pair of accessor methods—a getter and setter—for any CMR fields you declare. You declare these methods as abstract in the bean implementation class. The return type for the getter and parameter for the setter is a Collection for the "many" side of a one-to-many or many-to-many relationship. You can use implementations of Collection to suit the underlying needs of the relationship: TreeSet instances for ordered lists, Set instances for unique lists, and so on. Similarly, the type for the "one" side of a one-to-one or one-to-many relationship is the local interface.* The Book interface therefore has these methods:

```
public abstract Author getAuthor();

public abstract void setAuthor(Author auth);
```

Similarly, the Author interface includes:

```
public abstract Collection getBooks();

public abstract void setBooks(Collection bks);
```

In practice, you rarely want to set the whole list of books associated with an author at all once. Instead, you probably want to add books as new books are written. You can add other methods such as an addBook( ) method to support these needs. The EJB specification, however, demands that you write at least a getter and setter.

---

* In addition to remote interfaces, EJB 2.0 added the concept of local interfaces for reference within the container.

CMR magic

The beauty of EJB 2.0 CMR is its ability to manage the referential integrity of these relationships. If you assign one bean's collection of relationships to another bean, that collection is automatically removed from the first bean. If you delete the primary bean in a relationship marked in the descriptor with a `<cascade-delete>` tag, its dependent beans are also deleted.* In the sample descriptor, a `Book` will be deleted whenever its `Author` is deleted from the database to prevent us from having books with no authors.

EJB QL

Besides entity relationships, EJB 1.x CMP also had difficulties with searches. The main problem was that you had to write a different finder method to support every way you could possibly search for a bean or set of beans. Furthermore, the semantics of these finder methods left a lot to interpretation. For example, everyone knows what `getTitle()` and `setTitle()` do. Do you know what `findBooksByYear()` does? On the face of it, you would think it would provide all books published in a specific year. However, it can also mean find all books published after a specific year or before a specific year or even by authors born in a specific year. A container simply has no way to know from the EJB 1.x semantics.

Finders

EJB 2.0 introduced a query language called the EJBQL to address these searching issues. The best way to think of EJBQL is as SQL for EJBs. In other words, as SQL enables you to query tables in a relational database, EJBQL lets you query beans in your application.

You define EJBQL queries inside your deployment descriptor:

```
<ejb-jar>
  <enterprise-beans>
    <entity>
      <ejb-name>BookEJB</ejb-name>
      <local-home>com.imaginary.ora.BookHome</local-home>
      <local>com.imaginary.ora.Book</local>
      <cmp-version>2.x</cmp-version>
      <abstract-schema-name>Book</abstract-schema-name>
      <primkey-field>bookID</primkey-field>
      <cmp-field><field-name>title</field-name></cmp-field>
      <query>
        <query-method>
          <method-name>findByTitle</method-name>
          <method-params>
            <method-param>java.lang.String</method-param>
```

---

* This feature is also known as a *cascade delete*.

```
        </method-params>
      </query-method>
      <ejb-ql>
        SELECT OBJECT(b) FROM Book b WHERE b.title = ?1
      </ejb-ql>
    </query>
  </entity>
  ...
</enterprise-beans>
  ...
</ejb-jar>
```

The <query> tag introduces a query that applications can perform on the bean. It has two parts. The first part—<query-method>—describes the external interface, a finder method called findByTitle(String). The second part—<ejb-ql>—describes the actual query. It looks a lot like SQL but is different enough to make you tilt your head sideways.

The key to the EJB QL is the bean's *abstract schema name*. When you construct an EJB QL statement, you reference beans by their abstract schema names. In this example, the Book bean has the abstract schema name of Book. Thus, any time a book is referenced, it is referenced through the Book abstract schema name. Naturally, no two beans can share the same abstract schema name.

Two other pieces to the query are very much *un*-SQL. The first piece is the superfluous function OBJECT( ). It is supposedly an indicator to the container that you expect an EJB reference for that value. Of course, since you specified it as a Book, that desire is rather obvious. Just humor the container and use OBJECT( ) wherever you are referencing an EJB.

The last piece is the ?1 token. This token parallels JDBC prepared statement tokens. The major difference is that you add a parameter number after the ?. Thus ?1 represents the first parameter to the findByXXX( ) method, ?2 the second, and so on.

For the most part, the rest of EJB QL continues to look a lot like SQL—except with less functionality. It is missing many of the functions such as MAX( ) that are basic to SQL.* Furthermore, it has no concept of ordering. A full discussion of EJB QL's syntax is beyond the scope of this book.

You can define a finder method in your home interface to return single instances or collections. It will not matter to the container. It will generate the appropriate code for your finder based on the return type you specify in the interface's declaration for the finder.

---

* Some containers provide container-specific implementations of these missing functions.

Selectors

The audience for finders is external clients and other beans. EJB 2.0 also introduced a brand new class of query methods called selectors. Selectors support internal queries by a bean. In other words, you cannot call a selector externally.

Inside your bean implementation class, you provide abstract declarations for any selectors you desire:

```
public abstract Author ejbSelectWithBook( )
    throws FinderException;
```

This query—which could appear in any bean implementation class that needs it—identifies the author with the specified book. It is accompanied by a deployment descriptor with the following <query> tag:

```
<query>
  <query-method>
    <method-name>ejbSelectWithBook</method-name>
    <method-params>
      <method-param>com.imaginary.ora.Book</method-param>
    </method-params>
  </query-method>
  <ejb-ql>
    SELECT OBJECT(a) FROM Author a IN (a.books) bk WHERE bk = ?1
  </ejb-ql>
</query>
```

In addition to being another way to query for beans, selectors also enable you to query for data from beans:

```
SELECT b.title FROM Book b WHERE b.title LIKE '%rain%'
```

This code provides the titles of all books as a Collection of String instances for the books that have the substring "rain" in their titles.

 You cannot use query parameters in EJBQL LIKE comparisons.

Selectors and finders are very similar animals. As you can see from the ability of selectors to return partial bean data, however, selectors have slightly richer capabilities. The huge difference is their visibility. Selectors are not part of the remote or local bean interfaces; finders are. Finders are meant to enable external components to find beans matching some set of criteria. Selectors, on the other hand, are meant to enable a bean to perform its own arbitrary searches.

Beyond CMP

Container-managed persistence is the ideal. It enables you to build large-scale enterprise applications without worrying about the database. This chapter has described some best practices from a persistence perspective should you choose one of the two CMP models that EJB offers. However, EJB CMP is not a panacea. In the remaining chapters of this section, we will address the options out there that allow you to adhere to standard persistence models.

CHAPTER 6

EJB BMP

> *Beings are, so to speak, interrogated with regard to their being. But if they*
> *are to exhibit the characteristics of their being without falsification, they*
> *must for their part have become accessible in advance as they are in*
> *themselves. The question of being demands that the right access to being*
> *be gained and secured in advance with regard to what it interrogates.*
> —Martin Heidegger
> *Being and Time*

If you want something done right, sometimes you have to do it yourself. This is definitely true of building persistence into EJB 1.x systems. As you read in Chapter 5, EJB 1.x CMP is amazingly simple, but it is also amazingly simplistic. I have already spent enough time on the drawbacks of the model. To address these drawbacks, you may need to handle bean persistence yourself.

This chapter tells you how to handle persistence on your own using the EJB bean-managed persistence (BMP) model. Even if you are interested in some form of container-managed persistence, you should spend some time with this chapter since I cover many issues common to all three EJB persistence models in this chapter. Furthermore, through an understanding of the detailed mechanics of the BMP model, you will have a better understanding of the magic you are taking for granted under container-managed models.

EJBs Revisited

As in the chapters before this one, I here assume that you have a basic understanding of Enterprise JavaBeans. Chapter 9 provides an introduction to Enterprise JavaBeans that you should review if you do not have this foundation. Nevertheless, I want to start off with a review of the basic elements of the EJB architecture. If you have no experience with Enterprise JavaBeans, you will find this review lacking. I therefore recommend going through a book on the subject such as *Enterprise JavaBeans* (O'Reilly) by Richard Monson-Haefel to go in depth into EJB programming.

The Components of a Bean

Figure 6-1 is a UML class diagram that shows all of the elements of a single entity bean.

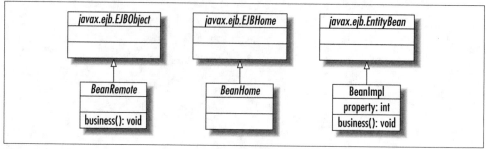

Figure 6-1. The classes that make up a single EJB

Each EJB requires three classes:

- A home interface
- A remote interface
- An implementation class

Though coding three classes to manage one basic business concept can be tedious, many IDEs manage that tedium for you these days.

The home interface identifies the metaoperations that control the bean at a class level. It manages the creation of new instances, the deletion of instances, and the searching for bean instances. It is basically your gateway to the bean.

The remote interface defines the public business operations supported by the bean. You include in this interface only those operations you want clients to be able to trigger.

Finally, the implementation class is where your attention should be focused. It is not an implementation of either the home or remote interfaces—though you do have to implement some of the methods they prescribe. The EJB container generates classes to implement your home and remote interfaces. Those container-generated classes delegate their behavior to the actual business logic that you write in the implementation class. It also handles the persistence operations I will be describing later in the chapter.

You create the server side of an EJB application by putting together a set of session and entity beans to support your business transactions and the logic behind them. Session beans manage the business transactions and entity beans manage the persistent concepts involved in those transactions. For example, in Chapter 5, I introduced two entity beans: a book and an author. If we were to create a library system that enabled you to manage books in a library, you might have a "front desk" session bean to handle check-in and check-out operations. Figure 6-2 illustrates these dynamics.

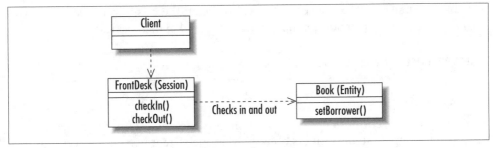

Figure 6-2. Session and entity beans working together

Kinds of Beans

The core persistent elements in any EJB system are the entity beans. They represent the concepts in your problem domain that transcend the particulars of workflow. If you were to build a travel reservations system, for example, you would have core concepts like a seat on a plane, a room in a hotel, or a rental car. No matter what kind of travel agency you have—business travel or leisure travel, major agency or a one-person shop—these concepts will not vary.

In an enterprise system, entity beans represent those timeless concepts that operate independent of the particulars of the workflows in which they are managed. What vary are the workflows that describe the way in which these timeless things interact. For example, the rules governing the booking of travel for business travel vary greatly from the rules for leisure travel. Session beans are the EJB tools for describing those rules.

Entity beans

Under the initial EJB paradigm published by Sun, an entity bean was any persistent object. As people began developing EJBs, they found that treating entity beans so narrowly resulted in unworkable applications. Looking back to the example of the card catalog from the previous chapter, a client application listing books might be inclined to call getBookID( ) and getTitle( ) on each book to display the list in a table.

While elegant in theory, this approach is unworkable in practice. The first problem is that long lists of entities end up being loaded into memory on the server when only a subset of data from a handful of them is required. For a travel reservations system in which a client will pull from a list of thousands of flights, the result is a system that cannot meet performance demands.

Another problem with this approach is the need to make multiple network calls to get the necessary data. For each book in the list, the client makes two network calls—one for each method. It also needs to make a network call for the initial bean lookup and another call for the subsequent book search.

These days, EJB developers hide entity beans from clients using a variety of techniques I will cover throughout this chapter. The entity bean is still the ultimate representation of transcendental business concepts. Instead of being the business concept as it was originally intended, it can now be thought of as the soul of the business concept.

BEST PRACTICE   Never access entity beans from client applications.

Session beans

As entity beans were designed as persistent business objects, session beans were designed as nonpersistent business objects. A nonpersistent business object is a business object that exists, at most, for the lifetime of the application instance. A user session in a web application is the eponymous example of a concept that should be represented as a session bean. The user session exists only as long as the user is logged in. When the user goes away, the session goes away.

As we shall see as we dive deeper into this chapter, session beans have become the windows through which client applications access the system. Through them, you execute transactions and gain access to the information encapsulated in entity beans.

Message-driven beans

The EJB 2.0 specification introduced a new kind of bean, the message-driven bean. Unlike regular beans, message-driven beans are asynchronous. In other words, a client calls one of their methods and returns immediately. The logic—generally involving sending messages to external systems—happens in another thread. Practically speaking, message-driven beans enable you to build EJB components that interact with Java Message Service (JMS) API–supported messaging services like IBM Websphere MQ.

BMP Patterns

The fundamental philosophy behind bean-managed persistence is that the EJB container manages the components and the transactions while you manage their persistence. The container tells you when interactions with the data store need to take place, and you make those interactions happen. The persistence patterns I described in Chapter 4 are therefore critical to bean-managed persistence. Figure 6-3 places the library business objects from Figure 6-2 into a real world BMP system.

To support three basic concepts, I have added a host of new classes. Some of them—such as the data access objects—provide direct support for bean-managed persistence. Others—like the value objects—are useful to real world EJB applications no matter what persistence model you follow.

As you can see from Figure 6-3, programming in an EJB context brings with it a lot of overhead. That overhead is necessary to support large-scale enterprise applications that require clustering, high-availability, and robust transaction management. If you have a fairly simple application, the use of EJBs will make that application unnecessarily complex.

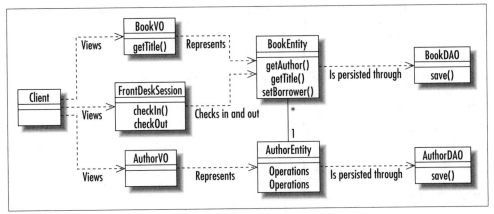

Figure 6-3. EJBs in the real world using BMP

BEST PRACTICE   Be certain Enterprise JavaBeans are the right tool for the job.

Looking back at Chapter 4, our application model included view logic, controller logic, business logic, data access logic, and data storage logic. As this book is about database programming, we assume the data storage logic is handled by a relational database. EJB does not address the view or controller logic. It is primarily concerned with the business logic. If you are using CMP, it cares about the data access logic. Under BMP, however, you provide the data access logic. In Figure 6-3, the data access objects—BookDAO and AuthorDAO—manage the data access logic.

The value objects in Figure 6-3 are not directly related to persistence. They are instead tools to help model entity beans and minimize the overhead that comes with entity beans. Because they do minimize database access, however, they are critical to the proper operation of a persistent EJB system.

Data Access Objects

I introduced the general concept of data access objects in Chapter 4. In the case of BMP, a data access object is a delegate for an EJB to handle its persistence operations. We can see how this works in practice by combining code from Chapter 4 and Chapter 5.

The persistence code under the CMP model for an AuthorBean looked like this:

```
public Long ejbCreate(Long bid, Long aid, String ttl) {
    bookID = bid;
    authorID = aid;
    title= ttl;
    return null;
}

public void ejbLoad() {
}
```

```
public void ejbPassivate( ) {
}

public void ejbPostCreate(Long bid, Long aid, String ttl) {
}

public void ejbRemove( ) {
}

public void ejbStore( ) {
}
```

The only thing remotely interesting was ejbCreate( ), which assigned initial values to a new bean. We could, of course, add the logic to create the book in the database inside the ejbCreate( ) method:

```
static private final String CREATE =
  "INSERT INTO Book ( bookID, authorID, title ) " +
  "VALUES ( ?, ?, ? )";

public Long ejbCreate(Long bid, Long aid, String ttl)
    throws CreateException {
    PreparedStatement stmt = null;
    Connection conn = null;

    bookID = bid;
    authorID = aid;
    title = ttl;
    try {
        Context ctx = new InitialContext( );
        DataSource  ds = (DataSource)ctx.lookup("jdbc/ora");

        conn = ds.getConnection( );
        stmt = conn.prepareStatement(CREATE);
        stmt.setLong(1, bookID.longValue( ));
        stmt.setLong(2, authorID.longValue( ));
        stmt.setString(3, title);
        if( stmt.executeUpdate( ) != 1 ) {
            throw new CreateException("Failed to add book: " + bookID);
        }
        return bookID;
    }
    catch( NamingException e ) {
        throw new EJBException(e);
    }
    catch( SQLException e ) {
        throw new EJBException(e);
    }
    finally {
        if( stmt != null ) {
            try { stmt.close( ); }
            catch( SQLException e ) { }
        }
        if( conn != null ) {
```

```
            try { conn.close( ); }
            catch( SQLException e ) { }
        }
    }
}
```

Though this example code works and is the way most books should teach you BMP, it is not how you want to build your beans in real world applications. In order to better divide the work of persistence, it helps to pull the database code out of our entity bean and place it into a data access object. With a data access object in place, the ejbCreate( ) method evolves into something much simpler:

```
static public final String AUTHOR_ID = "authorID";
static public final String BOOK_ID   = "bookID";
static public final String TITLE     = "title";

public Long ejbCreate(Long bid, Long aid, String ttl)
    throws CreateException {
    HashMap memento = new HashMap( );

    memento.put(BOOK_ID, bookID = bid);
    memento.put(AUTHOR_ID, authorID = aid);
    memento.put(TITLE, title = ttl);
    CommentDAO.create(memento);
    return bookID;
}
```

> **BEST PRACTICE**   Under EJB BMP, separate persistence logic from bean logic through the use of data access objects.

Each bean-managed EJB has at least four persistence operations. The code for each persistence operation is fairly involved and has little or nothing to do with the business logic that the bean represents. By moving persistence logic into a data access object, we have simplified the bean using a logical division of labor. Maintenance of persistence logic can now occur without requiring changes to the bean, and changes to business logic can now occur without requiring changes to the persistence handlers.

If you are wondering what the data access object code looks like for the bean, you are about to get another bonus of following this model: it looks exactly like the data access object from Chapter 4. In other words, using data access objects not only makes the maintenance of your application simpler, *it makes it possible to port an application between vastly different component models.*

Both the data access object and the memento from Chapter 4 combined to give the persistence logic total independence from the business logic—and vice versa. Thus, we are not only able to take our persistence logic from the homegrown component model of Chapter 4, we could also take our entity bean from this chapter and write a data access object to store the bean to an object database or a filesystem.

Value Objects

As we have already encountered, the distributed paradigm under which entity beans operate represent operational challenges for an EJB system. One of the tools for mitigating this problem is the value object—an object that encapsulates the state of an entity bean for a remote client.

Chapter 4 did not work under a distributed programming model. As a result, its components did not face the issues I have presented for entity beans. The component itself was, in a matter of speaking, its own value object.

Unfortunately, value objects violate the sensibility of object purists. This clash between object-oriented elegance and real world performance demands has resulted in a variety of approaches to building value objects. Which approach you prefer depends largely on where you sit on the object purity/convenience continuum.

> **BEST PRACTICE** Use value objects to share entity bean data with clients.

Simple value objects

Simple value objects sit strongly on the convenience side of the equation. You've seen the simplest form of a value object in the HashMap memento. Depending on the operation in question, your entity bean can shove the minimum amount of information necessary to support that operation into a HashMap and give it out to clients. One network call provides the client with everything it needs to know about an entity.

On the other hand, this approach throws most of the benefits of object-orientation out the window. You get absolutely no type safety and you risk chaos with calculated fields.

Complex value objects

Complex value objects basically attempt to be serializable mirrors of their entity bean counterparts. They have all of the methods and some of the business logic supported by the entity bean. As a result, type safety and encapsulation of logic are guaranteed.

Unfortunately, complex value objects are difficult to maintain. Any logic around getting and setting values must be maintained in two places—the entity bean and its value object—and you add yet another class to code for every single business concept you have in your domain model.

Other alternatives

Many alternatives to these two extremes exist. Examples include:

- Providing only methods to access value objects in the entity bean. You can thus maintain the business logic in only the complex value objects and avoid doing it in the entity bean.

- Having no primitive attributes in the entity bean, but instead storing the data in a value object in the bean.
- Managing the internal representation of the value object as a HashMap while providing an object-oriented wrapper around the HashMap.

Sessions as Transactions

Value objects are just one part of insulating entity beans.[*] Another approach is the use of sessions as the gateways into all server-side operations. In essence, any transaction—read or write—should go through a session bean. The session bean thus becomes a transactional business object.

> **BEST PRACTICE**   Use session beans to encapsulate all transactional logic.

When you think of transactions, you probably conjure up examples of transactions in which you are changing the state of the data store. Some of the most problematic transactions from a pure EJB perspective, however, are read transactions like searches and lookups.

Searches

If you remember the way searching occurs in EJB 1.x, you have to write finder methods for each kind of search you want to support. The finder methods then return collections of matching primary keys. When you want the data for those matching keys, the container will load each of the entities from which you request data. Searching under EJB 1.x is thus problematic for a variety of reasons:

- You have to write finder methods to match every conceivable manner of searching and place that logic inside your entity bean implementation class.
- You need to load a ton of entity beans just to get minimal information from each bean in a result set.
- You end up making many database calls just to support a simple search.

By placing searching logic into a session bean and combining this approach with the use of value objects, you can mitigate most problems. To find all books by Stephen King, we could create a session bean called BookSearch with a method that looks like this:

```
static private final String FIND =
   "SELECT title  FROM Book WHERE authorID = ?";

public Collection getTitles(Long aid) throws FinderException {
    PreparedStatement stmt = null;
```

---

[*] This section also applies to applications using container-managed persistence.

```
        Connection conn = null;
        ResultSet rs = null;

        try {
            Context ctx = new InitialContext( );
            DataSource ds = (DataSource)ctx.lookup("jdbc/ora");
            ArrayList results = new ArrayList( );

            conn = ds.getConnection( );
            stmt = conn.prepareStatement(FIND);
            stmt.setLong(1, aid.longValue( ));
            rs = stmt.executeQuery( );
            while( rs.next( ) ) {
                results.add(rs.getString(1));
            }
            return results;
        }
        catch( NamingException e ) {
            throw new EJBException(e);
        }
        catch( SQLException e ) {
            throw new EJBException(e);
        }
        finally {
            if( rs != null ) {
                try { rs.close( ); }
                catch( SQLException e ) { }
            }
            if( stmt != null ) {
                try { stmt.close( ); }
                catch( SQLException e ) { }
            }
            if( conn != null ) {
                try { conn.close( ); }
                catch( SQLException e ) { }
            }
        }
    }
```

You still have to write many finder methods to support a variety of needs. Neverthe-less, you get the entire overhead associated with entity beans out of the way. A more common approach than simply providing a title would be to provide the minimal information necessary for the client to support a list view plus a primary key. The client can then reference a specific bean by primary key if it wishes to drill down further or execute a write transaction.

Updates

Sessions are critical for updates as well as reads. In the context of an update, they help glue together all of the individual entities that are involved in a given transaction. Figure 6-4 shows how a session can be used to "glue together" two bank accounts into a transfer transaction.

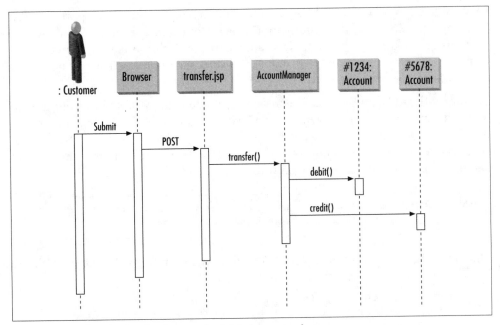

Figure 6-4. *Hiding the details of a transfer behind a session bean*

In this example, the client calls a single method, transfer( ) in the AccountManager session bean. That session bean, in turn, modifies the account balances for each account. The entire transaction succeeds or fails together.

It is important to note here that, although you are managing the persistence, you are not managing the transactions. While it is possible to manually handle transactions using bean-managed transactions, bean-managed transactions and bean-managed persistence are two distinct concepts. In general, you never want to use bean-managed transactions.

BEST PRACTICE   Avoid using bean-managed transactions.

State Management

As a developer of the persistence logic for a bean-managed bean, your job is to make sure that the state of the bean matches the state of the database. The container's role is simply to let you know when interesting things relating to the bean state occur.

Lazy-Loading

Loading a simple bean is fairly straightforward using the tools we have discussed in this chapter and previous chapters. One of the drawbacks I mentioned for container-managed persistence, however, was the inability to perform lazy-loading.

Lazy-loading is a tool that enables you to put off making queries to support complex bean relationships until that information is actually needed. An example of such a relationship includes a one-to-many relationship in which the many side requires a complex query or represents very many. Another example is an entity bean that stores a huge chunk of binary data.

For binary data like a Video bean representing a video clip, you do not want to load that video into memory for several reasons. First, it is a lot of data to load into memory. In fact, you never really want the whole clip to be in memory—you want to stream it. The other reason not to load it is because it will take a long time to load and thus hold up simple queries against the video's metadata.

> **BEST PRACTICE** Take advantage of lazy-loading when your entity bean stores large binary or text values or has complex object relationships.

The following code shows the ejbLoad( ) method (without using data access objects) for a Video bean implementation:

```
static private final String LOAD =
    "SELECT title, runningTime, size FROM Video WHERE videoID = ?";

public void ejbLoad( ) {
    PreparedStatement stmt = null;
    Connection conn = null;
    ResultSet rs = null;

    try {
        Context ctx = new InitialContext( );
        DataSource ds = (DataSource)ctx.lookup("jdbc/ora");
        Long id = (Long)context.getPrimaryKey( );

        conn = ds.getConnection( );
        stmt = conn.prepareStatement(LOAD);
        stmt.setLong(1, id.longValue( ));
        rs = stmt.executeQuery( );
        if( !rs.next( ) ) {
            throw new EJBException("No matching value.");
        }
        videoID = id;
        title = rs.getString(1);
        runningTime = rs.getString(2);
        size = rs.getLong(3);
        if( rs.next( ) ) {
            throw new EJBException("Multiple matching values.");
        }
    }
    catch( NamingException e ) {
        throw new EJBException(e);
    }
    catch( SQLException e ) {
```

```
            throw new EJBException(e);
        }
        finally {
            if( rs != null ) {
                try { rs.close( ); }
                catch( SQLException e ) { }
            }
            if( stmt != null ) {
                try { stmt.close( ); }
                catch( SQLException e ) { }
            }
            if( conn != null ) {
                try { conn.close( ); }
                catch( SQLException e ) { }
            }
        }
    }
}
```

The actual video is not loaded. The loading occurs when a client calls for it:

```
static private final String STREAM =
  "SELECT dataStream FROM Video WHERE videoID = ?";

public DistributedDataInputStream getStream( )  {
    PreparedStatement stmt = null;
    Connection conn = null;
    ResultSet rs = null;

    try {
        Context ctx = new InitialContext( );
        DataSource ds = (DataSource)ctx.lookup("jdbc/ora");
        DistributedDataInputStream is ;
        Clob clob;

        conn = ds.getConnection( );
        stmt = conn.prepareStatement(STREAM);
        stmt.setLong(1, videoID.longValue( ));
        rs = stmt.executeQuery( );
        if( !rs.next( ) ) {
            throw new EJBException("No matching value.");
        }
        clob = rs.getClob(1);
        is = new DistributedDataInputStream(clob.getBinaryStream( ));
        if( rs.next( ) ) {
            throw new EJBException("Multiple matching values.");
        }
        return is;
    }
    catch( NamingException e ) {
        throw new EJBException(e);
    }
    catch( SQLException e ) {
        throw new EJBException(e);
    }
```

```
        finally {
            if( rs != null ) {
                try { rs.close(); }
                catch( SQLException e ) { }
            }
            if( stmt != null ) {
                try { stmt.close(); }
                catch( SQLException e ) { }
            }
            if( conn != null ) {
                try { conn.close(); }
                catch( SQLException e ) { }
            }
        }
    }
}
```

For this example to work, of course, you need some kind of special streaming class that will send an input stream across the network to be read by a distributed client. That class is represented in the example by the DistributedDataInputStream class.

Depending on your database of choice, storing binary data in a database may be a bad idea. As a general rule of thumb, I recommend against storing any binary data in a database for a couple of reasons:

- Many database engines are incapable of properly streaming binary data. Even though they may support the JDBC Clob interface, they are really reading the entire binary value into memory and faking the streaming. If your database does not natively support streaming (for example, MySQL), this general rule of thumb should be an inviolable law.

- The database becomes an intermediary between your application and the data on the disk and thus slows down performance. At its core, this is exactly what a database is supposed to be. With binary data, however, the advantages of having this intermediary begin to be outweighed by the disadvantages.

Moving binary data to the filesystem, however, has its drawbacks. Most notably, you risk data integrity when you move the binary data directly to the filesystem. Your EJB must handle both the deletion of the metadata in the database and the file on the filesystem. More problematic, however, is the fact that you cannot do both as an atomic transaction.

> **BEST PRACTICE** Avoid storing binary data in the database; store it on the filesystem with pointers in the database.

Regardless of the approach you choose, lazy-loading can help you gain the optimal efficiency for managing large binary and character attributes.

To Store or Not to Store

Containers can be a little ejbStore( ) happy. If the container thinks there is the slightest possibility that a bean could have been modified during the course of a transaction, it will trigger a call to ejbStore( ). This approach is great when all of the beans involved in a transaction actually had state changes. In a transaction that touches dozens of beans yet modifies only one or two, however, this can seriously harm system performance.

A very common practice in EJB development with bean-managed persistence is to create a "dirty" flag and set it whenever a transaction actually modifies a bean. In our book example, we might have a setTitle( ) method that looks like this:

```
public void setTitle(String ttl) {
    title = ttl;
}
```

We can add a simple call to:

```
dirty = true;
```

This call will indicate to ejbStore( ) that the bean has, in fact, undergone a state change. We can then write ejbStore( ) like this:

```
public void ejbStore( ) {
    if( !dirty ) {
        return;
    }
    // perform the actual save
}
```

After a call to setTitle( ), ejbStore( ) saves the bean to the database. If the store-happy container, however, triggers ejbStore( ) without having modified the bean, nothing will happen. This trick thus saves at least one unnecessary trip to the database.

Exception Handling

The final piece in bean-managed persistence is exception handling. The EJB specification classifies three different exception conditions:

- Remote exceptions
- EJB exceptions
- Application exceptions

All bean interface methods throw remote exceptions—java.rmi.RemoteException. The underlying distributed computing architecture throws a remote exception whenever something goes wrong with the network. You should never throw one in your code.

EJB exceptions—javax.ejb.EJBException—are signals from your code to the container that something has gone wrong with the application outside of the normal application states. In the examples earlier in this chapter, I threw EJB exceptions for database errors and JNDI errors. As a developer, you should never catch an EJBException.

Anything that represents a flaw in the application state counts as an application exception. The container ignores application exceptions.

From the perspective of database access, your first task is to turn all data access exceptions into EJB exceptions as shown in the examples in this chapter. On the other hand, when you check for valid values, you will throw application exceptions to indicate a failure to match the required value. In the code to create a book, for example, I could have added the following check that throws a CreateException:

```
if( bookID.longValue( ) < 0L ) {
    throw new CreateException("Invalid  book ID.");
}
```

CHAPTER 7

JDO Persistence

> *Those who feel that liberation from tradition is a good thing rejoice at this change, while those who fear the results lament the loss of roots.*
> —David Kolb
> *The Critique of Pure Modernity*

JDBC provides your application with direct access to a relational data store. Though JDBC tries to objectify the data store using objects that represent relational database concepts, it does not provide an object-oriented picture of your problem domain. Your job in JDBC programming is to use information from those database objects to build an OO picture of your problem domain. This task is the problem of object-relational mapping we talked about in Chapter 4.

Also in Chapter 4, I introduced the concept of the data access object pattern. Using this pattern, business objects delegate their persistence to something else called a data access object. Chapter 4 then showed you how to use JDBC to build data access objects. Chapter 6 showed you how to use the data access object pattern in an EJB system to provide JDBC-based persistence.

You do not need to write the persistence layer for this pattern to be valid. EJB CMP "delegates" its persistence operations to the container. EJB CMP, however, is not the only automated persistence option for Java architects and developers. This chapter covers the major standard option to EJB CMP, the Java Data Objects (JDO) specification. If you are not familiar with this specification, Chapter 12 provides a tutorial to introduce you to JDO programming.

JDO or EJB?

This question is actually too simplistic. Your persistence options are much richer than JDO or EJB:

- JDBC
- JDO

- Alternative persistence systems
- Serialization
- EJB CMP
- EJB BMP + JDBC
- EJB BMP + JDO
- EJB BMP + alternative persistence systems
- EJB BMP + serialization

Each of these options—even serialization—can be the right answer for a particular persistence issue. EJB is overkill for small web applications. Using EJB will kill the performance of your small application and require significant effort to get initial functionality out the door. JDBC, on the other hand, is a bad solution for a programming team with limited database programming experience or with a significant number of persistent objects to code. JDO, finally, is poorly suited to teams with little understanding of transaction management or that require massive scalability. Table 7-1 describes different problems and the persistence mechanisms best suited to them. It is definitely not comprehensive and does not address the advantages of alternative persistence systems.

> **BEST PRACTICE**   Do not use a one-size-fits-all approach to persistence—choose the persistence option that fits the requirements and scale of your application.

Table 7-1. Sample applications and matching persistence models

Application	Persistence model	Rationale
Embedded PDA phone book	JDO	Enables the development of a persistent application with the lightest footprint besides serialization. Unlike serialization, however, the use of JDO preserves object relationships in the data store.
Enterprise CRM system	EJB + EJB 2.0 CMP	Supports the scalability needs of a massive enterprise system while hiding the complexities of transaction management and object-relational mapping. Also enables developers with less experience to be more productive in the development of the system—fewer bottlenecks created by architects and senior Java developers.
Medium-sized web application against a legacy database	JDBC	Provides the greatest ability to control the object-relational mapping for an application with light transactional and scalability demands.
Massive web application against a legacy database	EJB + JDBC	Provides the greatest ability to control the object-relational mapping for an application with heavy transactional and scalability demands.
Massive web application with a gradual migration from a legacy data store to a new data store	EJB + JDBC and JDO	Enables control over object-relational mapping in the short term with the advantages of automated persistence for simpler components while avoiding mixing CMP and BMP models.
Swing application that needs to save its state across executions	Serialization	Supports quick storage and retrieval of the JavaBeans representing your application state with none of the overhead of the other tools.

The issues in Table 7-1 are just the surface issues. In short, you really need to know your problem domain and the pluses and minuses of each persistence mechanism in order to choose the best tool to support your application. One of the purposes of this book is, of course, to arm you with an understanding of the different persistence options so you can make that decision for the systems you design and build.

The most fundamental distinction between the two persistence models, however, lies in the concept of transparency. In order to take advantage of EJB persistence— whether BMP or CMP—you must adhere to the EJB component model. Any components outside of that model cannot be made persistent. JDO, on the other hand, enables you to make any user-defined class persistent. In other words, the persistence model is transparent to the developer. Though you do not write any persistence code under EJB CMP, you are still writing your classes to adhere to the EJB CMP persistence.

> **BEST PRACTICE**   When not building your business objects to a specific component model such as Enterprise JavaBeans, design your business objects to the Java-Beans specification.

Basic JDO Persistence

Most JDO applications fall into the small-to-medium scale. In general, you have a simple to moderately complex domain model built into any one of the following kinds of architectures:

- Web application
- Server application
- Two-tier client/server

The tutorial in Chapter 12 covers the basics of building such an application.

Transaction Management

Though JDO persistence is designed to be transparent to the business component developer, it is not transparent to the application developer. The examples in Chapter 12 show only how to manage persistent objects in the main( ) method of a contrived application. In reality, you will be managing persistent objects through JSPs and servlets, Swing components, and even other persistent objects.

Figure 7-1 shows how JDO might interact with a web application. The JSP views perform queries and display data from the persistent objects. Controllers create, modify, and delete the persistent objects. In other words, the JSP pages perform the same role as the main( ) method from Chapter 12's examples.

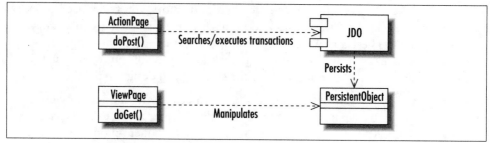

Figure 7-1. JDO in a simplistic web application

This approach works and you will see no problems from it until your domain model begins growing in complexity. One of the drawbacks of JDO, however, is that it does not manage object relationships automatically—you are responsible for maintaining the integrity of all relationships among persistent objects. When you embed the logic for the creation and deletion of persistent objects in views and controllers, you create a maintenance problem.

For example, your web application could have two controllers: one that deletes an author and another that deletes a book. Each controller would require code that not only calls deletePersistent( ), but that also protects the integrity of the relationship between Author and Book. If the rules governing this relationship change, you need to make sure you find all places in the application where the relationship is being managed and make the appropriate changes.

To diminish the risk of managing relationships in your application, you need to centralize the logic for managing your persistent object relationships. I recommend the creation of an EJB session bean–like class that performs metaoperations on your persistent classes. Example 7-1 shows such a class.

BEST PRACTICE   Centralize the logic for managing object relationships to preserve their integrity and the integrity of the underlying data store.

Example 7-1. A Bookshelf class to manage object relationships

```
package com.imaginary.ora;

import javax.jdo.*;

public abstract class Bookshelf {
    static private PersistenceManager getPersistenceManager() {
        PersistenceManagerFactory factory;
        Properties props = new Properties();

        // load JDO properties
        factory = JDOHelper.getPersistenceManagerFactory(props);
        return factory.getPersistenceManager();
    }
```

```
static public void createAuthor(Author auth) {
    PersistenceManager mgr = getPersistenceManager( );
    Transaction trans;

    trans = mgr.currentTransaction( );
    trans.setOptimistic(false);
    try {
        trans.begin( );
        mgr.makePersistent(auth);
        trans.commit( );
    }
    catch( Exception e ) {
        e.printStackTrace( );
    }
    finally {
        if( trans.isActive( ) ) {
            trans.rollback( );
        }
        mgr.close( );
    }
}

static public void deleteAuthor(Author auth) {
    PersistenceManager mgr = getPersistenceManager( );
    Transaction trans;

    trans = mgr.currentTransaction( );
    try { trans.setOptimistic(true); }
    catch( JDOUnsupportedOptionException e ) { }
    try {
        Iterator books = auth.getBooks( ).iterator( );

        trans.begin( );
        while( it.hasNext( ) ) {
            mgr.deletePersistent((Book)it.next( ));
        }
        mgr.deletePersistent(auth);
        trans.commit( );
    }
    catch( Exception e ) {
        e.printStackTrace( );
    }
    finally {
        if( trans.isActive( ) ) {
            trans.rollback( );
        }
        mgr.close( );
    }
}

static public void createBook(Author auth, Book book) {
    PersistenceManager mgr = getPersistenceManager( );
    Transaction trans;
```

```
        trans = mgr.currentTransaction( );
        try { trans.setOptimistic(true); }
        catch( JDOUnsupportedOptionException e ) { }
        try {
            trans.begin( );
            book.setAuthor(auth);
            auth.addBook(book);
            mgr.makePersistent(book);
            trans.commit( );
        }
        catch( Exception e ) {
            e.printStackTrace( );
        }
        finally {
            if( trans.isActive( ) ) {
                trans.rollback( );
            }
            mgr.close( );
        }
    }

    static public void deleteBook(Book book) {
        PersistenceManager mgr = getPersistenceManager( );
        Transaction trans;

        trans = mgr.currentTransaction( );
        try { trans.setOptimistic(true); }
        catch( JDOUnsupportedOptionException e ) { }
        try {
            trans.begin( );
            book.getAuthor( ).removeBook(book);
            mgr.deletePersistent(book);
            trans.commit( );
        }
        catch( Exception e ) {
            e.printStackTrace( );
        }
        finally {
            if( trans.isActive( ) ) {
                trans.rollback( );
            }
            mgr.close( );
        }
    }
}
```

This class performs two critical tasks:

- It clearly demarcates the boundaries of transactions involving Author and Book instances.

- It centralizes all logic relating to the management of Author and Book relationships.

It also has the hidden benefit of making the persistence model transparent to your controller classes. The JSP code to create a new author looks like this:

```
<% Bookshelf.createAuthor(new Author(firstName, lastName)); %>
```

This code also uses optimistic transaction management for optimal performance. In doing so, it checks for the possibility that the JDO implementation does not support optimistic transaction management. Not all JDO implementations support optimistic transaction management, and not all transactions are well suited to optimistic transaction management. In general, optimistic transaction management works when you are performing multiple operations and each operation targets a different object.

The exception in this example was the code to create a new Author. Because the operation touched only the Author class for a single operation, it is going to see better performance under data store transaction management.

> **BEST PRACTICE**   Use optimistic transaction management for long transactions involving multiple persistent objects.

Query Control

The previous section made the use of JDO transparent to controllers—views still use JDO queries to retrieve collections of persistent objects. This issue is not the maintenance problem that running creates and deletes in multiple locations produced. It would nevertheless be nice to centralize query logic to provide view pages with the same transparency as well as give us a single location to tweak query logic. The Bookshelf class looks like a good candidate. On the other hand, it probably makes more sense to have a one-to-one association between a persistent class and the class that manages its queries. Example 7-2 shows an AuthorFinder class to handle queries.

Example 7-2. A class that centralizes query logic for Author instances

```java
package com.imaginary.ora;

import java.util.*;

import javax.jdo.*;

public abstract class AuthorFinder {

    static private final String GENRE = "gen";
    static private final String YEAR  = "yr";

    static public Collection findByGenreYear(String gen, int yr) {
        Extent ext = mgr.getExtent(Author.class, true);
        Query query = mgr.newQuery(ext,
        "books.contains(book) & (book.year=yr & book.genre = gen)");
        HashMap params = new HashMap( );
```

```
        query.declareParameters("int yr, String gen");
        query.declareVariables("com.imaginary.ora.Book book");
        params.put(GENRE, gen);
        params.put(YEAR, yr);
        return(Collection)query.executeWithMap(params);
    }
}
```

This example provides a single query, but in reality it will likely contain a variety of queries to help support various Author searches. This particular query provides the application with a list of all authors who published a book of a specific genre in a specific year. Even though the search has only two parameters, I used executeWithMap( ) because it helps prevent any maintenance ugliness associated with matching parameter order.

BEST PRACTICE   Use executeWithMap( ) when executing multiparameter queries.

EJB BMP with JDO

From a JDO perspective, persisting EJBs as part of a bean-managed persistence model has little difference from persisting other kinds of objects. The most common difference is that you tend to be in a managed environment when working with EJBs; similarly, you tend to be in a nonmanaged environment when building other kinds of applications. You can, of course, build web applications in a managed environment and EJB applications that use bean-managed transactions.

One key differentiator between working with JDO in a managed J2EE container versus a nonmanaged environment—besides the obvious impact of transaction management—is the way you reference the PersistenceManagerFactory class. In a non-J2EE container or a nonmanaged environment, you pass a set of properties to the JDOHelper class. The JDOHelper class then hands you the appropriate PersistenceManagerFactory.

When working in a J2EE container, you can rely on JNDI to provide you with a PersistenceManagerFactory without worrying about properties:

```
    Context ctx = new InitialContext( );
    PersistenceManagerFactory factory;

    factory = (PersistenceManagerFactory)ctx.lookup("jdo/pmf");
```

Transaction Management

Because you are working in an EJB environment, transaction management issues disappear from your radar when using JDO as a bean-managed persistence tool. The

---

exception to this advantage comes when you decide to use bean-managed transactions. Managing your own transactions is one of the pitfalls of working with JDO in a nonmanaged environment. You definitely do not want to introduce that pitfall into this environment unless something makes bean-managed transactions your only option. If you do opt for bean-managed transactions, you should remember that it is a really bad idea to mix bean-managed and container-managed transactions. Chapter 5 has a detailed discussion of this topic.

> **BEST PRACTICE** Avoid bean-managed transactions unless there is an overriding need for them.

Persistence Strategies

In an EJB application, session beans perform the role we set aside for the Bookshelf class in the previous section. They may also create value objects for the entities that match any queries performed by the session bean. The entity beans, on the other hand, contain the business logic behind any persistent object. Depending on your EJB architecture philosophy, either the entity bean itself or its value object can be the JDO PersistenceCapable class. Using the value object, however, and having the entity bean delegate to the value object for all state information enables you to maintain state information in a single location.

If you take the approach of using the JDO instance as your value object, you need to take care that it is not involved in an uncommitted transaction when you serialize it to the client. Doing so may cause unpredictable exceptional conditions.

CHAPTER 8
Alternative Persistence Frameworks

*Reason must in all its undertakings subject itself to criticism; should it
limit freedom of criticism by any prohibitions, it must harm itself, drawing
upon itself a damaging suspicion. Nothing is so important through its
usefulness, nothing so sacred, that it may be exempted from this searching
examination, which knows no respect for persons. Reason depends on this
freedom for its very existence. For reason has no dictatorial authority, its
verdict is always simply the agreement of free citizens, of whom each one
must be permitted to express, without let or hindrance, his objection or
even his veto.*

—Immanuel Kant
The Critique of Pure Reason

As an enterprise application architect, you have more options than just choosing
between a persistence model blessed by Sun and rolling your own model. In fact,
alternative persistence models have been gaining in popularity recently for a variety
of reasons:

- EJBs are complex and heavy and they require an application server.
- JDBC is time-consuming and requires a significant degree of database programming skill.
- JDO is late on the scene and still lacking in implementations.

A quick search of the Internet will reveal a variety of alternative persistence systems.
Two of the most popular are the Castor JDO (not an implementation of the Sun JDO
specification) and Hibernate projects.[*] This chapter looks at Castor and Hibernate as
alternative XML object-relational mapping tools.

---

[*] Both are open source projects available at SourceForge (*http://www.sourceforge.net*).

Why Alternative Frameworks?

The Java philosophy is heavy on the idea that you adhere to the standards and compete on implementation. As a general rule of thumb in the Java world, you should avoid deviating from standards unless the standards in question simply do not meet your needs. Java's persistence models, however, are far from well-accepted standards. Part of the reason behind this divergence is that no single persistence model can support the needs of every application. Each approach to persistence requires design decisions that necessarily exclude features provided by other systems.

Each alternative framework brings its own advantages to database programming. As a general rule, alternative frameworks offer you:

- The ability to meet specific needs not addressed in the EJB or JDO standards.

- As with EJB and JDO, Hibernate and Castor rely on XML descriptor files for persistence mapping. This lends itself to providing a very easy to understand mapping file that describes complex database relationships.

- The alternatives in this chapter limit the amount of code developers need to write in order to make objects persistent.

- The alternatives in this chapter are open source. As such, they come with all of the benefits—and the drawbacks—of open source tools.

> **BEST PRACTICE** Use alternative persistence frameworks in applications designed for low-cost deployment environments or for applications that have niche requirements for which an alternative framework is uniquely suited.

Alternative persistence APIs are not without their own drawbacks:

- Alternative persistence APIs are simply that: an alternative. These APIs do not conform to recognized standards such as EJB 1.1, EJB 2.0, and JDO.

- Alternative persistence APIs do not provide a container-managed transaction system such as those provided by the EJB container. With EJBs, the transaction demarcation is done automatically by defining the transaction attributes in your deployment descriptor and is strictly enforced by the container.

The Open Source Model

The open source model is a model for distributing software based on the philosophy that the people who use software should have the right to the source code for the software, including the ability to modify the source code. Though it is often associated with the concept of free—meaning without cost—software, open source software describes itself as free, as in speech. In other words, open source software may or may not cost any money.

The benefits of open source software include:

- Greater control over your software, including the ability to improve the software instead of waiting for a vendor to fix it for you.
- Given a large contributor base, open source software tends to have a more diverse developer base than proprietary software.
- Open source software—even when it is not free—is generally cheaper than proprietary software since the business models for open source companies tend to be based on services around their software.

On the other hand, open source software has its drawbacks:

- Support for the software often depends on the whims of its developers rather than a solid service agreement.
- Releases of open source software without large developer bases are inconsistent and even prone to long periods of inactivity.
- The benefits of the greater control over your software can become liabilities if you lose the ability to maintain your changes.

BEST PRACTICE Do not use alternative frameworks for applications meant to be deployed in a variety of corporate environments. In such environments, adherence to standards is critical to the confidence of those who will be responsible for supporting the application.

Persistence Approach

As you have seen with all of the other automated persistence systems in this book, Castor and Hibernate both persist component attributes by reading an XML configuration file that defines persistence mapping. Table 8-1 shows the attributes of two business objects we might want to persist to a database.

> **BEST PRACTICE** Though each framework lets you specify all persistence mapping in a single XML file, you should limit each XML file to describing the mapping of a single class.

Table 8-1. The attributes of two business objects with the mapping type to be used

Class	Attribute	Type
Author	authorID	Long
	firstName	String
	lastName	String
	Publications	List
Book	bookID	Long
	Author	Author
	Title	String

Example 8-1 contains the code for the Author class described in Table 8-1.

Example 8-1. A persistent Author class

```
package book;

public class Author {
    private long    authorID;
    private String firstName;
    private String lastName;
    private Set     publications;

    public long getAuthorID () {
        return authorID;
    }

     public String getFirstName() {
        return firstName;
    }

    public String getLastName() {
        return lastName;
    }

    public Set getPublications () {
        return publications;
    }

    public void setAuthorID (long id) [
```

Example 8-1. A persistent Author class (continued)

```
        authorID   = id;
    }

    public void setFirstName(String fn) {
        firstName = fn;
    }

    public void setLastName(String ln) {
        lastName = ln;
    }

    public void setPublications (Set pubs) {
        publications = pubs;
    }
}
```

This business class is very simple—nothing but getters and setters to manage the attributes. No persistence code is present. Example 8-2 contains the basic code for the Book class.

Example 8-2. Book value object that contains an Author value object reference

```
package book;

public class Book {
    private Author author;
    private long    bookID
    private String title;

    public Author getAuthor () {
        return author;
    }

    public long getBookID () {
        return bookID;
    }

    public String getTitle () {
        return title;
    }

    public void setAuthor (Author auth) {
        author = auth;
    }

    public void setBookID (long id) {
        bookID =id;
    }
```

Example 8-2. Book value object that contains an Author value object reference (continued)

```
    public String setTitle (String ttl) {
        title = ttl;
    }
}
```

Castor Field Mapping

The key to Castor and Hibernate persistence is the XML file. Each API has it own definition language for defining the mapping between objects and a table. Example 8-3 shows how Castor maps the business objects to a database.

Example 8-3. Castor XML mapping descriptor

```xml
<?xml version="1.0"?>
<!DOCTYPE mapping PUBLIC "-//EXOLAB/Castor Mapping DTD Version 1.0//EN" "http://castor.
exolab.org/mapping.dtd">

<mapping>
    <class name="book.Author" identity="authorID" key-generator="MAX">
        <map-to table="AUTHOR"/>
        <field name="authorID" type="long">
            <sql name="AUTHORID"/>
        </field>
        <field name="firstname" type="java.lang.String">
            <sql name="FIRSTNAME"/>
        </field>
        <field name="lastname" type="java.lang.String">
            <sql name="LASTNAME"/>
        </field>
        <field name="publications" type="book.Book" collection="set">
            <sql many-key="authorid"/>
        </field>
    </class>

    <class name="book.Book" identity="bookID" key-generator="MAX">
        <map-to table="BOOK"/>
        <field name="bookID" type="long">
            <sql name="BOOKID"/>
        </field>
        <field name="title" type="java.lang.String">
            <sql name="TITLE"/>
        </field>
        <field name="author" type="book.Author">
            <sql name="AUTHORID"/>
        </field>
    </class>
</mapping>
```

For each class you wish to map, you have a class* entry in your XML-descriptor. This tag identifies the following:

- The name of the Java class being mapped.
- The name of the identity attribute (the attribute that uniquely identifies an instance of the class).
- The key generation tool to use to generate identity values. Both Castor and Hibernate provide several methods of generating unique values.

> **BEST PRACTICE** Choose the sequence generation method that best suits your persistence framework of choice.

Castor supports the following key generation algorithms:

HIGH-LOW
> This algorithm uses a mechanism similar to the custom sequence generation algorithm described in Chapter 4. It requires a special sequence table whose keys are the names of tables and whose columns are seed values for sequence generation. For more on seed values, look at the sequence generation part of Chapter 4.

IDENTITY
> The value generated is based on the value generated by the proprietary identity generation scheme of the underlying database engine. Supported databases include Hypersonic SQL, MS SQL Server, MySQL, and Sybase ASE/ASA.

MAX
> The value generated is one greater than the maximum value currently in the database.

SEQUENCE
> The value generated comes from the proprietary SEQUENCE concept of Interbase, Oracle, PostgreSQL, and SAP DB.

UUID
> This algorithm generates a globally unique value based on the IP address, current system time in milliseconds, and a static counter.

The SEQUENCE and HIGH-LOW algorithms require parameters. You can specify the parameters using the key-generator tag outside the class tag:

```
<key-generator name="HIGH-LOW">
  <param name="table" value="Sequence"/>
  <param name="key-column" value="name"/>
  <param name="value-column" value="seed"/>
  <param name="grab-size" value="1000000"/>
</key-generator>
```

---

* The use of the word class makes this XML dialect technically illegal since class is a reserved word in XML.

Within the <class></class> enclosure is the set of tags that defines the mapping of class attributes to database tables. The first tag in the group is the map-totable tag. As its name suggests, it specifies the name of the database table to which the attributes of this class map.

The rest of the tags define the actual field-to-column mappings. The tag of special interest is the one that defines how an Author relates to Book. Instead of identifying a column in the AUTHOR table, it identifies an attribute in the Book class. Castor then uses the mapping of this column to perform the appropriate joins.

Hibernate Field Mapping

Field mapping in Hibernate is quite similar. Example 8-4 shows the XML descriptor that defines that mapping of the sample classes to a database.

Example 8-4. Hibernate XML mapping descriptor

```
<?xml version="1.0"?>
<!DOCTYPE hibernate-mapping PUBLIC "-//Hibernate/Hibernate Mapping DTD//EN" "http://
hibernate.sourceforge.net/hibernate-mapping-1.1.dtd">

<hibernate-mapping >
    <class name="book.Author" table="AUTHOR">
        <id name="authorID" column="AUTHORID" type="long">
            <generator class="vm.long"/>
        </id>
        <property name="firstname" column="FIRSTNAME" type="string"/>
        <property name="lastname" column="LASTNAME" type="string"/>
        <set role="publications" lazy="true">
            <key column="AUTHORID"/>
            <one-to-many class="book.Book"/>
        </set>
    </class>
    <class name="book.Book" table="BOOK">
        <id name="bookID" column="BOOKID" type="long">
            <generator class="vm.long"/>
        </id>
        <property name="title" column="TITLE"/>
    </class>
</hibernate-mapping>
```

The Hibernate code is similar to the Castor code, yet different in many important ways. Again, Hibernate uses a class tag to define the persistence mapping for a specific Java class. Unlike Castor, Hibernate defines the table mapping as a tag attribute.

Within a class, you identity the ID, properties, and sets of the class. The ID is the primary key field. The id tag contains a generator tag to specify a key generation algorithm to use for automated key generation. This tag identifies a Java class that performs a key generation algorithm. If the algorithm requires parameters, they may be specified in the body of the generator tag as param tags:

```
<generator class="org.dasein.persist.Sequence">
  <param>sequence</param>
</generator>
```

The generator class is an implementation of cirrus.hibernate.id.Identifier-Generator. Hibernate provides the following built-in generators:

assigned

Enables the application to generate its own identifiers.

hilo.hex

This algorithm is the same as hilo.long, except the result is a string of 16 characters.

hilo.long

Generates unique long values using a HIGH-LOW algorithm. This generator should not be used in JTA environments or with user-supplied connections.

native

Generates a unique value based on the identity columns for DB2, MS SQL Server, MySQL, Sybase, and Hypersonic SQL.

seqhilo.long

Generates a unique long value for a named sequence using the HIGH-LOW algorithm.

sequence

Generates a unique value based on the SEQUENCE concept from DB2, Interbase, Oracle, PostgreSQL, and SAP DB.

uuid.hex

Generates a globally unique 32-character string.

uuid.string

Identical to uuid.hex, except it generates a 16-character ASCII string. This algorithm should not be used with PostgreSQL.

vm.hex

Generates unique strings based on hexadecimal digits. This algorithm should not be used in a cluster.

vm.long

Generates unique long values. This algorithm should not be used in a cluster.

Properties are the basic attributes of the class. Sets, on the other hand, represent the one-to-many or many-to-many mappings for the class. Again, our objects map one author to many books. Hibernate captures this relationship through the set tag.

Hibernate supports six different collection tags:

- `<array>`
- `<bag>`
- `<list>`
- `<map>`
- `<primitive-array>`
- `<set>`

For all of these set types except arrays, you can enable lazy-loading through the `lazy="true"` attribute. Using lazy-loading can greatly increase the speed of your application for operations such as searching. Additional approaches such as caching can also greatly increase the speed of your application. It is worthy to note that most alternative persistence APIs offer some type of built-in object caching that can be turned on or off.

Persistence Operations

The Author and Book classes in Examples 8-1 and 8-2 do not contain any persistence-related methods. Both Castor and Hibernate, however, require you to add code to trigger persistence operations.

With any database-intensive application, the flushing of new state to the database is a time-expensive process. One advantage to controlling when the flushing of your data occurs is that you can manage this expense.

With both persistence systems, persistence operations are done by loading the mapping files, obtaining a database connection, calling for an object to be persisted, and closing out the transaction. Abstracting the persistence code with a data access object will help you create a cleaner implementation.

> **BEST PRACTICE**   Encapsulate persistence operations using both frameworks in data access objects similar to those we have used in other persistence models in this book. This will allow you to easily refactor your code to an alternative persistence system such as EJBs.

Castor Persistence

In our example, we need the ability to add a new book to an author's list of books. In Castor, the method to perform this task might look like this:

```
public Book addBook (Book book) throws Exception {
    JDO jdo = new JDO("alternativepersistencedb");
    jdo.loadConfiguration("database.xml");
    Database db = jdo.getDatabase( );
    db.begin( );
    db.create(book);
    db.commit( );
    db.close( );
    return book;
}
```

> **BEST PRACTICE**   Using a singleton to manage the loading and parsing of your persistence configuration files will increase the speed of your persistence operations.

This code references a new XML file, the *database.xml* configuration file. It describes your database connections to enable Castor to access a JDBC data source. Example 8-5 shows what such a file looks like.

Example 8-5. Castor database connection descriptor

```
<!DOCTYPE databases
  PUBLIC "-//EXOLAB/Castor JDO Configuration DTD Version 1.0//EN"
         "http://castor.exolab.org/jdo-conf.dtd">

<database name="aps" engine="sql-server">
    <driver class-name="net.sourceforge.jtds.jdbc.Driver" url="jdbc:jtds:sqlserver://
localhost:1433/aps">
        <param name="user" value="aps"/>
        <param name="password" value="research"/>
    </driver>
    <mapping href="mapping.xml"/>
</database>
```

With the connection information defined, a database session is established by calling the JDO class method getDatabase( ). To start a transaction, the begin( ) method is called on the Database session. The Book class is now ready to be persisted. This is accomplished by calling create( ) on the Database session. The new Book has been persisted, and connection cleanup needs to be performed by closing the transaction with `commit( )` and `close( )` on the Database session. If a transaction error occurs, a `TransactionAbortedException` will be thrown by the Database session.

Hibernate Persistence

Hibernate persistence works very much like Castor persistence. You basically have to make calls to methods with similar names in different classes:

```
public Book addBook (Book book) throws Exception {
    Datastore ds = Hibernate.createDatastore( );
    ds.storeFile("hibernate.xml");
    SessionFactory sessionFactory = ds.buildSessionFactory( );
    Session session = sessionFactory.openSession( );
    session.beginTransaction( );
    session.saveOrUpdate(book);
    session.flush( );
    session.connection( ).commit( );
    session.close( );
}
```

The first line of code calls `createDatastore( )`, which loads the Hibernate connection descriptor (an example is provided in Example 8-6). An XML-based connection descriptor is also available.

Example 8-6. Hibernate database connection descriptor

```
hibernate.connection.driver_class=net.sourceforge.jtds.jdbc.Driver
hibernate.connection.url=jdbc:jtds:sqlserver://localhost:1433/aps
hibernate.connection.username=aps
hibernate.connection.password=research
```

With the connection information loaded, the `storeFile( )` method then reads in the mapping descriptor. The `SessionFactory` is used to manage session connections across the application. For our example, we are creating the `SessionFactory` with each request. To start a transaction, the `beginTransaction( )` method on the current `Session` is called. The `saveOrUpdate( )` method is then called to create or update any object that needs to be persisted. The `flush( )` must be called at the end of any transaction cycle. Flushing is used to synchronize the database with persistent objects in memory. To close the transaction, the `commit( )` method is called, and the transaction is closed with the `close( )` method. Transaction errors will throw a `SQLException`.

BEST PRACTICE	Both frameworks support database connection pooling or the use of JNDI data sources. Take advantage of this support in your database applications.

Searches

Searching with both persistence systems looks similar to JDO. They both use object-based query languages and leverage a similar API set.

Castor Searches

Castor uses the Object Query Language (OQL). OQL queries are similar to standard ANSI SQL but use object names in place of column fields. Example 8-7 details the implementation of a book search with Castor.

Example 8-7. Searching for a book by title with Castor

```
public Book findBookByTitle(String title) throws Exception {
    JDO jdo = new JDO("alternativepersistencedb");
    jdo.loadConfiguration("database.xml");
    Database db = jdo.getDatabase();
    db.begin();
    OQLQuery query = db.getOQLQuery("SELECT b FROM book.Book b WHERE
        title=$1");
    query.bind("Alternative Persistence Systems");
    QueryResults results = query.execute();
    // assume the first book found is the desired book
    Book book = (Book) results.next();
    db.commit();
    db.close();
    return book;
}
```

As before, all configuration information needs to be loaded and ready before any database operations can be performed. Once the connection has been established, the OQLQuery and QueryResults classes are used for searching. The most important line here is the getOQLQuery() method. This particular search looks for all entities that have a title value equal to the title attribute supplied by the calling method. If no results exist when next() is called, a NoSuchElementException will be thrown.

Hibernate Searches

Searching with Hibernate is almost identical to that with Castor. Example 8-8 details the implementation of searching with Hibernate.

Example 8-8. Searching for a book by title with Hibernate

```
public Book findBookByTitle(String title) throws Exception {
    Datastore ds = Hibernate.createDatastore();
    ds.storeFile("hibernate.xml");
    SessionFactory sessionFactory = ds.buildSessionFactory();
    Session session = sessionFactory.openSession();
```

Example 8-8. Searching for a book by title with Hibernate (continued)

```
    Book book = null;
    List results = session.find("from o in class book.Book where title =
        ?", title, Hibernate.STRING);
    if (results.isEmpty()) {
        throw new Exception ("Entity not found: " + title);
    } else {
        book =  results.get(0);
    }
    session.close();
    return book;
}
```

The difference with Hibernate is that rather than throwing an exception when no entities are found, the framework supplies the method isEmpty() to determine if your search yielded no results.

Beyond the Basics

A full discussion of the details of each alternative framework is well beyond the scope of this book. Furthermore, Castor and Hibernate are not your only alternatives. You should now, however, have an appreciation of how these two frameworks operate, some things to look for, and the role of alternative persistence frameworks in database programming.

PART III

Tutorials

The first two sections of the book cover a variety of technologies. You should be familiar with many of the them, but you may not be familiar with all of them. As an EJB programmer, you probably know J2EE technologies like EJB and JNDI well, but you may not be familiar with JDO. This section provides a JDO tutorial just for you. Because you know EJB and JNDI so well, however, you will find no use for the J2EE tutorial.

In short, not every tutorial chapter is for every reader of this book. Some advanced readers, in fact, will have no use for any of the tutorial chapters. I do expect most readers will find the need to reference at least one of these chapters before tackling a chapter earlier in the book. If you have no experience in JDO, for example, you probably want to look at the JDO tutorial before reading the chapter on JDO persistence. If you have no EJB experience, read the J2EE chapter before tackling either of the EJB persistence chapters. Finally, you need to understand the material in the JDBC and SQL tutorials to appreciate just about any chapter in Part I or Part II.

CHAPTER 9

J2EE Basics

We must know the secret union of soul and body, and the nature of both
these substances; by which the one is able to operate, in so many instances,
upon the other.
—David Hume
An Enquiry Concerning Human Understanding

Most of the time when you are working with a database in a Java environment, you are working in some aspect of the J2EE framework. Rarely will you build a pure JDBC application with no reliance on the J2EE platform. It is therefore no surprise that many of the chapters in this book assume some level of appreciation for the J2EE APIs.

This tutorial is far from a comprehensive how-to on building J2EE applications. If you are looking to learn J2EE, then you should pick up a book dedicated to the subject. In this chapter, I offer an overview of the most important concepts in the J2EE platform so that you can tackle the subject matter of this book's first eight chapters.

The Platform

A platform provides application developers with a full abstraction of a generic computing environment. The Windows platform, for example, is a suite of APIs that enables developers to write desktop applications for any system running Windows, regardless of the underlying hardware they are using. The main Java platform, Java 2 Standard Edition (J2SE), does the same thing except its abstraction spans all desktop systems.

Whereas the J2SE platform creates a standard for desktop programming independent of hardware and operating system, the J2EE platform provides a standard for enterprise systems. It is a superset of J2SE. It adds the following abstractions:

- Enterprise JavaBeans (EJB)
- Java Servlets
- JavaServer Pages (JSP)

- Java Naming and Directory Interface (JNDI)
- Java Transaction Architecture (JTA)
- Java Message Service (JMS)
- Java Mail
- J2EE Connector API
- XML support

Two APIs critical to the J2EE platform, JDBC Data Access and Remote Method Invocation (RMI), predate the J2EE platform and exist in the J2SE platform.

The focus of this book is simply one aspect of J2EE programming, application persistence through relational databases. A full discussion of the J2EE platform is thus beyond the scope of this book. Nevertheless, as a database programmer, a foundation in a few of these APIs is important. I provide an overview of JNDI, JavaServer Pages, RMI, and Enterprise JavaBeans here. Later in the book, I provide a more detailed tutorial on JDBC.

Java Naming and Directory Interface

The Java Naming and Directory Interface API provides a single set of classes for accessing any kind of naming or directory service. If you are intent on learning just one enterprise API, you should learn JNDI with it; it is the door through which you will have to work to program in an enterprise environment.

> **BEST PRACTICE**   If you intend to work with the J2EE APIs, make sure you learn JNDI.

Naming and Directory Services

Naming and directory services are among the most fundamental tools of computing. They enable us to access computing resources using human-friendly names. It would be hard to imagine using a computer in which you had to access a file on a hard drive by its physical location or select a printer for a print job based on its I/O port. Instead, you have a filesystem that lets you use a name that is automatically translated to a physical location on request. Before you can access just about any resource—local or remote—you need to access a naming or directory service.

A *naming service* is nothing more than a database that associates familiar names with technical values. A very simple example of a naming service is the Internet Domain Name Service (DNS). DNS associates computer names with IP addresses. If you want to access my web site, you type in *www.imaginary.com* and the application checks with a DNS server to translate that name value to the IP address that provides the actual location of my server on the Internet. Not only is *www.imaginary.com* easier to remember than a quad of numbers; the use of an easy-to-remember name enables me to change the physical location of the server without impacting your ability to access it.

A *directory service* is simply an extension of a naming service that enables you to structure data in a hierarchical namespace. In other words, not only does a directory service support access to some network object by an easy-to-remember name, but it also enables you to create a tree of information in which that object is stored. A domain object, for example, could contain many hosts. Microsoft's Active Directory Service (ADS) is among the newest examples of directory services. In ADS, Windows 2000 stores a variety of network resources, including users, computers, domains, and printers.

You may be wondering what the differences are between a directory service storing user information and a relational database storing user information. Both directory services and relational databases are specific kinds of databases. A directory service stores information in a hierarchical format and a relational database in a more complex format consistent with relational theory. A directory service is best suited to read-heavy, hierarchical data. By *read-heavy*, I mean that access to that data is mostly read access with occasional writes.

When writing database applications, you will deal with a variety of directory services. The most common directory services include:

- ActiveDirectory
- LDAP
- NIS

The most common directory service you will access, however, is the directory service built into your J2EE application server. It may use LDAP or some other directory service, or it may follow a proprietary format. You will use it to look up J2EE resources such as JDBC data sources.

JNDI Architecture

JNDI is the J2EE gateway into different naming and directory services. Using JNDI, an application can store information in and retrieve information from naming and directory services. Like other Java enterprise APIs, the beauty of JNDI is that the application does not care what kind of naming or directory service is being used. The same API serves to access LDAP directories, OpenDirectory, ADS, NIS+, NDS, DNS, and more. Sun even provides an implementation of JNDI that stores information in a regular filesystem.

Some of the J2EE APIs serve as abstractions for common kinds of architectural components in enterprise systems. JNDI is one of these architectural abstractions.

Enterprise applications talk to a JNDI service provider using the generic JNDI API. Figure 9-1 illustrates this architecture.

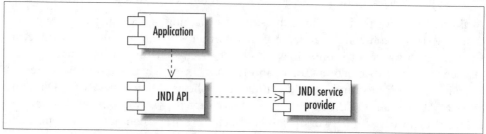

Figure 9-1. The JNDI architecture

No matter what naming or directory service you are using, your application will use the exact same JNDI calls to perform the exact same functions. The JNDI classes know how to find the service providers for different services based on the application's runtime configuration. These service providers implement an API called the JNDI Server Provider Interface (SPI). The SPI is specifically a set of Java interfaces that a service provider must implement in order to give JNDI access to its directory service. The advantage of this approach is that you can literally switch an application from NIS to ActiveDirectory simply by changing configuration information—no code changes are required. For the most current list of service providers, visit *http:// java.sun.com/products/jndi/serviceproviders.html*.

The Basics of JNDI Programming

A Java application basically wants to do one of two things with a directory service:

- Find objects stored in the directory service
- Bind new or modified objects to the directory service

Because a directory service is a read-heavy data store, applications really spend most of the time looking up objects stored in the directory.

InitialContext

The first JNDI code you write in any JNDI application is code that creates an initial context. A context is simply a base from which everything is considered relative. In your local phone book, for example, the context is your country code and often an area code. The numbers in the phone book do not mention their country code or area code—you just assume those values from the context. A JNDI context performs the exact same function. The initial context is simply a special context to get you started with a particular naming and directory service. The simple form of initial context construction looks like this:

```
Context ctx = new InitialContext( );
```

In this case, JNDI grabs its initialization information from your system properties. In using this format, you make it possible for an application to be directory service–independent. You can, however, specify your own initialization values by passing the properties to the InitialContext constructor:

```
Properties props = new Properties();
Context ctx;

// Specify the name of the class that will serve
// as the context factory
props.put(Context.INITIAL_CONTEXT_FACTORY,
          "com.sun.jndi.fscontext.RefFSContextFactory");
ctx = new InitialContext(props);
```

This code will create an initial context for the filesystem provider. You can now use this context to bind Java objects to the filesystem or to look them up. The most common configuration properties are:

java.naming.factory.initial (Context.INITIAL_CONTEXT_FACTORY)

This property identifies the service provider to be used by specifying the fully qualified class name of the factory class that creates the initial context object.

java.naming.language (Context.LANGUAGE)

This property stores the language preferences of the user accessing the naming or directory service. This value can be a colon-separated list of language tags. If left unspecified, the service provider determines the language preference.

java.naming.security.authentication (Context.SECURITY_AUTHENTICATION)

This property stores the security level to be used by the service provider. Its value must be one of the following strings: "none", "simple", or "strong". The security level is dependent on the service provider when this property is not specified.

java.naming.security.credentials (Context.SECURITY_CREDENTIALS)

This property stores whatever data will help authenticate the user (principal) to the naming or directory service. For example, this property could store a user's password or X.509 certificate.

java.naming.security.principal (Context.SECURITY_PRINCIPAL)

This property identifies the principal using the naming or directory service. The actual value depends on the authentication scheme being used. For example, with username/password authentication, this property will store the username.

java.naming.security.protocol (Context.SECURITY_PROTOCOL)

This property stores text identifying the security protocol to be used. For example, it might contain the text "ssl" to specify SSL (Secure Sockets Layer). If left unspecified, the service provider can interpret this property as it sees fit.

When you create a new InitialContext, the InitialContext class—which implements the Context interface—asks the service provider's initial context factory for an initial context. That object then delegates to the service provider's initial context to handle any operations.

Lookups

Lookups under JNDI are very simple. The following code finds a printer using the fileservice provider:

```
Printer p = (Printer)ctx.lookup("printers/laser");
```

This code will do a search in the directory for the object with the matching DN. If the matching object is not a printer, then you will see a ClassCastException.

Names are one of the tricky parts of JNDI. Specifically, each naming and directory service has its own name format. Examples from different domains include:

- *cn=George Reese,ou=Web,dc=imaginary,dc=com*
- *c=us,o=imaginary,ou=Web,cn=Sal*
- */usr/local/bin/python*

Of course, there are also names that span multiple directory services. The URL *http://www.imaginary.com/Java/index.html*, for example, references the file */prd/www/html/Java/index.html* (a filename) on the machine *www.imaginary.com* (a DNS name). JNDI provides the Name class to help abstract away from naming service–specific conventions. All Context methods that look for a name as an argument will accept either a String representation of the name or a Name object representation.

Before you can look and object up in JNDI, it must first be bound to the directory. The task of assigning an object to a DN is called binding:

```
Printer = new Printer();
Context ctx = new InitialContext(props);

p.setManufacturer("HP");
p.setModel("LaserJet 4ML");
ctx.bind("printers/Laser", p);
ctx.close();
```

References

This code shows JNDI returning a Java Printer object from the directory. JNDI supports two different ways of storing Java objects in a directory:

- Directly via Java serialization
- Indirectly using special reference objects

The direct method stores the Java object in a directory as binary data representing the serialized form of the Java object. Many directory services, however, do not understand serialization. Furthermore, not all applications accessing a directory service are written in Java. JNDI therefore supports an alternate mechanism for storing Java objects in a directory in the form of references.

The JNDI Reference class enables a directory service to save the internal state of a Java object to a directory. A Reference also knows how to instantiate a copy of the desired Java object from data in the directory. In order to enable your Java objects to be stored by reference instead of serialization, they need to implement the Referenceable interface. This interface prescribes a single method: getReference( ). The job of this method is to create a Reference instance populated with the attributes to be stored. Example 9-1 shows how a User object might accomplish this task.

Example 9-1. Implementing Referenceable for storage in JNDI

```java
import javax.naming.NamingException;
import javax.naming.Reference;
import javax.naming.Referenceable;
import javax.naming.StringRefAddr;

public class User implements Referenceable {
    private String email  = null;
    private String userID = null;

    public User(String uid, String em) {
        super( );
        userID = uid;
        em = email;
    }

    public String getEmail( ) {
        return email;
    }

    public Reference getReference( ) throws NamingException {
        String cname = UserFactory.class.getName( );
        Reference ref =
            new Reference(getClass( ).getName( ),     cname, null);

        ref.add(new StringRefAddr("email", email));
        ref.add(new StringRefAddr("userID", userID));
        return ref;
    }

    public String getUserID( ) {
        return userID;
    }
}
```

The UserFactory class referenced in the User class is used by the service provider to create a User instance when an application reads a User object from the directory service. Example 9-2 provides an implementation of this class.

Example 9-2. A factory for User instances

```
import java.util.Hashtable;
import javax.naming.NamingException;
import javax.naming.Reference;
import javax.naming.spi.ObjectFactory;

public class UserFactory extends ObjectFactory {
    public UserFactory() {
        super();
    }

    public Object getObjectInstance(Object ob,m Name nom,
                                    Context ctx, Hashtable env) {
        if( ob instanceof Reference ) {
            Reference ref = (Reference)ob;

            if( ref.getClassName().equals(User.class.getName()) ) {
                RefAddr tmp = ref.get("userID");
                String uid, em;

                if( tmp != null ) {
                    uid = (String)tmp.getContent();
                }
                tmp = ref.get("email");
                if( tmp != null ) {
                    em = (String)tmp.getContent();
                }
                return new User(uid, em);
            }
        }
        return null;
    }
}
```

Attribute manipulation

Reading from a directory means more than doing straight lookups. An application will also look up object attributes. In such cases, your application should get a specific kind of context, the directory context. A directory context is represented by the JNDI class DirContext:

```
DirContext ctx = new InitialDirectoryContext();
```

You can then grab the attributes associated with a DN using the following code:

```
Attributes atts =
    ctx.getAttributes("cn=Sal,ou=Web,dc=imaginary,dc=com");
```

The Attributes class is a collection holding all of the attributes associated with an object in the directory. You can get a specific attribute from the collection using the get( ) method:

```
Attribute pw = attrs.get("password");
```

Finally, you can access the actual attribute value using the `Attribute` class's `get( )` method:

```
System.out.println("Your password is: " + pw.get( ));
```

Though getting attributes from a directory is pretty straightforward, changing them can be downright bizarre. You have to create a `ModificationItem` instance with an `Attribute` representing the attribute to modify. Finally, you tell the directory context to make the change:

```
ModificationItem[ ] changes = new ModificationItem[1];
BasicAttribute attr = new BasicAttribute("password", "secret");

changes[0] = new ModificationItem(DirContext.REPLACE_ATTRIBUTE,
                                  attr);
ctx.modifyAttributes("cn=Sal,ou=Web,dc=imaginary,dc=com",
                     changes);
```

All of this code does nothing more than change Sal's password to "secret". Under this paradigm, however, you can change multiple attributes for the same object at once. You need only add more elements to the changes array. In addition to replacing an attribute, you can use this API to add a new attribute or delete an obsolete attribute:

```
ModificationItem[ ] changes = new ModificationItem[2];
BasicAttribute tel, cell;

tel = new BasicAttribute("telephone", "+1.763.555.1778");
cell = new BasicAttribute("cellphone");
changes[0] = new ModificationItem(DirContext.ADD_ATTRIBUTE,
                                  tel);
changes[1] = new ModificationItem(DirContext.REMOVE_ATTRIBUTE,
                                  cell);
ctx.modifyAttributes("cn=Sal,ou=Web,dc=imaginary,dc=com",
                     changes);
```

Searching the directory

`Attributes` instances are also critical to searching the directory for objects. To perform a simple search, you construct an instance of `BasicAttributes`—which implements the `Attributes` interface—and specify the attributes on which you wish to search:

```
DirContext ctx = new DirContext( );
Attributes attrs = new BasicAttributes(true);
NamingEnumeration res;

attrs.put(new BasicAttribute("favoriteColor", "red"));
res = ctx.search("ou=Web", attrs);
while( res.hasMoreElements( ) ) {
    // process matching element
}
```

The result, of course, is a list of all of the people in the web department whose favorite color is red. The true parameter passed to the `BasicAttributes` constructor says that we do not want case sensitivity in our attribute matching. Each element in the resulting enumeration is actually an instance of a class called `SearchResult`. The `SearchResult` represents the object bound in the directory service. If you want the actual object, you can call `getObject( )`. On the other hand, you can just grab its attributes if that is all you are after:

```
while( res.hasMoreElements( ) ) {
    SearchResult sr = (SearchResult)res.nextElement( );
    Attributes attrs = sr.getAttributes( );
    Attribute cn = attrs.get("cn");

    System.out.println(cn.get( ) + " likes red!");
}
```

This simple search is not particularly interesting. You may want to ask questions like "Who has a Social Security number starting with 042?" or "Who has a last name of Smith?" For these more complex searches, you need to use search filters. If you are familiar with regular expressions from languages like Perl or Python, JNDI search filters will be at least somewhat familiar to you. Specifically, JNDI relies on RFC 2254 for defining its matching rules. Table 9-1 lists the symbols included in this RFC with their meanings.

Table 9-1. JNDI search filter symbols from RFC 2254

Symbol	Name	Description
&	Conjunction	The expression is true if all component expressions are true.
|	Disjunction	The expression is true if only one component expression is true.
!	Negation	Negates the truth-value of the expression.
=	Equality	The expression is true if the attribute matches the specified value in accordance with the matching rules for that attribute.
~=	Approximate equality	The expression is true if the attribute comes close to matching the specified value in accordance with the matching rules for that attribute.
>=	Greater than	The expression is true if the attribute is greater than the specified value in accordance with the matching rules for that attribute.
<=	Less than	The expression is true if the attribute is less than the specified value in accordance with the matching rules for that attribute.
=*	Presence	The attribute has a value, but the actual value is unimportant.
*	Wildcard	Matches zero or more characters in its position.
\	Escape	Escapes special symbols, including (and), when they appear in a filter.

The format of the search filters is a bit unintuitive. Each expression is enclosed by parentheses. Two expressions may be joined by a & or | symbol. For example:

```
(&(cn=* Reese)(favoriteColor=red))
```

This expression translates to all objects in which the cn ends with "Reese" (i.e., a last name of Reese) and the favoriteColor value is "red". You can end up with some fairly LISP-like* expressions on complex search filters. The following code performs a search using a more complex search filter:

```
NamingResult res;
String flt;

flt = "(&(favoriteColor=red)(|(cn=* Reese)(cn=* Viega)))";
res = ctx.search("ou=Web", flt, null);
while( res.hasMoreElements( ) ) {
    // process results
}
```

Access to Enterprise Components via JNDI

If you have done any JDBC programming, you know what a nightmare it can be to connect to the database. Your application must both register a vendor-specific class with JDBC and provide connection information specific to that driver, including such information as the driver-specific URL, user ID, and password. In short, your application needs to know a lot about the specific connection requirements of a specific vendor tool to access a specific database. The result is a cumbersome connection process that is too easily tied to proprietary components.

In a robust architecture, components reference one another by name only. Just as the IP address for my web server can change without affecting your ability to reach my web site because you are using a name via a naming service, you can code your application to find other architectural components by name by registering them with some sort of naming service. For JDBC, you can store database configuration information in a directory service under a specific name. An application seeking a database connection then accesses the desired database by name. As a result, system administrators can change configuration information in the directory service without any impact on the production application.

JNDI is probably the single most important API on the J2EE platform exactly because most APIs rely on a directory service to store information about enterprise resources. The best way to access JDBC and RMI is through JNDI. The only way to access EJB is through JNDI.

JNDI and JDBC

On the J2EE platform, an application gains access to a database via JDBC's DataSource class. A DataSource instance contains all of the information necessary to

---

* If you missed out on the joys of LISP in college, it is a rather odd programming language in which all notation is in reverse-polish notation, the format shown in the examples.

make a connection. Using this class, an application can connect using the following simple code:

```
Connection conn;
DataSource ds;

// some code to get a DataSource instance goes here
conn = ds.getConnection();
```

So where does the application get a DataSource instance? Naturally, it retrieves it from a directory service via JNDI. At deployment time, a system administrator goes into the administrative tool appropriate for the directory service being used and enters information about the database to which the DataSource should connect. The system administrator then assigns a name to this DataSource and saves the configuration.

How the configuration actually works is naturally dependent on the directory service being used. Ideally, this information will be stored in a serialized DataSource object in the directory service. If the directory service is incapable of storing serialized Java objects, then the configuration tool will use an alternative mechanism. Either way, your application does not care. The earlier missing code looks like this:

```
Context ctx = new InitialContext();
Connection conn;
DataSource ds;

ds = (DataSource)ctx.lookup("enterpriseExamples");
conn = ds.getConnection();
```

JNDI and EJB

EJB, like JDBC, has a special class through which applications access the system. Unlike JDBC, an application does not seek access to the EJB application server as a whole, but instead to specific business objects within the application server. The special class through which these business objects are accessed is called their home. A Flight business object, for example, would have a FlightHome home.

Homes are configured during the process of deploying an Enterprise JavaBeans application. The EJB application server takes the information from the deployment process and creates an entry in its directory service. A client then uses the application server's JNDI implementation to gain access to the deployed EJB.

In order to access a specific Flight instance, you need to know only the name under which the home is registered and the primary key for the flight being sought:

```
Context ctx = new InitialContext();
FlightHome home;
Flight flight;

home = (FlightHome)ctx.lookup("FlightHome");
flight = home.findByPrimaryKey(somePK);
```

JNDI and other enterprise components

You should see a pattern emerging here. Everywhere one enterprise component needs to access another, it does so via JNDI. All of the information required for that access is stored in a JNDI-supported directory. This architecture enables components to change drastically without any effect on the other components in the system. The freedom to reconfigure components in a runtime is critical to scalability. For example, an application that was launched with the web server, application server, and database server all on the same physical machine can be reconfigured to run on three different machines without requiring any code changes or regression testing.

JavaServer Pages

JavaServer Pages are the Java way to build web-based user interfaces using Java as a scripting language for generating dynamic XHTML.[*] In other words, JSP enables you to embed Java code inside your XHTML so that the full content of the XHTML page can be dependent on the state of the system when a user requests a page. Example 9-3 shows your obligatory "Hello World" application as a JSP page.

Example 9-3. A simple JSP page

```
<%@ page info="Hello World" %>

<% String msg = "Hello World!"; %>

<html>
  <head>
    <title><%=msg%></title>
  </head>

  <body>
    <h1><%=msg%></h1>
    <p>
      Though this example is largely uninteresting, it does
      demonstrate how Java can be embedded in an XHTML page to
      generate content dynamically.
    </p>
  </body>
</html>
```

As with any "Hello World" application, this one is mind-numbingly dull. What you should take from it, however, is the basic structure that enables you to call methods in Java objects and drive content from Java values. Though I used a simple `String` instance in this example, the `<title>` and `<h1>` values could have been drawn from a database.

---

[*] JSPs are not limited to XHTML. They can generate HTML, XML, or any other kind of textual markup.

The web server or application server in which the JSP runs interprets anything between <% and %> as Java code and anything between <%= and %> as values to be printed out. When a request is made for a JSP page, that page is turned into a Java object. Your embedded Java code becomes part of that compilation. The XHTML in your page becomes a string to send out. The server then executes the method into which your Java code was compiled.

This compile happens only once as long as the server remains running and no one changes the JSP source. If you make a change to the JSP source, however, the server will recompile it the next time it is requested.

JSPs become interesting when you hook them up to an EJB system or a database. Naturally, we will be doing just that throughout Part II of this book. This section simply describes the basics behind JavaServer Pages.

Page Structure

A JSP page consists of static content, JSP directives, Java code, and JSP tags:

Static content
> Static content is the XHTML into which your JSP code is embedded.

JSP directives
> These elements appear between <%@ and %> markers. They indicate directives to the server prior to compiling the JSP page.

Java code
> Java code is everything between <% and %> and between <%= and %> tags. This code is executed for each page view.

JSP tags
> A JSP tag is an XML-like interface into a library of Java code. The JSP specification prescribes a core set of tags, but you can add your own through custom tag libraries.

As a general rule, the fewer lines of Java code in your JSP page, the better. When you add a lot of Java code to a JSP page, you, in a sense, defeat the purpose of using JSPs over the Java Servlet API. Specifically, defining your user interface as a set of JSPs enables you to transfer the work of user interface writing to XHTML programmers instead of Java programmers. This transfer hopefully results in more creative resources being responsible for UI development.

JSP Programming

Example 9-4 provides a more typical JSP page than the "Hello World" code in Example 9-3.

Example 9-4. A JSP page that drives content from a content management database

```jsp
<%@ page info="Page Loader" %>
<%@ page import="org.dasein.tractatus.jsp.ErrorLog" %>
<%@ page import="org.dasein.tractatus.jsp.Tractatus" %>

<%@ taglib uri="/WEB-INF/tld/tractatus.tld" prefix="tractatus" %>

<jsp:useBean id="user" scope="session" class="org.dasein.security.User"/>
<% pageContext.setAttribute(Tractatus.USER, user); %>
<% user.setPreferredLocale(request.getLocale()); %>

<tractatus:setTarget/>

<% pageContext.setAttribute("template", target.getTemplate()); %>
<% if( target.getContent() != null ) { %>
  <% pageContext.setAttribute("contentTemplate",
                              target.getContent().getTemplate()); %>
<% } else { %>
  <% pageContext.setAttribute("contentTemplate", null); %>
<% } %>

<tractatus:authorize>
  <tractatus:allowed>
    <tractatus:isNull name="template">
      <tractatus:true>
        <tractatus:isNull name="contentTemplate">
          <tractatus:true>
            <tractatus:printContent/>
          </tractatus:true>
          <tractatus:false>
 <jsp:include page="<%=target.getContent().getTemplate().getRelativeURL()%>"/>
          </tractatus:false>
        </tractatus:isNull>
      </tractatus:true>
      <tractatus:false>
        <jsp:include page="<%=target.getTemplate().getRelativeURL()%>"/>
      </tractatus:false>
    </tractatus:isNull>
  </tractatus:allowed>
  <tractatus:denied>
    <% String msg = "<p class=\"error\">Access denied.</p>"; %>
    <jsp:include page="page.jsp">
      <jsp:param name="target"
       value="<%=target.getSite().getErrorPage().getPageID()%>"/>
      <jsp:param name="error" value="<%=ErrorLog.storeException(msg)%>"/>
    </jsp:include>
  </tractatus:denied>
  <tractatus:unauthenticated>
    <%
      response.sendRedirect(target.getSite().getLoginPage().getRelativeURL() +
```

```
                              "&previous=" + target.getPageID( ));
    %>
  </tractatus:unauthenticated>
</tractatus:authorize>
```

Though all of the content for this page is dynamically generated, very little of it is direct Java code. It starts out with three directives:

```
<%@ page info="Page Loader" %>
<%@ page import="org.dasein.tractatus.jsp.ErrorLog" %>
<%@ page import="org.dasein.tractatus.jsp.Tractatus" %>

<%@ taglib uri="/WEB-INF/tld/tractatus.tld" prefix="tractatus" %>
```

The first directive provides metainformation about the JSP page for tools. The second and third directives tell the server what Java import statements to use for this page when compiling it. The final one tells the server where to find definitions for the custom tags in use in this page.

Only the last directive requires any elaboration. When you build a library of Java objects that can serve as JSP tags, you need to create an XML descriptor file that maps tag names to Java classes. The uri value for the taglib directive points to this XML file. The prefix value then names what prefix will appear for the tags in this JSP page. In this case, the prefix is *tractatus*.

You will use the tag in the next line of code, <jsp:useBean>, in almost all of your JSP pages. It enables you to store and access a regular JavaBean as part of the user session information. In this case, I am storing a User object representing the site visitor.

The next two lines are the first bit of actual Java code:

```
<% pageContext.setAttribute(Tractatus.USER, user); %>
<% user.setPreferredLocale(request.getLocale( )); %>
```

You probably gather that the user variable in the second line comes from the call to <jsp:UseBean>. On the other hand, it is entirely unclear where the pageContext variable comes from. A JSP page defines several page-level variables to which you have access. The two you will most commonly use are pageContext and request. The pageContext variable represents information about the context of the page execution. In this example, I am setting an attribute that can be used by my custom tags. The Tractatus.USER constant is simply a String constant for "user".[*]

The other variable you will commonly need, request, represents the HTTP request coming in from the browser. It contains information about the requester and the

---

[*] I believe it is a good solid practice never to have literal values in your source code, except as constant definitions. This line reflects that practice.

headers of the request. In the second line, I am looking for internationalization information from the request. Specifically, I am trying to find out what locales the browser is set to accept.

The next line is the first custom tag in this JSP page:

```
<tractatus:setTarget/>
```

Behind this tag's simplicity is some complex Java code for setting a variable named target to a custom Java object of type org.dasein.tractatus.Page based on the request sent to the server. For example, if the URL was *http://www.imaginary.com/ page.jsp?target=5*, then the <tractatus:setTarget> tag will go to the database, find the Page with a pageID of 5, and then set the target variable to that Page instance.

Perhaps you can imagine the level of complexity I would have added to this page had I not hidden everything behind a JSP tag. Now, XHTML programmers do not need to know anything about looking up custom objects hidden in a database. They simply include this one empty tag and they are all set.

The rest of the code is mostly custom tags with a small mix of Java code. In short, it does the following:

1. Verifies that the user has access to the requested page.
2. Verifies that the user is disallowed, allowed, or not yet authenticated:
   - If disallowed, the user is redirected to a page telling him he does not have the proper permissions.
   - If allowed, the user is shown the actual content through the <jsp:include> tags.
   - If the user has yet to be authenticated and the web page is not open to the public, the user is redirected to a login page.

Custom Tags

The power of JavaServer Pages lies in the ability to build reusable Java components and then hide them behind custom tags. The creation of custom tags is quite simple. You write a class that implements a specific API and then map that class to a tag name via an XML descriptor file. A simple custom tag looks like Example 9-5.

Example 9-5. A simple custom tag

```
package org.dasein.tractatus.jsp;

import java.io.IOException;
import java.util.Locale;

import javax.servlet.ServletRequest;
import javax.servlet.jsp.JspException;
import javax.servlet.jsp.tagext.TagSupport;
```

Example 9-5. A simple custom tag (continued)

```
import org.dasein.persist.PersistenceException;
import org.dasein.security.User;
import org.dasein.tractatus.Page;

public class HTMLTitleTag extends TagSupport {
    public int doEndTag( ) throws JspException {
        try {
            Page p = (Page)pageContext.getAttribute(Tractatus.TARGET);
            User u = (User)pageContext.getAttribute(Tractatus.USER);
            Locale def = p.getSite( ).getDefaultLocale( );
            String ttl;

            ttl = "<title>" + p.getTitle(u.getPreferredLocale(def))
                + "</title>";
            pageContext.getOut( ).println(ttl);
        }
        catch( IOException e ) {
            throw new JspException(e.getMessage( ));
        }
        catch ( PersistenceException e ) {
            throw new JspException(e.getMessage( ));
        }
        return EVAL_PAGE;
    }
}
```

This custom tag extends the TagSupport class from the JSP API and implements a single method, doEndTag( ). This method is triggered when the server reaches the end tag of your custom tag. Because this particular tag is an empty tag, the end happens right after the start. In this example, the tag finds the current target value (previously set by <tractatus:setTarget>) as well as the current user value (previously set by <jsp:useBean>). It then prints out the XHTML for the page's title translated into the user's preferred language.

To add this tag to the web site, you need to edit the XML tag library descriptor file to map a tag name to this class. If this tag were the only tag in the tag library, the descriptor file would look like Example 9-6.

Example 9-6. Sample tag descriptor

```
<?xml version="1.0" encoding="ISO-8859-1" ?>
<!DOCTYPE taglib
PUBLIC "-//Sun Microsystems, Inc.//DTD JSP Tag Library 1.1/EN"
"http://java.sun.com/j2ee/dtds/web-jsptaglibrary_1_1.dtd">

<taglib>

  <tlibversion>1.0</tlibversion>
  <jspversion>1.1</jspversion>
  <shortname>tractatus</shortname>
```

Example 9-6. Sample tag descriptor (continued)

```
<tag>
  <name>htmlTitle</name>
  <tagclass>org.dasein.tractatus.jsp.HTMLTitleTag</tagclass>
  <bodycontent>empty</bodycontent>
</tag>
```

```
</taglib>
```

The code in bold shows the definition of the custom tag. It maps the name `htmlTitle` to the class `org.dasein.tractatus.jsp.HTMLTitleTag` and establishes the constraint that the tag should be an empty tag. Consequently, whenever the server encounters the following in a JSP page:

```
<tractatus:htmlTitle/>
```

The server prints out the title of the page referenced by the `target` variable localized for the user.

Custom tags do get more complicated. Some contain XHTML code, while others contain other custom tags. A full description of this API is well beyond the scope of this book. For more information, take a look at *JavaServer Pages* (O'Reilly) by Hans Bergsten.

Remote Method Invocation

The object is the center of the Java world. Distributed object technologies provide the infrastructure that enables two objects running on two different machines to talk to each other using an object-oriented paradigm. Using traditional networking, you need to write IP socket code to let two objects on different machines communicate. While the socket-based approach works, it is prone to error. The ideal solution is to let the Java virtual machine do the work. You call a method in an object, and the virtual machine determines where the object is located. If it is a remote object, it will perform all the dirty network work for you.

Several technologies, like the Common Object Request Broker Architecture (CORBA), predate Java. CORBA enables developers to provide a clean, distributed programming architecture. CORBA has a very wide reach and is wrought with complexities associated with its grandiose goals. For example, it supports applications whose distributed components are written in different languages. In order to support everything from writing an object interface in C to handling more traditional object languages such as Java and Smalltalk, it has built up an architecture with a very steep learning curve.

CORBA does its job very well, but it does a lot more than you need in a pure Java environment. This extra functionality has a cost in terms of programming complexity. Unlike other programming languages, Java has distributed support built into its core. Borrowing heavily from CORBA, Java supports a simpler, pure Java distributed object solution called RMI.

The Structure of RMI

RMI is an API that enables you to ignore the fact that you have objects distributed all across the network. You write Java code that calls methods in remote objects using the same semantics you use in calling local methods. The biggest problem with providing this kind of API is that you are dealing with two separate virtual machines existing in two separate memory address spaces. Consider, for example, the situation in which you have a Bat object that calls hit( ) in a Ball instance. Located together on the same virtual machine, the method call looks like this:

```
ball.hit( );
```

You want RMI to use the exact same syntax when the Bat instance is on one machine and the Ball instance is on another. The problem is that the Ball instance does not exist inside the client's memory. How can you possibly trigger an event in an object to which there is no reference? The first step is to get a reference.

Remote object access

I am going to co-opt the term *server* for a minute and use it to refer to the virtual machine that holds the real copies of one or more distributed objects. In a distributed object system, you can have a single host (generally called an application server) act as an object server—a place from which clients get remote objects—or you can have all systems act as object servers. Clients simply need to be aware of where the object server(s) is located.* An object server has a single defining function: to make objects available to remote clients.

A special program called *rmiregistry* that comes with the JDK listens to a port on the object server's machine. The object server in turn binds object instances to that port using a special URL so clients can later find it. The format of the RMI URL is *rmi:// server/object*. A client then uses that URL to find a desired object. For the previous bat and ball example, the ball would be bound to *rmi://athens.imaginary.com/Ball*. An object server binds an object to a URL by calling the static rebind( ) method of java.rmi.Naming:

```
Naming.rebind("rmi://athens.imaginary.com/Ball", new BallImpl( ));
```

---

* Using JNDI, they do not even need to know where the server is. Clients just look up objects by name, and the naming and directory service knows where the server is. You will see this in practice later in the chapter when you read about EJB.

The *rmi://athens.imaginary.com* portion of the preceding URL is self-evident; you cannot bind an object instance to a URL on another machine in a secure environment. Naming allows you to rebind an object using only the object name for short:

```
Naming.rebind("Ball", new BallImpl());
```

 In RMI, binding is the process of associating an object with an RMI URL. The rebind() method specifically creates this association. At this point, the object is registered with the *rmiregistry* application and is available to client systems. Reference by any system to its URL is thus specifically a reference to the bound object.

The rebind() methods make a specific object instance available to remote objects that do a lookup on the object's URL. This is where life gets complicated. When a client connects to the object URL, it cannot get the object bound to that URL. That object exists only in the memory of the server. The client needs a way to fool itself into thinking it has the object while routing all method calls in that object over to the real object. RMI uses Java interfaces to provide this sort of hocus-pocus.

Remote interfaces

All Java objects that you intend to make available as distributed objects must implement an interface that extends the RMI interface java.rmi.Remote. You call this step making an object remote. You might do a quick double take if you look at the source code for java.rmi.Remote. It looks like this:

```
package java.rmi;

public interface Remote {
}
```

No, there is no typo there. The interface prescribes no methods to be implemented. It exists so that objects in the virtual machines on both the local and remote systems have a common base class they can use for deriving all remote objects. They need this base class since the RMI methods look for subclasses of Remote as arguments.

When you write a remote object, you have to create an interface that extends Remote and specify all methods that can be called remotely. Each of these methods must throw a RemoteException in addition to any application-specific exceptions. In the bat and ball example, you might have had the following interface:

```
public interface Ball extends java.rmi.Remote {
    void hit() throws java.rmi.RemoteException;

    int getPosition() throws RemoteException;
}
```

The BallImpl class implements Ball. It might look like:

```
import java.rmi.RemoteException;
import java.rmi.server.UnicastRemoteObject;

public class BallImpl
extends UnicastRemoteObject implements Ball {
    private int position = 0;

    public Ball( ) throws RemoteException {
        super( );
    }

    public int getPosition( ) {
        return position;
    }

    public void hit( ) {
        position += calculateDistance( );
    }

    protected int calculateDistance( ) {
        return 10;
    }
}
```

The java.rmi.server.UnicastRemoteObject class that the BallImpl extends provides support for exporting the ball; that is, it allows the virtual machine to make it available to remote systems. This may look like what the Naming class does, but it has a different purpose. Naming ensures that the object is bound to a particular URL, while exporting an object enables it to be referenced across the network. This means that you can pass the object as a method argument or return it as a return value. It also means that you can use Naming.rebind( ) to make the object available through a URL lookup. A URL lookup looks like this:

```
ball = (Ball)Naming.lookup("rmi://athens.imaginary.com/Ball");
```

 Because you have just read about JNDI, you might wonder why RMI forces you to know where the object is located instead of using a simple JNDI name. The answer is simple: RMI predates JNDI. JNDI now, however, offers a service provider supporting RMI lookups.

Because you may not have the option of extending UnicastRemoteObject, you can export your objects another way using this syntax in the object constructor:

```
public BallImpl( ) throws RemoteException {
    super( );
    UnicastRemoteObject.exportObject(this);
}
```

Both approaches are equally valid. The only difference is the structure of your inheritance tree.

After writing both classes, you compile them just like any other object. This will, of course, generate two *.class* files, *Ball.class* and *BallImpl.class*. The final step in making the `BallImpl` class distributed is to run the RMI compiler, *rmic*, against it. In this case, run *rmic* using the following command line:

```
rmic BallImpl
```

Like the *java* command—and unlike the *javac* command—*rmic* takes a fully qualified class name as an argument. This means that if you had the `Ball` class in a package called baseball, you would run *rmic* as:

```
rmic -d classdir baseball.Ball
```

In this case, *classdir* represents whatever the root directory for your baseball package class files is. This directory will likely be in your CLASSPATH. The output of *rmic* will be two classes: *Ball_Skel.class* (the *skeleton*) and *Ball_Stub.class* (the *stub*). These classes will be placed relative to the *classdir* you specified on the command line.

Stubs and skeletons

I have introduced a couple of concepts, stub and skeleton, without any explanation. They are two objects you should never have to concern yourself with, but they do all of the heavy lifting that makes remote method calls work. In Figure 9-2, I show where these two objects fit in a remote method call.

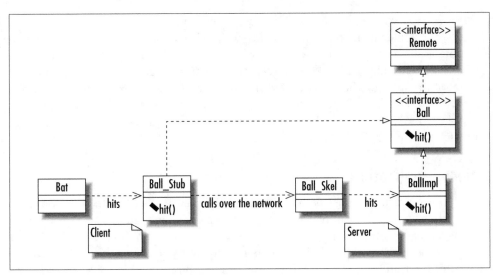

Figure 9-2. The process of calling a method in a remote object

The process of translating a remote method call into network format is called *mar-shaling*; the reverse is called *unmarshaling*. When you run the *rmic* command on your remote-enabled classes, it generates two classes that perform the tasks of mar-shaling and unmarshaling. The first of these is the stub object, a special object that implements all of the remote interfaces implemented by the remote object. The dif-ference is that where the remote object actually performs the business logic associ-ated with a method, the stub takes the arguments to the method and sends them across the network to the skeleton object on the server. In other words, it marshals the method parameters and sends them to the server. The skeleton object, in turn, unmarshals those parameters; it takes the raw data from the network, translates it into Java objects, and then calls the proper method in the remote object.

The skeleton and stub perform the reverse roles for return values. The skeleton takes the return value from the method and sends it across the network. The client stub then takes the raw socket data and turns it into Java data, returning that Java data to the calling method.

Remote exceptions

All methods that can be called remotely and all constructors for remote objects must throw a special exception called `java.rmi.RemoteException`. The methods you write will never explicitly throw this exception. Instead, the local virtual machine will throw it when you encounter a network error during a remote method call. Exam-ples of such situations include one of the machines crashing or a loss of connectivity between the two machines.

A `RemoteException` is unlike any other exception. When you write an application to be run on a single virtual machine, you know that if your code is solid, you can pre-dict potential exceptional situations and where they might occur. You can count on no such predictability with a `RemoteException`. It can happen at any time during the course of a remote method call, and you may have no way of knowing why it hap-pened. You therefore need to write your application code with the knowledge that at any point your code can fail for no discernible reason and have contingencies to sup-port such failures.

Object Serialization

Not all objects that you pass between virtual machines are remote. In fact, you need to be able to pass the primitive Java data types as well as many basic Java objects, such as `String` or `HashMap`, that are not remote. When a nonremote object is passed across virtual machine boundaries, it gets passed by value using object serialization instead of the traditional Java RMI way of passing objects, by reference. Object seri-alization is a feature that enables you to turn objects into a data stream that you can use the way you use other Java streams—send it to a file, over a network, or to standard output. What is important about this method of passing objects across virtual machines is that changes you make to the object on one virtual machine are not reflected in the other virtual machine.

Most of the core Java classes are serializable. If you wish to build classes that are not remote but need to be passed across virtual machines, you need to make those classes serializable. A serializable class minimally needs to implement java.io.Serializable. For almost any kind of nonsensitive data you may want to serialize, just implementing Serializable is enough. You do not even need to write a method; Object already handles the serialization for you. It will, however, assume that you do not want the object to be serializable unless you implement Serializable. Example 9-7 provides a simple example of how object serialization works. When you run it, you will see the SerialDemo instance in the second block display the values of the one created in the first block.

Example 9-7. A simple demonstration of object serialization

```java
import java.io.*;

public class SerialDemo implements Serializable {
    static public void main(String[ ] args) {
        try {
            { // Save a SerialDemo object with a value of 5
                FileOutputStream f = new FileOutputStream("/tmp/testing.ser");
                ObjectOutputStream s  = new ObjectOutputStream(f);
                SerialDemo demo = new SerialDemo(5);

                s.writeObject(demo);
                s.flush( );
            }
            { // Now restore it and look at the value
                FileInputStream f = new FileInputStream("/tmp/testing.ser");
                ObjectInputStream s = new ObjectInputStream(f);
                SerialDemo demo = (SerialDemo)s.readObject( );

                System.out.println("SerialDemo.getVal( ) is: " +
                                    demo.getVal( ));
            }
        }
        catch( Exception e ) {
            e.printStackTrace( );
        }
    }

    int test_val = 7; // value defaults to 7

    public SerialDemo() {
        super( );
    }
```

Example 9-7. A simple demonstration of object serialization (continued)

```
public SerialDemo(int x) {
    super();
    test_val = x;
}

public int getVal() {
    return test_val;
}
}
```

Enterprise JavaBeans

RMI is a distributed object API. It specifies how to write objects so that they can talk to one another no matter where on the network they are found. I could write dozens of business objects that can, in principal, talk to your business objects using RMI. At its core, however, RMI is nothing more than an API to which your distributed objects must conform. RMI says nothing about other characteristics normally required of an enterprise-class distributed environment. For example, it says nothing about how a client might perform a search for RMI objects matching some criteria. It also says nothing about how those objects might work together to construct a single transaction.

What is missing from the picture is a distributed component model. A component model is a standard that defines how components are written so that systems can be built from components by different authors with little or no customization. You may be familiar with the JavaBeans component model. It is a component model that defines how you write user interface components so that they may be plugged into third-party applications. The magic thing about JavaBeans is that there is very little API behind the specification—you neither implement nor extend any special classes and you need call no special methods. The force of JavaBeans is largely in conformance with an established naming convention.

Enterprise JavaBeans is a more complex extension of this concept. While there are API elements behind Enterprise JavaBeans, it is much more than just an API. It is a standard way of writing distributed components so that the components I write can be used with the components you write in someone else's system. RMI does not support this ability for several reasons. Consider all of the following issues RMI does not address:

Security

RMI says nothing about security. RMI alone basically leaves your system wide open. Anybody who has access to your RMI interfaces can forge access to the underlying components. Unless you write some complex security checks to authenticate clients and verify access, you will have no security. Your components are therefore unlikely to interoperate with my components unless we agree to share some sort of security model.

Searching

RMI provides the ability to do a lookup for only a specific, registry-bound object. It says nothing about how you find unbound objects or perform searches for a group of objects meeting certain requirements. Writing a banking application, you might want to support the ability to find all accounts with negative balances. In order to do this in an RMI environment, you would have to write your own search methods in bound objects. Again, your custom approach to handling searches simply won't work with someone else's custom approach to searching without forcing clients to deal with both search models.

Transactions

Perhaps the most important piece to a distributed component model is support for transactions. RMI says absolutely nothing about transactions. When you build an RMI-based application, you will need to address how you will support transactions. In other words, you will need to keep track of when a client begins a transaction, what RMI objects that client changes, and committing and rolling back those changes when the client is done. This problem is compounded by the fact that most distributed object systems are supporting more than one client at a time. Different transaction models are even more incompatible than different search or security models. While client coders can get around differences in search and security models by being aware of those differences, transaction models can almost never be made to work together.

Persistence

RMI says nothing about how RMI objects persist across time. Over the course of this book, I will introduce several different persistence models. EJB is behind three of these persistence models.

Enterprise JavaBeans addresses all of these points and more so that you can literally pick and choose the best designed business components from different vendors and make them work and play well with one another in the same environment. EJB is now the standard component model for capturing distributed business components. It hides from you the details you might have to worry about yourself if you were writing an RMI application.

EJB Roles

One of the benefits of the EJB approach is that it separates different application development roles into distinct parts so that everything one role does is usable by any possible player of any of the other roles. EJB specifically defines the following roles:[*]

---

[*] Any given role may be played by multiple players on a project. Similarly, one person may play multiple roles.

The EJB provider

> The EJB provider is an expert in the problem domain in question and develops Java objects that capture the business concepts that make up the problem domain. The EJB provider worries about nothing other than business logic programming.

The application assembler

> The application assembler is an expert in the processes that make up a business and in building user interfaces that employ the EJB provider's business components.

The deployer

> The deployer is an expert in a specific operating environment. The deployer takes an assembled application and configures it for deployment in the runtime environment.

The EJB server provider

> A server provider supports one or more services, such as a JDBC driver supporting database access.

The EJB container provider

> The container is where EJB components live. It is the runtime environment in which the beans operate. The container provider is a vendor that builds the EJB container.

The system administrator

> The system administrator manages the runtime environment in which EJB components operate.

An EJB provider captures each of the business components that model a business in Java code. The EJB specification breaks down each of these business components into three pieces: the home interface, the remote interface, and the bean implementation. Your job as the EJB provider is thus to write these three classes for each business component in your system.

Kinds of Beans

EJB specifies two kinds of beans: *entity beans* and *session beans*. The distinction between the two is that entity beans are persistent and session beans are transient. In other words, entity beans save their states across time while session beans do not. Most business concepts will work best as entity beans—they are the entities that make up your business. Entity beans are shared by all clients.*

---

* This is not necessarily true of all environments. Specifically, EJB allows for a clustered environment in which multiple application servers work together to serve up beans. In such an environment, the same entity may appear on different servers and serve different clients. The containers are responsible in those situations for making the system appear as if the clients share the same entity reference.

Session beans are unique to each client. They come to life only when requested by a client. When that client is done with them, they go away. An example of a session bean might be a `Registration` class that represents the registration of a person for some event. The `Registration` exists for a specific client to associate a person with an event. It manages the business logic associated with a registration, but it goes away once the registration is complete. The persistent data is in the `Person` and `Event` classes.

 The word *bean* is a heavily overloaded term in Java. Even within the EJB specification, the word *bean* has different meanings in different contexts. It can mean one of the three classes called the bean implementation or it can mean the business concept as a whole. I take the approach of using the term *bean* alone to mean the business component represented by the three EJB classes and the term *bean implementation* to mean the one class that implements the business logic.

The home and remote interfaces for both kinds of beans are RMI remote interfaces. That is, they are indirectly derived from the `java.rmi.Remote` interface and are exported for remote access. The class extended by a remote interface is `EJBObject`. If, for example, you wanted to turn the `Ball` object from earlier in the chapter into an entity bean, you would create a `BallHome` interface, a `Ball` interface, and a `BallBean` implementation. The `Ball` interface would extend `javax.ejb.EJBObject`, which in turn extends `java.rmi.Remote`. The result might be a class that looks like this:

```
public interface Ball extends javax.ejb.EJBObject {
    void hit( ) throws java.rmi.RemoteException;

    int getPosition( ) throws RemoteException;
}
```

This interface looks a lot like the RMI example from earlier in the chapter. In fact, the only difference is that this one extends `Remote` indirectly via `EJBObject`. The interface specifies only those methods that should be made available to the rest of the world.

The home interface is where you go to find or create instances of the bean. It specifies different versions of `create( )` or `findXXX( )`[*] methods that enable a client to create new instances of the bean or find existing instances. If you think about the problem of a banking system, they might have account beans, customer beans, and teller beans. When the bank attracts a new customer, its enterprise banking system needs to create a `Customer` bean to represent that customer. The bank manager's Windows application that enables the registration of new customers might have the following code for creating a new `Customer` bean:

```
InitialContext ctx = new InitialContext( );
CustomerHome custhome;
```

---

[*] Only entity beans have finder methods.

```
Customer cust;

custhome = (CustomerHome)ctx.lookup("CustomerHome");
cust = custhome.create(ssn);
```

This code provides you with your first look at JNDI support in EJB. Using a JNDI initial context, you look up an implementation of the customer bean's home interface. That home interface, CustomerHome, provides a create( ) method that enables you to create a new Customer bean. In the preceding case, the create( ) method accepts a String representing the customer's Social Security number.* The EJB specification requires that a home interface specify create( ) signatures for each way to create an implementation of that bean. The CustomerHome interface might look like this:

```
public interface CustomerHome extends EJBHome {
    Customer create( ) throws CreateException, RemoteException;

    Customer create(String ssn)
    throws CreateException, RemoteException;

    Customer findByPrimaryKey(CustomerKey pk)
    throws FinderException, RemoteException;

    Customer findBySocialSecurityNumber(String ssn)
    throws FinderException, RemoteException;
}
```

The finder methods provide ways to look up Customer objects. All except the findByPrimaryKey( ) method can be named however you wish to name them, and they should return either a remote reference to the bean in question or a Collection.

The findByPrimaryKey( ) method is a special finder for EJBs. Each entity bean instance has a primary key that uniquely identifies it. The primary key can be any serializable Java class you write. The only requirement is that the class must implement the equals( ) and hashCode( ) in an appropriate fashion. For example, if your beans have a unique numeric identifier, you might create your own CustomerKey class that stores the identifier as a long. If you do the latter, your CustomerKey class should look something like the following:

```
public class CustomerKey implements Serializable {
    private long objectID = -1L;

    public CustomerKey(long l) {
        objectID = l;
    }

    public boolean equals(Object other) {
        if( other instanceof CustomerKey ) {
            return ((CustomerKey)other).objectID == objectID;
```

---

* A Social Security number is a U.S. federal tax identifier.

```
        }
        return false;
    }

    public int hashCode( ) {
        return (new Long(objectID)).hashCode( );
    }
}
```

You can even use primitive wrapper classes instead of custom primary key classes. The following example, for instance, could just as easily have used the Long class for its primary keys.

You do not actually write the class that implements the Customer or CustomerHome interfaces—that is the task of the EJB container. Generally, the EJB container will have tools that enable a deployer to automatically create and compile implementation classes for the home and remote interfaces. These automatically generated classes handle issues such as security and then delegate to your bean implementation class. The bean is where you write your business logic.

The bean class must implement the following methods:

- It must implement every method in the class it implements: EntityBean for entity beans and SessionBean for session beans.

- It must implement every method in the remote interface using the exact same signatures found in the remote interface.

- It must implement a variation of the methods in the home interface.* For create( ) methods, it must implement counterparts called ejbCreate( ) that each takes the same arguments but returns a primary key object. Similarly, the findXXX( ) counterparts for entities are ejbFindXXX( ) methods that each takes the same arguments and returns either a primary key object or a collection of primary keys.

Consider that the Customer remote interface for the previous home interface looks like this:

```
public interface Customer extends EJBObject {
    String getSocialSecurityNumber( ) throws RemoteException;
}
```

A skeleton of the bean implementation might look something like this (minus the method bodies):

```
public class CustomerBean implements EntityBean {
    private transient EntityContext context = null;
    private          String        ssn    = null;
```

---

* This applies only to beans using bean-managed persistence. For container-managed beans, the creates and finds are implemented by the container.

```java
public void ejbActivate() throws RemoteException {
    // you will mostly leave this method empty
    // activation of resources required by
    // an object of this type independent of the
    // customer it represents belong here
    // an example might be opening a file handle
    // for logging
}

public CustomerKey ejbCreate() throws CreateException {
    // this method creates a primary key for the
    // customer and inserts the customer into the
    // database
}

public CustomerKey ejbCreate(String ssn)
throws CreateException {
    // this method works the same as ejbCreate()
}

public CustomerKey ejbFindByPrimaryKey(CustomerKey pk)
throws FinderException, RemoteException {
    // this method goes to the database and performs
    // a SELECT and returns the PK if it is in the
    // database
}

 public CustomerKey ejbFindBySocialSecurityNumber(String ssn)
throws FinderException {
    // this method goes to the database and performs
    // a SELECT and returns the PK of the row
    // with a matching SSN
}

public void ejbLoad() throws RemoteException {
    // this method goes to the database and selects
    // the row that has this object's primary key
    // and then populates this object's fields
}

public void ejbPassivate() throws RemoteException {
    // this method is generally empty
    // you should release any system resources held
    // by this object here
}

public void ejbPostCreate() {
    // this is called to let you do any initialization
    // for this object after ejbCreate() is called and
    // a primary key is assigned to the object
}
```

```
public void ejbRemove() throws RemoteException {
    // this method goes to the database and deletes
    // the record with a primary key matching this
    // object's primary key
}

public void ejbStore() throws RemoteException {
    // this method goes to the database and saves
    // the state of this bean
}

public String getSocialSecurityNumber() {
    // this method is from the Customer remote interface
    return ssn;
}

public void setEntityContext(EntityContext ctx)
throws RemoteException {
    // this method assigns an EntityContext to the
    // bean
    context = ctx;
}

public void unsetEntityContext()
throws RemoteException {
    // this method removes the EntityContext assignment
    context = null;
}
}
```

JDBC comes into play under the bean-managed persistence model in the ejbCreate( ), ejbFindXXX( ), ejbLoad( ), ejbStore( ), and ejbRemove( ) methods. Chapter 6 describes the details of bean-managed persistence. Under container-managed persistence, you do not worry about any persistence issues. EJB supports two distinct container-managed persistence models. The old model, EJB 1.x persistence, did not work well at all. The newer model, EJB 2.x persistence, is very promising though not yet widely implemented in production systems. Chapter 5 covers container-managed persistence.

The book *Enterprise JavaBeans* (O'Reilly) by Richard Monson-Haefel contains a more complete discussion of EJB development.

CHAPTER 10

SQL

Being a part of a sentence is a Normal condition for proper performance of every elementary sentence part. But it is also more than a Normal condition. It is a necessary condition. For just what each element is supposed to do cannot be defined except in relation to the rest of the sentence.

—Ruth Garrett Millikan
Language, Thought, and Other Biological Categories

SQL—often apocryphally referred to as the Structured Query Language—is the vehicle for communication with relational databases. Once you learn SQL, you are in command of the basic tool for talking to Oracle, DB2, MySQL, SQL Server, Ingres, PostgreSQL, Informix, mSQL, Sybase, Access, and any other relational database engine. Other query languages like OQL (Object Query Language) exist, but they tend to support interaction with other kinds (i.e., not relational) of databases. Even when you are accessing your database through a GUI tool or a higher-level abstraction, somewhere under the hood SQL is probably in play.

SQL is a sort of "natural" language. In other words, an SQL* statement should read—at least on the surface—like a sentence of English text. This approach has both benefits and drawbacks, but the end result is a language unlike traditional programming languages such as Java and C.

Background

SQL is "structured" in the sense that it follows a very specific set of rules. A computer program can parse a formulated SQL query easily. In fact, the O'Reilly book *lex & yacc*

---

* SQL is pronounced "ess-que-el." Some people get very offended when you mispronounce it. A sufficient number of people do mispronounce it nevertheless. Consequently, the mispronunciation "sequel" is nearly as valid as the proper pronunciation in spite of the protests of purists

by John Levine, Tony Mason, and Doug Brown implements an SQL grammar to demonstrate the process of writing a program to interpret a programming language! A query is a fully specified command sent to the database server. The database server then performs the requested action. Here's an example of an SQL query:

```
SELECT name FROM Person WHERE name LIKE 'Stac%';
```

This statement reads almost like a form of broken English: "Select names from a list of persons where the names are like 'Stac'." SQL uses few of the formatting and special characters generally associated with computer languages.

The SQL Story

IBM invented SQL in the 1970s, shortly after Dr. E. F. Codd invented the concept of a relational database. From the beginning, SQL was an easy-to-learn yet powerful language. It resembles a natural language, so it is less daunting to a nontechnical person. In the 1970s, even more than today, this advantage was important. There were no casual hackers; you were a hardcore programmer or did not program at all. The people who programmed computers knew everything about how a computer worked. SQL was aimed at the army of nontechnical accountants and business and administrative staff who would benefit from accessing the power of a relational database.

SQL was so popular with its target audience, in fact, that in the 1980s, the Oracle Corporation launched the world's first publicly available commercial SQL system. Oracle SQL was a huge hit and it spawned an entire industry built around SQL. Sybase, Informix, Microsoft, and several other companies have since come forward with their implementations of SQL-based relational database management systems (RDBMSs).

When Oracle and its competitors first hit the scene, SQL was still relatively new and no standard existed. It was only in 1989 that the ANSI standards body issued the first public SQL standard. These days, that standard is often referred to as SQL89. Unfortunately, the standard did not go far enough into defining the technical structure of the language. Thus, even though the various commercial SQL languages were drawing closer together, differences in syntax still made it nontrivial to switch among implementations. It was not until 1992 that the ANSI SQL standard came into its own.

People refer to the 1992 standard as both SQL92 and SQL2. The SQL2 standard expanded the language to accommodate as many of the proprietary extensions added by the commercial vendors as possible. Many cross-DBMS tools—including JDBC—have standardized on SQL2 as their mode of communication with relational databases. Due to the extensive nature of the SQL2 standard, however, relational databases that implement the full standard are very complex beasts.

SQL2 is not the last word on the SQL standard. With the growing popularity of object-oriented database management systems (OODBMS) and object-relational database management systems (ORDBMS), there has been increasing pressure to capture support for object-oriented concepts in relational databases. The recent SQL3 (SQL99) standard is the answer to this problem.

SQL2 defines several levels of compliance to address its complexity. The most important level—the one required by JDBC—is SQL92, entry level. Entry level defines the core SQL syntax. If your goal is to write portable applications, you should go no further in the SQL specification than entry level.

Database Interaction

Any number of methods exists for sending SQL to a database engine and retrieving the results of your command. Throughout most of this book, you are using Java's JDBC API to handle that interaction. For the purposes of this chapter, however, you will need to use a tool that interactively sends SQL to your database. Each database engine comes with at least one such tool. In general, there are both command-line and GUI-interactive SQL tools. MySQL, for example, provides the *mysql* commands line utility. PostgreSQL similarly provides a similar tool called *psql*. Before going any further in this chapter, I recommend you find out the tool that comes with your database so you can try the examples that come later.

When you run a command-line program like *mysql*, it prompts you for SQL:

```
[09:04pm] carthage$  mysql -u root -p jtest
Enter password:
Welcome to the MySQL monitor.  Commands end with ; or \g.
Your MySQL connection id is 3 to server version: 3.22.29
Type 'help' for help.
mysql>
```

The previous *mysql* command says to connect to the MySQL server on the database jtest on the local machine as the user root (the -u option) with the client prompting you for a password (the -p option). Another option, -h, enables you to connect to MySQL servers on remote machines:

```
[09:04pm] carthage$ mysql -u root -h db.imaginary.com -p jtest
```

Once *mysql* is running, you can enter your SQL commands all on a single line or split them across multiple lines. MySQL waits for a semicolon or the \g sequence before executing the SQL:

```
mysql> SELECT book_number
    -> FROM book
    -> ;
```

```
+-------------+
| book_number |
+-------------+
|           1 |
|           2 |
|           3 |
+-------------+
3 rows in set (0.00 sec)
```

GUI utilities generally provide you with a text box into which you can enter SQL. Pressing Enter or clicking a button to send the SQL to the database will execute the SQL for you. The tool then displays the results in a graphical table. In some cases, you can even manipulate the table and the tool will create and send to the database SQL that updates the underlying database.

Basic Syntax

As I mentioned earlier, SQL resembles a human language more than a computer language because it has a simple, defined imperative structure. Much like an English sentence, individual SQL commands—called *queries*—can be broken down into language parts. Consider the following examples:

```
CREATE     TABLE Person      ( name CHAR(10) );
verb       direct object     adjective phrase

INSERT     INTO Person       ( name )              VALUES ( 'me' );
verb       indirect object   adjective phrase      direct object

SELECT     name              FROM people           WHERE name like '%e';
verb       direct object     indirect object       adjective phrase
```

Most SQL implementations are case-insensitive. In other words, it does not matter how you type SQL keywords as long as the spelling is correct. The previous CREATE example is just as valid when written like this:

```
cREatE TAblE Person ( name ChAr(10) );
```

This case-insensitivity extends only to SQL keywords.* In some database engines, identifiers are also case-insensitive. For others, they are case-sensitive. Still, the case-sensitivity of other database engines like MySQL depends on the underlying operating system. Most MySQL identifiers are case-sensitive; however, table names and database names are case-sensitive only on operating systems whose filesystems are case-sensitive. It is therefore good practice to assume that your identifiers are case-sensitive in order to guarantee portability of your SQL across all database engines.

---

* For the sake of readability, I capitalize all SQL keywords in the book. I also recommend this convention as a solid best-practice technique for all production code.

The first element of an SQL query is always a verb. The verb expresses the action you wish the database engine to take. The most commonly used verbs are:

CREATE
> Creates an object in the database

DELETE
> Deletes data from a database table

INSERT
> Inserts new data into a database table

SELECT
> Retrieves data from the database

UPDATE
> Modifies data in a database table

Although what follows the verb varies depending on the verb used, they all follow the same general format: you name the object upon which you are acting and then describe the data you are using for the action. For example, the query CREATE TABLE people (name CHAR(10)) uses the verb CREATE, followed by the object TABLE. The rest of the query describes the table to be created.

An SQL query originates with a client application. The client constructs a query based on user actions and sends the query to the database engine. The database engine must then process the query and perform the specified action. Once the server has done its job, it returns some value or set of values to the client.

Because the primary focus of SQL is to communicate actions to the database server, it does not have the flexibility of a general-purpose language. Most of the functionality of SQL concerns input to and output from the database: adding, changing, deleting, and reading data. SQL provides other functionality, but always with an eye toward how it can be used to manipulate data within the database.

 In order to execute the SQL in this chapter, you will need the proper access rights. Different actions naturally demand different levels of access. For example, you should have no problem executing basic queries. Unless you have the DBA password, however, it is unlikely you will be able to create database instances.

Database Creation

The first thing you do with any database engine is to create a database instance to work with. It is therefore quite ironic that no standard mechanism for creating database instances is supported. For the most part, you can create a database instance in most database engines using some variation of the CREATE DATABASE statement. Its simplest form is common to all database engines:

```
CREATE DATABASE name
```

In essence, this statement creates a brand new, blank database instance. It is all you need to create a MySQL or PostgreSQL database. PostgreSQL does offer the option of specifying where you place the database files for the instance:

```
CREATE DATABASE name WITH LOCATION = 'path'
```

The more complex database engines require more complex database creation statements. Oracle, for example, allows you to specify options such as log file specifications, datafile specifications, and character set information. When in doubt, you can get away with the basic syntax listed earlier. However, you rarely will find any default database creation values suitable to a production environment. In places like this, you will find the help of a good DBA (database administrator) with expertise in your database engine of choice invaluable.

Once you have a database to work with, you can work with that database using the CONNECT statement:

```
CONNECT [TO]
DEFAULT | { [server] [AS name] [USER user] }
```

For example, to connect to the PostgreSQL database instance library on the server carthage, you would execute the following SQL:

```
CONNECT TO library@carthage AS libconn USER webuser
```

In MySQL, this statement is slightly different:

```
CONNECT dbname [server [AS user]]
```

Oracle also provides an alternate syntax:

```
CONNECT [ [user/password] [AS [SYSOPER | SYSDBA] ] ]
```

You are now set to begin using your new database instance. In the examples in this chapter, I will be using a database called jtest.

Once you are done with a database and no longer have use for the data it contains, you can get rid of the instance from your server using the DROP DATABASE command:

```
DROP DATABASE dname
```

 Dropping databases—or anything else for that matter—from a database is a very destructive operation. The only way to recover from an accidental DROP command is to restore from a backup!

Oracle, however, does not support the DROP DATABASE command. To get rid of a database in Oracle, issue the CREATE DATABASE command with no parameters using the name of the existing database that should be dropped.

Table Management

Now that you have a clean, new database instance and have connected to it, it is time to create the structures that will hold your data. The most basic of these structures is the table. Before adding data to a table, you must first create it in the database.

The Basics of Table Creation

The act of creating a table defines the data the table holds and any constraints placed on that data. The basic elements of the table structure are the names of its columns, their data types, and their constraints. SQL data types are similar to data types in other languages. The full SQL standard allows for a large range of data types. The general form for creating a table is:

```
CREATE TABLE tblname (
    colname type [modifiers]
    [, colname type [modifiers]]
)
```

A table may have any number of columns, but too many columns can render the table inefficient. Good database design can help you avoid unwieldy table structures. By creating properly normalized* tables, you can join tables together and perform searches for data across multiple tables. We discuss the mechanics of a join later in the chapter.

Consider, for example, the table structure of the User table in Table 10-1.

Table 10-1. The structure for a User table

Column name	Data type	Constraints
userID	INT UNSIGNED	NOT NULL PRIMARY KEY
name	CHAR(10)	NOT NULL UNIQUE INDEX
lastName	VARCHAR(30)	
firstName	VARCHAR(30)	
office	CHAR(2)	NOT NULL

You can create the table shown in Table 10-1 using the following SQL:

```
CREATE TABLE User (
    userID    INT UNSIGNED   NOT NULL,
    name      CHAR(10)       NOT NULL,
    lastName  VARCHAR(30),
    firstName VARCHAR(30),
    office    CHAR(2)        NOT NULL DEFAULT `NY'
)
```

---

* See Chapter 2 for a full discussion of database design and normalization.

This statement creates a table called User with five columns: userID, name, lastName, firstName, and office. After each column comes the data type for the column and some modifiers. In this example, we describe only the NOT NULL constraints as part of the CREATE statement. We will define the indexes later.

The NOT NULL modifier indicates that the column may not contain any NULL values. If you attempt to assign a NULL value to that column, the database will issue an error. A couple of exceptions exist for this rule. First, if the column is some kind of sequence column,* the database will automatically generate a unique value for the column. The second exception is when you specify a default value for a column as we did for the office column. When you insert a NULL value into a NOT NULL column with a default value, the default value is inserted in place of the NULL.

To get rid of your newly created table (with the exception of Oracle users), use the DROP statement:

```
DROP TABLE User
```

Data Types

In a table, each column has a data type. As I mentioned earlier, SQL data types are similar to data types in other languages. While many languages define a bare minimum set of types necessary for completeness, SQL goes out of its way to provide types such as DATE that will be useful to everyday users. You could store a date value in a column with a more basic numeric type, but having a type specifically dedicated to the nuances of date processing adds to SQL's ease of use—one of SQL's primary goals.

In dealing with data types, you really need to know your database engine of choice. All databases share a small subset of data types and then extend beyond that core set. Furthermore, two databases may have data types of the same name that behave differently. Whatever the database you are using, however, some basic best practices can assist you in your database programming.

Before you create a table, you should know what kind of data you intend to store in the table's columns. Beyond obvious decisions about whether your data is character-based or numeric, you should also know the approximate size of the data you wish to store. If it is a numeric field, what is the maximum possible value that could make sense? What is the minimum possible value? Could that range change in the future? Answering these questions will enable you to choose a data type sufficient for storing your data without wasting disk space or RAM.

---

* Sequence columns are columns for which the database automatically generates values. The mechanics of sequence columns vary from database to database with very little in common between any two.

You should always strive for the smallest possible type capable of storing your value range. If, for example, you have a field that represents the population of a state, use an unsigned numeric type if your database supports unsigned types. As long as no state has a negative population, your database will operate well. Furthermore, a 32-bit numeric type will be sufficient for a state's population. It would take a state population roughly the size of the current population of Earth to get you in trouble with this choice of data type.

Numeric types

Numeric data types store uninterpreted number values. Such values can range from simple integers to complex, high-precision decimals. Your choice of numeric data type depends on what you expect the largest possible value to be, what you expect the smallest value to be, and how precise you expect that value to be. Table 10-2 shows the major numeric types for MySQL and Oracle.

Table 10-2. Numeric types in MySQL and Oracle

Database	Type	Description
MySQL	TINYINT	Whole 7-bit numbers in the range −128 to 127.
	SMALLINT	Whole 8-bit numbers in the range −32758 to 32,757.
	MEDIUMINT	Whole 16-bit numbers in the range −8,388,608 to 8,388,607.
	INT	Whole 32-bit numbers in the range −2,147,483,548 to 2,147,483,547.
	BIGINT	Whole 64-bit numbers in the range −9,223,372,036,854,775,808 to 9,223,372,036,854,775,807.
	DECIMAL(p,s)	Decimal values with s as the scale and p as the precision.
	DOUBLE(p,s)	Double-precision values with s as the scale and p as the precision.
	FLOAT(p)	Floating point numbers with a precision of 8 or less.
Oracle	INTEGER(n)	Whole numbers capable of storing up to n digits.
	NUMBER(p,s)	Any number where p specifies the precision and s the scale. The precision may be between 1 and 38 and the scale between −84 and 127.
	FLOAT(p)	Floating point numbers with a precision up to 126.

Character types

Managing character types is much more complicated that managing numeric types. Not only do you have to worry about minimum and maximum lengths, but you have to worry about the average size, variation, and character set of the strings. Indexing, which I will cover in the next section, also complicates the choice of character type. It generally works best when you choose a fixed-length data type for indexed character columns. If your column has little or no variation in the length of its strings, the fixed-length CHAR data type is probably your best bet. An example of a solid candidate for the CHAR data type is a column holding a country code. The International Standards

Organization (ISO) provides a comprehensive list of standard two-character codes for countries (e.g., US for the United States, FR for France, etc.). Because the codes are always two characters, a CHAR(2) is the best way to maintain a column holding country codes.

A value does not have to have a constant length to be held in a CHAR column. It should, however, have very little variance. Phone numbers, for example, will fit in a CHAR(13) column even though phone number lengths vary from nation to nation. The variance is small enough that there is no point in making the string variable length. The problem with a CHAR field, however, is that it always takes up the exact same amount of storage no matter what you store in it. In a CHAR(20) column, the strings "A" and "ABCDEFGHIJKLMNO" all occupy the same amount of storage space. Anything under 20 characters is padded with spaces. Though the minimal potential waste for phone number values is an acceptable trade-off for the efficiency of fixed-length searches, it is not acceptable for strings with greater variance.

Variable-length fields address the needs of strings that have a significant variance between their minimum and maximum lengths. A good, common example of such a value is a web URL. A URL can be as simple as *http://www.imaginary.com* or as long as *http://code.law.harvard.edu/filtering/test.asp?URL=http%3A%2F%2Fwww.slashdot.org*. If you create a column with a fixed-width field large enough to hold the latter URL, you will waste a lot of space with the majority of values that look more like the former.

Most character types require you to specify a maximum length for the string. In most databases, the database truncates any strings that exceed the maximum length. If, for example, you insert the string "happy birthday" into a CHAR(4) field, the database will store only "happ".

Table 10-3 contains the most common character types for MySQL and Oracle.

Table 10-3. Character types for MySQL and Oracle

Database	Type	Description
MySQL	CHAR(n)	Fixed-length character type that holds exactly n characters. Shorter strings are padded with spaces to n characters.
	NCHAR(n)	Same as CHAR, except for Unicode strings.
	VARCHAR(n)	Variable-length strings that may store up to n characters. Any excess characters are discarded.
	NVARCHAR(n)	Same as VARCHAR, except for Unicode strings.
Oracle	CHAR(n)	Fixed-length character type that holds exactly n characters. Shorter strings are padded with spaces to n characters.
	NCHAR(n)	Same as CHAR, except for Unicode strings.
	VARCHAR2	Variable-length strings up to 4000 characters in length.
	NVARCHAR2	Same as VARCHAR2, except for Unicode strings.

Other types

SQL supports many other types, from dates and times to binary data and more. The most recent ANSI SQL, SQL99, adds support for user-defined data types in the mold of object-oriented programming languages. You should check the documentation for your database of choice to understand the full range of data types available to you.

Indexing

Indexes assist the database in identifying specific rows in a table. Without an index, a search for a specific row in a table containing a million rows would require the engine to walk through every single row. An index provides the database with hints about the location of the row and how many possible matches might exist for your search criteria.

The cost of an index is storage space. The most efficient use of indexes is therefore to create indexes for the columns you intend to search on. You can create an index using the following basic syntax:

```
CREATE [UNIQUE] INDEX idxname ON tblname ( colname [, colname] )
```

As with just about any other SQL statement, each database carries its own variations on this syntax. Nevertheless, you can create the unique index for the name column in the User table referenced earlier in any database engine using the following syntax:

```
CREATE UNIQUE INDEX userName ON User ( name )
```

Some databases also let you create an index while creating the table:

```
CREATE TABLE User (
    userID    INT UNSIGNED      NOT NULL,
    name      CHAR(10)          NOT NULL,
    lastName  VARCHAR(30),
    firstName VARCHAR(30),
    office    CHAR(2)           NOT NULL DEFAULT 'NY',
    UNIQUE INDEX ( name )

)
```

When the database now searches for a row having a specific name value, it knows how to narrow its search to a subset of the table. Furthermore, because the index is unique, it knows to stop the search when it finds the matching value.

ANSI SQL also supports a special kind of index called a *primary key*. A relational table can have at most a single primary key. The primary key is a unique index that signifies the preferred mechanism for uniquely identifying a row in that table. In all technical respects, the primary key is indistinguishable from a unique index. You are allowed to specify single-column primary keys on the same line as the column definition in a table CREATE statement:

```
CREATE TABLE cities (id      INT  NOT NULL PRIMARY KEY,
                     name    VARCHAR(100),
                     pop     INT,
                     founded DATE)
```

Before you create a table, determine which fields, if any, should be keys. As I mentioned earlier, any fields that support joins are good candidates for primary keys.

You will commonly want to specify multicolumn indexes and primary keys. For example, a translation table for book titles requires the book ID and language to uniquely identify a title translation:

```
CREATE TABLE BookTitleTrans (
    bookID     INTEGER(9)   NOT NULL,
    language   CHAR(2)      NOT NULL,
    title      VARCHAR2(255) NOT NULL,
    PRIMARY KEY ( bookID, language ));
```

Data Management

The first thing you will probably want to do with a newly created table is add data to it. Once the data is in place, you need to maintain it—add to it, modify it, and perhaps even delete it.

Inserts

Creating a row in a table is one of the more straightforward concepts in SQL. The standard form of the INSERT statement is:

```
INSERT [INTO] table_or_view_name (column1, column2, ..., columnN)
{ [DEFAULT] VALUES | VALUES (value1, value2, ..., valueN)
| select_statement }
```

You specify the columns followed by the values to populate those columns for the new row. When inserting data into numeric fields, you can insert the value as is; for all other fields, you must wrap them in single quotes. For example, to insert a row of data into a table of addresses, you might issue the following command:

```
INSERT INTO Address (name, address, city, state, phone, age)
VALUES('Robert Smith', '123 Fascination St.', 'New London', 'CT',
    '(800) 555-1234', 43)
```

In addition to the direct specification of the values to add, you can populate the table with a new row containing default values or even from the results of some other query. For example, to insert the results from a query as new rows in a table, you might execute the following SQL:

```
INSERT INTO FavoriteSong ( id, name, album, artist )
SELECT Song.id, Song.name, Album.title, Artist.name
FROM Song, Album, Artist
```

```
WHERE Song.ranking > 4
AND Song.album = Album.id
AND Album.artist = Artist.id
```

You should note that the number of columns in the INSERT call matches the number of columns in the SELECT call. In addition, the data types for the INSERT columns must match the data types for the corresponding SELECT columns. Finally, the SELECT clause in an INSERT statement cannot contain an ORDER BY modifier and cannot be selected from the same table in which the INSERT occurs.

Primary Keys

The best kind of primary key is one that has absolutely no meaning in the database except to act as a primary key. When you use information such as a username or an email address as a primary key, you are in effect saying that the username or email address is somehow an intrinsic part of who that person is. If that person ever changes the username or email address, you will have to go to great lengths to ensure the integrity of the data in the database. Consequently, it is a better design principle to use meaningless numbers as primary keys.

You thus need a mechanism for generating meaningless, yet unique, numbers every time you insert a new row. Every database provides some kind of extremely proprietary tool for generating unique identifiers. They differ so vastly that I cannot even begin to provide a generic description of unique identifier generation as I can with most SQL elements. Because of how greatly they differ, it is a good idea to simply avoid the proprietary database tools. Chapter 4 provides a database-independent approach to sequence generation.

Updates

The insertion of new rows into a database is just the start of data management. Unless your database is read-only, you will probably also need to make periodic changes to the data. The standard SQL modification statement looks like this:

```
UPDATE table_or_view_name
SET column1={DEFAULT |value} [, ... ]
[WHERE clause]
```

You specifically name the table you want to update and the values you want to assign in the SET clause and then identify the rows to be affected in the WHERE clause. If you fail to specify a WHERE clause, the database will update every row in the table.

In addition to assigning literal values to a column, you can also calculate the values. You can even calculate the value based on a value in another column:

```
UPDATE Project
SET end_year = begin_year+5
```

This command sets the value in the end_year column equal to the value in the begin_year column, plus 5, for each row in that table.

The WHERE Clause

The previous section introduced one of the most important SQL concepts, the WHERE clause. In SQL, a WHERE clause enables you to pick out specific rows in a table by specifying a value (like a primary key) that must be matched by the column in question. For example:

```
UPDATE Band
SET leadSinger = 'Ian Anderson'
WHERE id = 8
```

This UPDATE specifies that you should change only the leadSinger column for the row where id is 8. If the specified column is not a unique index, the WHERE clause may match multiple rows. Many SQL commands employ WHERE clauses to help pick out the rows on which you wish to operate. Because the columns in the WHERE clause are columns on which you search, you should generally have indexes created around whatever combinations you commonly use. We discuss the kinds of comparisons you can perform in the WHERE clause later in the chapter.

Deletes

Deleting data is a straightforward operation. You simply specify the table followed by a WHERE clause that identifies the rows you want to delete:

```
DELETE FROM table_name [WHERE clause]
```

As with other commands that accept a WHERE clause, the WHERE clause is optional. If you omit it, you will delete all of the records in the table! Of all the destructive commands in SQL, this is the easiest one to issue by mistake.

Queries

The last common SQL command, SELECT, enables you to view the data in the database. This action is by far the most common action performed in SQL. While data entry and modifications do happen on occasion, most databases spend the vast majority of their lives serving up data for reading. The general form of the SELECT statement is as follows:

```
SELECT [ALL | DISTINCT] column1 [, column2, ..., columnN ]
FROM table1 [, table2, ..., tableN ]
[JOIN condition]
[WHERE clause]
[GROUP BY column_list]
```

```
[HAVING condition]
[ORDER BY column_list [ASC | DESC]]
```

The SELECT statement enables you to identify the columns you want from one or more tables. The WHERE clause identifies the rows with the data you seek.

Basic queries

The variations on this syntax are numerous. The simplest form is:

```
SELECT 1;
```

This simple, though completely useless query returns a result set with a single row containing a single column with the value of 1. A more useful version of this query might be the MySQL query that tells you what database you are using:

```
mysql> SELECT DATABASE();
+------------+
| DATABASE() |
+------------+
| jtest      |
+------------+
1 row in set (0.01 sec)
```

The expression DATABASE() is a MySQL function that returns the name of the current database. I will cover functions in more detail later in the chapter. Nevertheless, you can see how simple SQL can provide a quick-and-dirty way of finding out important information.

Most of the time, however, you should use slightly more complex queries that help you pull data from a table in the database. The first part of a SELECT statement enumerates the columns you wish to retrieve. You may specify a * to say that you want to select all columns. The FROM clause specifies which tables those columns come from.

The other optional clauses all determine what rows you are selecting and how to display the results. By now, you should feel comfortable with the WHERE clause. In the case of a SELECT statement, the WHERE clause tells the database to return only the rows that match the specified clause. I will cover the more complex clauses later in this chapter.

Aliasing

When you use column names that are fully qualified with their table and column names, the names can grow to be quite unwieldy. In addition, when referencing SQL functions (which will be discussed later in the chapter), you will likely find it cumbersome to refer to the same function more than once within a statement. You can get around these issues by using aliases. An alias is usually a shorter and more descriptive way of referring to a cumbersome name. You can use it anywhere in the same SQL statement in place of the longer name. For example:

```
# A column alias
SELECT long_field_names_are_annoying AS myfield
```

```
FROM table_name
WHERE myfield = 'Joe'

# A table alias
SELECT people.names, tests.score
FROM tests, really_long_people_table_name AS people
```

Ordering

The results from a SELECT are, by default, indeterminate in the order they will appear. You can tell a database to order any results you see by a certain column. For example, if you specify that a query should order the results by last_name, then the results will appear alphabetized according to the last_name value. Ordering is handled by the ORDER BY clause:

```
SELECT last_name, first_name, age
FROM people
ORDER BY last_name, first_name
```

In this situation, we are ordering by two columns. You can order by any number of columns.

If you want to see things in reverse order, add the DESC (descending) keyword:

```
ORDER BY last_name DESC
```

The DESC keyword applies only to the field that comes directly before it. If you are sorting on multiple fields, only the field directly before DESC is reversed; the others are sorted in ascending order.

Grouping

Grouping lets you group rows with matching values for a specific column into a single row in order to operate on them together. You usually do this to perform aggregate functions on the results. I will go into functions a little later in the chapter.

Consider the following:

```
mysql> SELECT name, rank, salary FROM people;
+--------------+----------+--------+
| name         | rank     | salary |
+--------------+----------+--------+
| Jack Smith   | Private  |  23000 |
| Jane Walker  | General  | 125000 |
| June Sanders | Private  |  22000 |
| John Barker  | Sergeant |  45000 |
| Jim Castle   | Sergeant |  38000 |
+--------------+----------+--------+
5 rows in set (0.01 sec)
```

If you want to get a list of different ranks, you can use the GROUP BY clause to get a full account of the ranks:

```
mysql> SELECT rank FROM people GROUP BY rank;
+----------+
| rank     |
+----------+
| General  |
| Private  |
| Sergeant |
+----------+
3 rows in set (0.01 sec)
```

You should not, however, think of these results as simply a listing of the different ranks. The GROUP BY clause actually groups all of the rows matching the WHERE clause (in this case, every row) based on the GROUP BY clause. The two privates are thus grouped together into a single row with the rank Private. The two sergeants are similarly aggregated. With the individuals grouped according to rank, you can find out the average salary for each rank. Again, we will further discuss the functions you see in this example later in the chapter.

```
mysql> SELECT rank, AVG(salary) FROM people GROUP BY rank;
+----------+-------------+
| rank     | AVG(salary) |
+----------+-------------+
| General  | 125000.0000 |
| Private  |  22500.0000 |
| Sergeant |  41500.0000 |
+----------+-------------+
3 rows in set (0.04 sec)
```

Here you see the true power of grouping. This query uses an aggregate function, AVG( ) to operate on all of the rows grouped together for each row. In this case, the salaries of the two privates (23000 and 22000) are grouped together in the same row, and the AVG( ) function is applied to them.

The power of ordering and grouping combined with the utility of SQL functions enables you to do a great deal of data manipulation even before you retrieve the data from the server. However, you should take great care not to rely too heavily on this power. While it may seem more efficient to place as much processing load as possible onto the database server, this is not really the case. Your client application is dedicated to the needs of a particular client, while the server is shared by many clients. Because of the greater amount of work a server already has to do, it is almost always more efficient to place as little load as possible on the database server.

Operators

So far, we have used the = operator for the obvious task of verifying that two values in a WHERE clause equal each other. Other fairly basic operators include <>, >, <, <=, and >=. Note that though ANSI SQL requires the use of <> to check for inequality, most database engines also support !=. Table 10-4 contains a full set of ANSI SQL operators.

 Not all databases support all operators. In addition, MySQL and SQL Server support various bitwise operators, including &, |, ^, <<, and >>.

Table 10-4. ANSI SQL Operators

Operator	Context	Description
+	Arithmetic	Addition (also works for date addition on some database engines)
–	Arithmetic	Subtraction
*	Arithmetic	Multiplication
/	Arithmetic	Division
=	Comparison	Equal
<>	Comparison	Not equal
<	Comparison	Less than
>	Comparison	Greater than
<=	Comparison	Less than or equal to
>=	Comparison	Greater than or equal to
BETWEEN	Comparison	Between two values
IN	Comparison	Membership in a list
LIKE	Comparison	Similarity
AND	Logical	And
OR	Logical	Or
NOT	Logical	Negation
+	Unary	Positive
–	Unary	Negative
~	Unary	Complement

ANSI SQL operators have the following order of precedence:

1. + - ~ (unary)
2. NOT
3. * / %
4. + - (arithmetic)
5. < <= > >= = <> IN LIKE
6. BETWEEN IN
7. AND
8. OR

Precedence moves from left to right for operators of equal precedence. You can override the rules of precedence through the use of parentheses, in which case elements within the parentheses have higher precedence. For expressions with nested parentheses, the innermost parentheses are evaluated first.

Logical operators

SQL's logical operators—AND, OR, and NOT—let you build more dynamic WHERE clauses. The AND and OR operators specifically let you add multiple criteria to a query:

```
SELECT name
FROM User
WHERE age > 18 AND status = 'RESIDENT';
```

This sample query provides a list of all users who are residents and are old enough to vote. In other words, it finds every resident 18 years or older.

You can build increasingly complex queries and override SQL's order of precedence with parentheses. The parentheses tell the database which comparisons to evaluate first:

```
SELECT name
FROM User
WHERE (age > 18 AND status = 'RESIDENT')
OR (age > 18 AND status = 'APPLICANT');
```

In this more complex query, we are looking for anyone currently eligible to vote as well as people who might be eligible in the near future. You can also use the NOT operator to negate an entire expression:

```
SELECT name
FROM User
WHERE NOT (age > 18 AND status = 'RESIDENT');
```

In this case, negation provides all the users who are not eligible to vote.

Comparisons with NULL

NULL is a tricky concept for most people new to databases to understand. As in other programming languages, NULL is not a value, but the absence of a value. This concept is useful, for example, if you have a customer-profiling database that gradually gathers information about your customers as they offer it.

When you first create a record, for example, you may not know how many pets the customer has. You want that column to hold NULL instead of 0 so you can tell the difference between customers with no pets and customers whose pet ownership is unknown.

The concept of NULL gets a little funny when you use it in SQL calculations. Many programming languages use NULL as simply another kind of value. In Java, the following syntax evaluates to true when the variable is NULL and false when it is not:

```
str == NULL
```

The similar expression in SQL, col = NULL, is neither true nor false—it is always NULL, no matter what the value of the COL column. The following query will therefore not act as you might expect:

```
SELECT title FROM Book WHERE author = NULL;
```

Because the WHERE clause will never evaluate to true no matter what value is in the database for the author column, this query always provides an empty result set— even when you have author columns with NULL values. To test for "nullness," use the IS NULL and IS NOT NULL operators:

```
SELECT title FROM Book WHERE author IS NULL;
```

Membership tests

Sometimes applications need to check whether a value is a member of a set of values or within a particular range. The IN operator helps with the former:

```
SELECT title FROM Book WHERE author IN ('Stephen King', 'Richard Bachman');
```

This query will return the titles of all books written by Stephen King.* Similarly, you can check for all books by authors other than Stephen King with the NOT IN operator.

To determine whether a value is in a particular range, use the BETWEEN operator:

```
SELECT title FROM Book WHERE bookID BETWEEN 1  AND 100;
```

Both of these simple examples could, of course, be replicated with the basic operators. The Stephen King check, for example, could have been done by using the = operator and an OR:

```
SELECT title
FROM Book
WHERE author = 'Stephen King' OR author = 'Richard Bachman';
```

The check on book IDs could also have been done with an OR clause using the >= and <= or > and < operators. As your queries get more complex, however, membership tests can help you build both readable and better-performing queries than those you might create with the basic operators.

---

* Richard Bachman is a pseudonym used by Stephen King for some of his books.

Functions

Functions in SQL are similar to functions in other programming languages such as C and Perl. A function takes zero or more arguments and returns some value. For example, the function SQRT(16) returns 4. Within an SQL SELECT statement, functions may be used in one of two ways:

As a value to be retrieved

This form involves a function in the place of a column in the list of columns to be retrieved. The return value of the function, evaluated for each selected row, is part of the returned result set as if it were a column in the database.[*]

This query selects the name of each event and today's date for all events more recent than the given time:

```
SELECT name, CURRENT_DATE( )
FROM Event
WHERE time > 90534323
```

This query selects the title of a paper, the full text of the paper, and the length of the text in bytes for all of the papers authored by Douglas Adams. The LENGTH( ) function returns the character length of a given string:

```
# The LENGTH( ) function returns the character length of
# a given string.
SELECT title, text, LENGTH(text)
FROM Paper
WHERE author = 'Douglas Adams'
```

As part of a WHERE clause

This form involves a function used in place of a constant when evaluating a WHERE clause. The value of the function is used for comparison for each row of the table.

This query randomly selects the name of an entry from a pool of 35 entries. The RAND( )function generates a random number between 0 and 1. This random value is then multiplied by 34 to turn the value into a number between 0 and 34. Incrementing the value by 1 provides a number between 1 and 35. The ROUND( ) function rounds the result to the nearest integer. The result is a whole number between 1 and 35 and will therefore match one of the ID numbers in the table:

```
SELECT name
FROM Entry
WHERE id = ROUND( (RAND( )*34) + 1 )
```

You may use functions in both the value list and the WHERE clause. This query selects the name and date of each event less than a day old:

---

[*] You can use aliasing, covered earlier in the chapter, to give the resulting columns "friendly" names.

```
SELECT name
FROM Event
WHERE time > (CURRENT_TIMESTAMP( ) - (60 * 60 * 24) )
```

You may also use the value of a table field within a function. This example returns the names of people who used their names as passwords. The ENCRYPT( ) function from MySQL returns a Unix password-style encryption of the specified string using the supplied two-character salt. The LEFT( ) function returns the leftmost *n* characters of the specified string:

```
SELECT name
FROM People
WHERE password = ENCRYPT(name, LEFT(name, 2))
```

Though there is a basic set of ANSI SQL functions, the number of non-ANSI functions in any database engine likely outnumbers their ANSI counterparts. When programming in SQL, it is therefore always a good idea to have a reference specific to your database at your side.

Joins

Joins put the "relational" in relational databases by enabling you to relate the data in one table with data in other tables. The basic form of a join is sometimes described as an inner join. Joining tables is a matter of specifying equality in columns from two tables:

```
SELECT Book.title, Author.name
FROM Author, Book
WHERE Book.author = Author.id
```

This query pulls columns from two different tables when a relationship exists between rows in the two tables. Specifically, this query looks for situations in which the value of the Author column in the Book table matches the id value in the Author table. Consider a database in which the Book table looks like Table 10-5, and the Author table looks like Table 10-6.

Table 10-5. A Book table

ID	Title	Author
1	Slaughterhouse 5	4
2	Last Rites	2
3	The Vampire Lestat	3
4	The Shining	1

Table 10-6. An Author table

ID	Name
1	Stephen King
2	Terry Pratchett
3	Anne Rice
4	Kurt Vonnegut
5	Douglas Adams

An inner join creates a virtual table by combining the fields of both tables for rows that satisfy the query in both tables. In our example, the query specifies that the author field of the Book table must be identical to the id field of the Author table. The query's result would look like Table 10-7.

Table 10-7. Query results based on an inner join

Book title	Author name
The Shining	Stephen King
Last Rites	Terry Pratchet
Slaughterhouse 5	Kurt Vonnegut
The Vampire Lestat	Anne Rice

Douglas Adams is nowhere to be found in these results. He is left out because there is no value for his Author.id value found in the author column of the Book table. In other words, he did not write any of the books in our database! An inner join contains only those rows that match the query exactly.

Just about every database supports inner joins via the WHERE clause. Nevertheless, this approach violates the ANSI standard. ANSI-compliant joins—inner and otherwise—occur in the JOIN clause of your SELECT statement. The book query is properly written in ANSI SQL as:

```
SELECT Book.title, Author.name
FROM Author
JOIN Book ON Author.id = Book.author
```

What you get in your result set involving a join depends on the *join type*. You have already seen how an inner join fails to show Douglas Adams since he has no books listed in the Book table. ANSI SQL supports the following kinds of joins:

Inner join

An inner join is the default kind of join. Under an inner join, any rows that do not match from either table are discarded from the result set.

Left join

A left join enables us to see that we have Douglas Adams in the database with no books. In short, all rows from the left side of the join are included in the results regardless of whether they match a row from the right side of the join. Where no match exists, NULL values are shown for fields from the table on the right side of the join.

Right join

Right and left joins are variations of a single kind of join known as an *outer join*. As a left join provides all the rows from the left side of the join, a right join provides all the rows from the right side.

 Because these two joins are only semantically different, MySQL has chosen not to support right joins. If you need a right join, you can simply restate your SQL as a left join in order to achieve the same results.

Full join

A full join is a combination of a right and left join. In other words, all rows from both tables appear in the result set. If no match exists for each side, NULL values appear in the result set.

Natural join

A natural join looks for columns in the joined tables having identical names, data types, and values. For example, the inner join we performed on the Book and Author tables could be made a natural join if the author column in the Book table were renamed authorID and the id column in the Author table renamed authorID:

```
SELECT Book.title, Author.name
FROM Author
NATURAL JOIN Book;
```

Cross join

A cross join provides the full data from the joined two tables and is the same as specifying no JOIN or WHERE clause at all. I cannot think of any reason why you would want to perform a cross join.

The left outer join that gives us Douglas Adams in our results looks like:

```
SELECT Book.title, Author.name
FROM Author
LEFT JOIN Book ON Book.author = Author.id
```

The results of the outer join would therefore look like this:

```
+--------------------+----------------+
| Book.title         | Author.name    |
+--------------------+----------------+
| The Shining        | Stephen King   |
| Last Rites         | Terry Pratchett|
| The Vampire Lestat | Anne Rice      |
| Slaughterhouse 5   | Kurt Vonnegut  |
| NULL               | Douglas Adams  |
+--------------------+----------------+
```

CHAPTER 11

JDBC

These common thoughts are expressed in a shared public language,
consisting of shared signs… a sign has a "sense" that fixes the reference
and is "grasped by everybody" who knows the language…
—Noam Chomsky
Language and Thought

JDBC is one of the oldest programming APIs in the Java platform. In fact, it is the first of the enterprise APIs that eventually became the J2EE platform. Its goal is to create a shared public language for Java access to any database engine.

SQL lies at the heart of the JDBC API. I therefore assume a basic knowledge of SQL in this chapter. Chapter 10 contains a SQL tutorial if you need some background.

Architecture

Working with leaders in the database field, Sun developed JDBC as a unified API for database access. As part of the JDBC design process, they kept in mind three main goals:

- JDBC should be an SQL-level API.
- JDBC should capitalize on the experience of existing database APIs.
- JDBC should be relatively simple.

As an SQL-level API, JDBC enables you to construct SQL statements and embed them inside API calls. You are essentially using JDBC to make a smooth transition between the SQL and Java. Your application sends a query to the database as SQL and gets the results back through a Java object. Any database error you encounter is thrown to your application as a Java exception.

Database programming in most languages today is very different from what it was just seven years ago. It used to be that each database engine had its own proprietary C API. If you were programming against Sybase, you had to learn Sybase's API. On the other hand, you had to learn a very different Oracle API if you needed to talk to Oracle. For programming in languages other than C, you had to write a bridge to the C API.

JDBC leverages several attempts to provide unified database APIs, including ODBC and X/OPEN SQL. ODBC (Open Database Connectivity) was initially created as a Windows API for open database access. Although the industry has accepted ODBC as a standard, it does not translate well into the Java world:

- ODBC is primarily a Windows API and best suited for applications on the Windows platform.
- ODBC has an overly complex design with a steep learning curve.

In addition to ODBC, the X/OPEN SQL Call Level Interface (CLI) heavily influenced JDBC. Sun wanted to reuse the key abstractions from both ODBC and X/OPEN in order to ease acceptance of the API by database vendors and thus capitalize on the existing knowledge capital in the incumbent APIs. In addition, Sun realized that deriving an API from existing ones can provide quick development of solutions for database engines supporting only the old protocols. Specifically, Sun worked in parallel with Intersolv to create an ODBC bridge that maps JDBC calls to ODBC calls. Consequently, every Java VM has the ability to talk to any ODBC-supported database using this bridge.

 The JDBC-ODBC bridge is a great tool for developers who are interested in learning JDBC but may not want to invest in anything beyond the Microsoft Access database that comes with Microsoft Office. When developing for production sites, however, you almost certainly want to move to a JDBC driver that is native to your deployment database engine.

JDBC attempts to remain as simple as possible while providing developers with maximum flexibility. A key criterion employed by Sun is simply asking whether database applications read well. The simple and common tasks use simple interfaces, while more uncommon or bizarre tasks are enabled through specialized interfaces. For example, a handful of method calls in three interfaces manage the vast majority of database access. This list of key methods and interfaces has changed very little since the first JDBC specification in March 1996. JDBC nevertheless provides many other interfaces for handling more complex and unusual tasks.

The Core Interfaces

JDBC accomplishes its goals through a set of Java interfaces, each implemented differently by individual vendors. The set of classes that implements the JDBC interfaces for a particular database engine combine into a tool called a JDBC driver. In building a database application, you do not have to think about the implementation of these underlying classes at all; the whole point of JDBC is to hide the specifics of each database and enable you to focus on your application logic. Figure 11-1 illustrates the JDBC architecture.

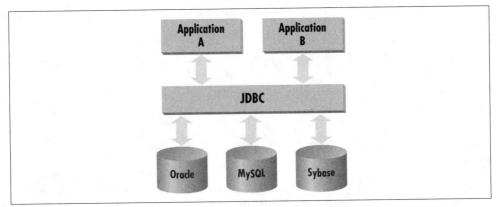

Figure 11-1. The JDBC architecture

If you think about a database query for any database engine, it requires you to connect to the database, issue your SELECT statement, and process any results. Example 11-1 is the JSP code for a very simple SELECT call that pulls all rows from a table in a MySQL database. It gets a connection from a data source configured in a JNDI directory service and then uses that connection to execute the query. The values in each row then appear in the generated HTML.

Example 11-1. A simple JSP page displaying the data in a table

```
<%@ page info="Table Results Page""%>

<%@ page import="java.sql.*""%>
<%@ page import="java.naming.*""%>
<%@ pagge import="javax.sql.DataSource""%>

<html>
  <head>
    <title>Table Results Page</title>
  </head>
  <body>
    <table>
      <tr>
        <th>ID</th>
        <th>Value</th>
      </tr>
      <%
        InitialContext ctx = new InitialContext();
        DataSource ds = ctx.lookup("jdbc/ora");
        Connection conn = ds.getConnection();
        Statement stmt = conn.createStatement();
        ResultSet rs;
```

```
        rs = stmt.executeQuery("SELECT id, val FROM test");
        while( rs.next( ) ) {
    %>
    <tr>
      <td><%=rs.getint(1)%></td>
      <td><%=rs.getString(2)%></td>
    </tr>
    <%
      }
      conn.close( );
    %>
  </table>
 </body>
</html>
```

If you are an experienced JSP programmer, you should be able to follow the flow of
this JSP page without knowing any JDBC. No references to any vendor-specific procedures exist in the sample code. Instead, this page uses only JDBC interfaces to provide an abstraction of the DBMS-specific implementation. The JDBC
implementation, in turn, performs the actual database access somewhere behind the
scenes. Figure 11-2 is a UML class diagram of the basic JDBC classes and interfaces.

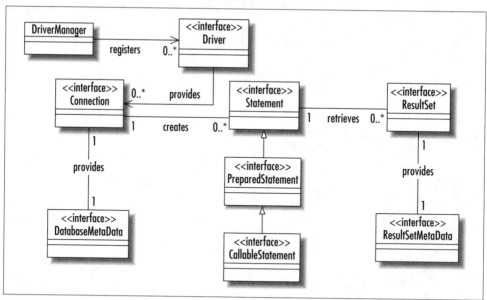

Figure 11-2. The basic classes and interfaces of the JDBC API

In the simple JSP page of Example 11-1, the JSP code asks JNDI for a DataSource
object stored in the directory service under the name *jdbc/ora*. Someone should have
configured your directory service to hold the information JDBC needs to make a
database connection. We will talk more about this configuration later in the chapter.

The JSP page then gets a `Connection` instance from the `DataSource`. This `Connection` is the JDBC representation of a physical connection to your database. You can use it to execute all the SQL you like.

Databases and Drivers

Before you can get a connection from JNDI, you need to have a database to connect to. Whatever database you have the most immediate access to will work. If you do not have access to a database, I recommend using an open source database like MySQL (*www.mysql.com*) or PostgreSQL (*www.postgresql.org*). Both are free and will enable you to learn JDBC and develop solid database applications. PostgreSQL has the advantage of supporting a fuller range of JDBC features, whereas MySQL has the advantage of being easier to install and set up.

Once your database engine is installed and your database is all set up, you will need a JDBC driver to connect to that database engine. Whatever your database of choice, it should be very simple to find a driver free of charge. Most commercial databases ship with a JDBC driver. Other database engines allow you to download a driver from their web site. In addition, you can opt for a commercially developed driver that probably performs better than the vendor-supported driver.

JDBC drivers come in four distinct categories. Sun has named the categories types 1–4.

Type 1
> A type 1 driver is a bridge between JDBC and another database-independent API like ODBC. The JDBC-ODBC driver that comes with the Java SDK is the primary example of a type 1 driver.

Type 2
> A type 2 driver translates JDBC calls into a native API provided by the database vendor.

Type 3
> Type 3 drivers are network bridges that enable an application to take advantage of the WORA (Write Once, Run Anywhere) capabilities of type 4 drivers even when your database of choice supports only type 2 drivers.

Type 4
> A type 4 driver talks directly to a database using a network protocol. Because it makes no native calls, it can run on any JVM.

For a list of all currently known drivers, their types, and the version of JDBC they support, visit *http://industry.java.sun.com/products/jdbc/drivers*.

Simple Database Access

At this point, you have the basics for connecting to a database. Example 11-1, however, did not really do much. It showed you how to make a database connection and perform simplistic result set management. You are unlikely to ever have such basic functionality in your applications. The basic database behavior common to most applications, however, does not require significantly more complex code.

The Connection

JDBC represents a connection to a database through the Connection interface. Thus, connecting to a database requires you to get an instance of the Connection interface from your JDBC driver. JDBC supports two ways of getting access to a database connection:

- Through the JDBC DataSource (as shown in Example 11-1)
- Using the JDBC DriverManager

The data source method is the preferred approach to database connectivity. Data sources, however, tend to be usable only in application server contexts. You should therefore understand both forms of connectivity since you can rely on DriverManager connectivity no matter what environment you are working in.

Connection Troubles

The JDBC connection process is the most difficult part of JDBC to get right. The API itself is very straightforward, but many "gotchas" hide right beneath the surface in the configuration of your environment. If you used the data source approach, you are less likely to run into configuration problems. Unfortunately, this approach is only commonly available to applications running inside a J2EE application server. If you do run into problems making a connection, check whether these problems match the following:

Connection fails with the message "Class not found"

This message usually results from not having the JDBC driver in your CLASSPATH. You should remember to enter *.zip* and *.jar* files explicitly in your CLASSPATH. If you put all of your application *.class* files and your driver *.jar* file (for this example, *driver.jar*) in *C:\lib*, your CLASSPATH should read *C:\lib;C:\lib\driver.jar*.

Connection fails with the message "Driver not found"

You did not register your JDBC driver with the DriverManager class. This chapter describes several ways to register your JDBC driver.

DataSource connectivity

Data source connectivity is very simple. In fact, the following code makes a connection to any database for any application:

```
Context ctx = new InitialContext();
DataSource ds = (DataSource)ctx.lookup("jdbc/dsn");
Connection conn = ds.getConnection();
```

The only requirement is that you have a JNDI-supported directory service containing a DataSource configured with the name *jdbc/dsn*.

The first line gets an InitialContext object in accordance with the JNDI* specification. If your environment isn't set up properly, you catch a javax.naming.NoInitial-ContextException. The InitialContext enables you to navigate a directory service. You use it in your database applications to look up a JDBC DataSource instance. Finally, once you have found that DataSource, you use it to make a connection.

Technically, DataSource connectivity does not require a directory service. Instead, you can serialize a configured DataSource instance out to a filesystem or load one in some other fashion. You will nevertheless find that the most common situation you will encounter is looking one up in a directory service via JNDI.

You may be wondering how the DataSource gets into the directory service so you can look it up. JNDI does provide a process for binding objects into a directory service:

```
SomeDataSourceClass ds = new SomeDataSourceClass();
Context ctx = new InitialContext();

// configure the data source through various setter methods
ctx.bind("jdbc/dsn", ds);
```

I have two bits of magic in this code. First, the class SomeDataSourceClass is an implementation of javax.sql.DataSource—generally written by your database or application server vendor. Next, the configuration of your data source—the step I commented out—is highly dependent on the DataSource implementation you are using. In some cases, you may configure a user ID, password, database name, and server name. You will likely specify much more.

Fortunately, few programmers actually write code to bind data sources to JNDI directory services. You will mostly encounter the need to configure a data source via XML or some other means. A sample *data-sources.xml* file from the Orion application server looks like this:

```
<?xml version="1.0"?>
<!DOCTYPE data-sources PUBLIC
  "Orion data-sources"
```

---

* You should not be too concerned if you are not familiar with JNDI. For the purposes of basic JDBC connectivity, the preceding three lines of JNDI code are all you need to know. The only thing that changes from application to application is the name of the data source.

```
        "http://www.orionserver.com/dtds/data-sources.dtd">

    <data-sources>
        <data-source class="com.evermind.sql.DriverManagerDataSource"
                      name="dsn"
                      location="jdbc/dsn"
                      xa-location="jdbc/xa/HypersonicXADS"
                      ejb-location="jdbc/HypersonicDS"
                      connection-driver="org.gjt.mm.mysql.Driver"
                      username="dvl"
                      password="dvl"
                      url="jdbc:mysql://localhost/dvl"
                      inactivity-timeout="30"/>
    </data-sources>
```

This configuration file places a `DataSource` instance in the application server's directory service that enables me to connect to a MySQL database named "dvl" on the *localhost* using the user ID "dvl" and password "dvl".

DriverManager connectivity

One of the few implementation classes in the `java.sql` package is the class `DriverManager`. It maintains a list of implementations of the `java.sql.Driver` interface and provides you with connections based on a JDBC URL that you provide. This JDBC URL comes in the form *jdbc:protocol:subprotocol*. This URL tells a `DriverManager` which database engine you wish to connect to and provides the `DriverManager` with enough information to make a connection.

 JDBC uses the word "driver" in multiple contexts. When lowercase, a JDBC driver is the collection of classes that together implement the JDBC specification. When uppercase, the `Driver` is the class that implements `java.sql.Driver`. Finally, JDBC provides a `DriverManager` that can be used to keep track of all the different `Driver` implementations.

The protocol part of the URL refers to a given JDBC driver. The protocol for the GNU MySQL driver, for example, is *mysql*. The subprotocol provides the implementation-specific connection information. Most drivers minimally require the name of a database to connect to. It is also common to specify a host and even a port number in the subprotocol.

Each driver's JDBC URL is different, and so I cannot say anything more explicit that will tell you what the proper URL is for your driver. Your driver documentation, however, should have easy-to-find documentation describing the exact form of its JDBC URL. Whatever the format of the URL, the primary function of the URL is to uniquely identify the driver needed by the application and pass that driver any information it needs to make a connection to the proper database.

Before you can use a URL to get a connection from the DriverManager, you first need to register your Driver implementation with the DriverManager. You have two main options for registering a Driver:

- Specify the names of the Driver implementation classes you want to register on the command line of your application using the *jdbc.drivers* property:

  ```
  java -Djdbc.drivers=com.caucho.jdbc.mysql.Driver MyAppClass
  ```

- Explicitly load the class in your program using a new statement or a Class. forName():

  ```
  Class.forName("com.caucho.jdbc.mysql.Driver").newInstance();
  ```

For portability's sake, I recommend that you put all configuration information in some sort of configuration file, such as a properties file, then load the configuration data at runtime. By taking this approach, your application will not rely on a particular database or JDBC driver. You can simply change the values in the configuration file to move from one driver to another or one database to another.

Once you register a driver, you can ask the DriverManager for a Connection by calling the getConnection() method in the driver with the information identifying the desired connection. This information minimally includes a JDBC URL, a user ID, and a password:

```
Connection conn =
    DriverManager.getConnection("jdbc:mysql:/localhost/Web",
                                "userID", "password");
```

This code returns a connection to the MySQL database named *Web* using the GNU MySQL driver. This connection occurs under the permissions of the user "userID" identified by the password "password".

An alternative signature to this method enables you to specify a Properties object that may contain values beyond the basic user ID and password:

```
Properties p = new Properties();
Connection conn;

p.put("user", "userID");
p.put("password", "password");
p.put("encoding"", "UTF-8");
conn = DriverManager.getConnection("jdbc:mysql:/localhost/Web", p);
```

Example 11-2 provides a full example that connects to a MySQL database.

Example 11-2. Using the DriverManager to make a connection

```
import java.sql.*;
import java.util.Properties;

public class Connect {
    static public void main(String[] args) {
        Connection conn = null;
```

Example 11-2. Using the DriverManager to make a connection (continued)

```
        try {
            String url = "jdbc:mysql:/localhost/Web";
            Properties p = new Properties( );

            Class.forName("org.gjt.mm.mysql.Driver").
                newInstance( );
            p.put("user", "dvl");
            p.put("password", "password");
            conn = DriverManager.getConnection(url, p);
        }
        catch( SQLException e ) {
            e.printStackTrace( );
        }
        finally {
            if( conn != null ) {
                try { conn.close( ); }
                catch( SQLException e ) { }
            }
        }
    }
}
```

In this example, I have hardcoded the driver name and connection information in the application. The only reason this is acceptable is because it is an example showing all of the elements of making a connection. In practice, you will always want to follow the best practices in the next section that avoid hardcoding these values.

Portability through properties

Java is a language based on the concept of portability. To most people, portability means that you do not write code that will run on only one platform. In the Java world, however, portability means no proprietary dependencies—and that means no database dependencies.

I touched earlier on how the JDBC URL and Driver implementation classes are driver-specific. Because both values are simple strings, you can pass them as command-line arguments or applet parameters. Unfortunately, this approach is hardly elegant since it requires users to remember long command lines or to pass authentication credentials as HTML to an applet tag.

You could, of course, prompt the user for this information. However, this approach demands that the user know a JDBC URL and driver name. The elegant approach is the use of properties files. Java supports the concept of properties-based application configuration through java.util.ResourceBundle and its subclasses.

Using a properties file, you can store all configuration information like the JDBC URL, driver class, user ID, and password and change it as the runtime environment changes. Example 11-3 is a sample properties file.

Example 11-3. A properties file containing driver configuration data

```
url=jdbc:mysql:/localhost/Web
driver=org.gjt.mm.mysql.Driver
user=dvl
password=dvl
```

You can now turn Example 11-2 into a portable example of making a connection as shown in Example 11-4.

Example 11-4. Using a properties file to achieve portability

```
import java.sql.*;
import java.util.*

public class Connect {
    static public void main(String[ ] args) {
        Connection conn = null;

        try {
            ResourceBundle bdl = ResourceBundle.getBundle("connect");
            String url = bdl.getString("url");
            Properties p = new Propertes( );;
            Enumeration keys = bdl.keys( );

            while(  keys.hasMoreElements( ) ) {
                String prop = (String)keys.nextElement( );
                String val = bdl.getString(prop);

                p.setProperty(prop, val);
            }
            Class.forName(bld.getString("driver")).newInstance( );
            conn = DriverManager.getConnection(url, p);
        }
        catch( SQLException e ) {
            e.printStackTrace( );
        }
        finally {
            if( conn != null ) {
                try { conn.close( ); }
                catch( SQLException e ) { }
            }
        }
    }
}
```

We no longer have any code specific to MySQL or the GNU driver. This code will now work against any database engine using any JDBC driver, simply through changing the properties file.

Query Execution

The most basic element of communication over a Connection is the Statement. Your application encapsulates SQL queries into a Statement or one of its subclasses and processes the results. An SQL query can be an INSERT, UPDATE, DELETE, or any other valid SQL statement.

Simple queries

The Connection class enables you to create Statement instances via the createStatement( ) method:

```
Statement stmt = conn.createStatement();
```

You can then use that statement to send SQL to the database:

```
stmt.executeUpdate("UPDATE test SET val = 'cheese' WHERE id = 1");
```

In this case, we are sending SQL that modifies the database. If the SQL returned results, however, we would use the executeQuery( ) method and get back an instance of ResultSet:

```
ResultSet rs = stmt.executeQuery("SELECT id, val FROM test");
```

Example 11-5 shows a query returning results and the processing of those results.

Example 11-5. A query that returns results for processing

```
Connection conn = null;

try {
    Statement stmt = conn.createStatement();
    ResultSet rs = stmt.executeQuery("SELECT id, val FROM test");

    while( rs.next() ) {
        System.out.println("ID: " + rs.getInt(1) + ", rs.getString(2));
    }
}
```

The query in Example 11-5 retrieves every row from the table test. The JDBC code loops through those rows and displays the values for each row's columns.

SQL NULL Versus Java null

SQL and Java do not match up the way they treat the absence of value—null. Specifically, any SQL value can be NULL. In Java, however, only object types can have null values. After retrieving a value from a ResultSet, your Java application needs to ask the ResultSet if the value retrieved is a driver representation of NULL. For example, a call to rs.getInt( ) might return 0 even though the underlying database value for the column is NULL. To find out if the value is actually 0 or NULL, you should call rs.wasNull( ).

Until the first call to next( ), the result set does not point to any row returned by the query. The first call makes the result set point to the first row. Until the next call to next( ), any operations you perform on the result set act on that row. Subsequent calls to next( ) move the result set forward through the rows in the result set. In this example, I move through each row until the next( ) method returns false. A return value of false indicates that there is no next row to move the result set to.

Dealing with a row means retrieving the values for its columns. Whatever the value in the database, you can retrieve it using a getter method in the ResultSet interface. In Example 11-5, I used getInt( ) to retrieve the id column and getString( ) to retrieve the val column. These getter methods can accept either the number of the column—starting with 1—or the column name. You should, however, avoid retrieving columns by name because it is generally much slower than retrieving them by number.

Scrollable result sets

By default, you are limited to simple forward navigation through a result set. JDBC does, however, provide a tool for navigating backward and forward through a result set; it is called a *scrollable result set*. You can get scrollable result sets back from your queries if you indicate that you want a scrollable result set when you create your statement:

```
Statement stmt = conn.createStatement(ResultSet.TYPE_SCROLL_SENSITIVE,
                        ResultSet.CONCUR_READ_ONLY);
```

The first argument indicates that you want a scrollable result set. The second argument indicates that you want a read-only result set. Non-read-only result sets are an advanced topic beyond the scope of this chapter.

With a scrollable result set, you can make calls to:

previous( )
> To navigate backward through the result set. previous( ) moves the result set over one row—except it moves the result set to the row *before* the current row. It will return false if there is no previous row to move to.

absolute( )
> To move to an arbitrary row (similar to next( )). absolute( ) requires the number of the row to which you want to navigate,

relative( )
> To move to an arbitrary row (similar to next( )). relative( ) moves the number of rows you specify forward or backward. A negative number moves the result set backward, and a positive number forward. Thus, relative(1) is like next( ), and relative(-1) is like previous( ).

Transactions

Chapter 3 covered the role of transactions in database programming. The critical job of a transaction is to take the database from one consistent state to another. Your database handles many of the complexities of transaction management. When you modify a table, the underlying database acquires the appropriate locks and guarantees that your changes do not conflict with those of another client.

In order for the database to properly manage your transactions, your application needs to tell it what operations constitute a single transaction. By default, JDBC treats every distinct SQL execution as a transaction. This default is called *auto-commit*. In other words, each statement is committed the minute it completes unless there is application logic to the contrary. The following code updates the balance of a bank account in the default auto-commit mode:

```
float ob = account.getBalance( );
Connection conn = null;

account.calculateInterest( );
try {
    Statement stmt = null;

    conn = ds.getConnection( );
    stmt = conn.createStatement( );
    stmt.executeUpdate("UPDATE account SET balance = " +
        account.getBalance( ) +
" WHERE id = " + account.getId( ));
}
catch( SQLException e ) {
    account.resetBalance(ob);
}
catch( Error e ) {
    account.resetBalance(ob);
    throw e;
}
catch( RuntimException e ) {
    account.resetBalance(ob);
    throw e;
}
finally {
    if( conn != null ) {
        try { conn.close( ); }
        catch( SQLException e ) { }
    }
}
```

From a JDBC perspective, nothing in this sample code differs from what you have done so far. What differs is the exception handling so that your application returns to a state consistent with the database. In this case, when an exception occurs, the account object gets its balance set back to the value prior to calculating interest.

Basic transaction management

Rarely are transactions as simplistic as the previous one. A given transaction can make numerous modifications that need to occur together or not at all. The classic example of such a transaction is a transfer of funds from your savings account to your checking account. This transaction includes the following steps:

1. Debit the savings account.
2. Credit the checking account.

If the credit to the checking account fails for whatever reason, you as the account holder certainly want that money recredited to the savings account. In JDBC's default auto-commit mode, there is no sure way to achieve this consistency. You therefore need to turn auto-commit off and manually tell JDBC where to commit the transaction. You also need to handle errors so that it will get rolled back in exceptional conditions. The following code shows this account transfer:

```
float sb = savings.getBalance( );
float cb = checking.getBalance( );
Connection conn = null;
boolean success = false;

savings.transfer(checking, 10.00);
try {
    Statement stmt = null;

    conn = ds.getConnection( );
    conn.setAutoCommit(false);
    stmt = conn.createStatement( );
    stmt.executeUpdate("UPDATE account SET balance = " +
                        savings.getBalance( ) +
                    " WHERE id = " + asavings.getId( ));
      stmt.executeUpdate("UPDATE account SET balance = " +
                        checking.getBalance( ) +
                    " WHERE id = " + achecking.getId( ));
    success = true;
}
catch( SQLException e ) {
    e.printStackTrace( );
}
finally {
    if( conn != null ) {
        if( success ) {
            try { conn.commit( ); }
            catch( SQLException e ) {
                savings.resetBalance(sb);
                checking.resetBalance(cb);
                try { conn.rollback( ); }
                catch( SQLException e ) { }
            }
        }
        else {
```

```
                savings.resetBalance(sb);
                checking.resetBalance(cb);
                try { conn.rollback( ); }
                catch( SQLException e ) {  }
            }
            try { conn.close( ); }
            catch( SQLException e ) { }
        }
    }
```

The bold sections illustrate what changes for multi-statement transactions. First, you need to turn off auto-commit using setAutoCommit(false). You then execute transactions as you always would. When done, you either commit the transaction (using commit( )) or roll it back (using rollback( )). In this sample, I have tracked the success or failure of the transaction and I perform the commit and rollback in the finally block.

Savepoints

As described earlier, transactions work well when you have a very straightforward beginning state with only one possible consistent end state. In other words, the database starts with one set of values and should end up with another specific set of values when the transaction completes. Some situations, however, allow for multiple possible consistent end states dependent on the events that occur during the course of the transaction. Such transactions require a much more fine grained approach to transaction management than the commit/rollback scheme allows. JDBC manages these transactions through savepoints.

A savepoint is a JDBC tool for marking a database state as a possible final consistent state for a transaction. Specifically, you can execute a statement and then establish a savepoint with the connection. Depending on what happens in the transaction, you can commit the transaction, roll it back, or roll it back to the savepoint. If you roll back to the savepoint, you can chose to commit that work or execute an alternative flow for the transaction.

The mechanics of savepoints are simple:

```
Connection conn = ds.getConnection( );
Statement stmt = conn.createStatement( );
Savepoint sp;

stmt.executeUpdate(
    "INSERT INTO test ( id, val ) VALUES ( 1, 'test')");
sp = conn.setSavepoint("safety");
stmt.executeUpdate(
    "INSERT INTO other ( id, name ) VALUES ( 32, 'sample')");
try {
    stmt.executeUpdate("UPDATE test SET other = 32 WHERE id = 1");
}
catch( SQLException e ) {
```

```
        conn.rollback(sp);
    }
    conn.commit();
```

The application sets the savepoint after the first SQL. It can now guarantee that no matter what else happens, it can return the database to a state in which a new row is in the test table without missing references or unreferenced values in the other table. If an error occurs in the SQL updating the test table so that the new test value points to the new other value, then the transaction is rolled back so that the test value exists alone in the database.

This example begs the question: why not simply commit after the first statement? One reason is performance. You do not need to release and reacquire any locks to execute the transaction. The other reason, however, would be in more complex transactions in which some branches of logic after the savepoint is set need to roll back completely while others need to roll back only to the savepoint.

To illustrate the kind of logic to which savepoints apply, consider a game in which you toss marbles into a jar. The goal of the game is to end up with the most marbles in the jar. You start the game with no marbles and continue tossing marbles into the jar until your fourth miss or you call it quits. Your score is the number of marbles in the jar after your fourth miss.

The trick behind scoring, however, is that missing two in a row returns your marble count to its number after your first miss. If you miss three in a row, the jar is emptied and your final score is whatever you can get in the jar before your next miss.

In transactional terms, the following events occur:

- First miss: set a savepoint.
- Second consecutive miss: roll back to the savepoint.
- Third consecutive miss: roll back the entire transaction.
- Fourth miss: commit.

Error Handling and Cleanup

All JDBC method calls can throw `SQLException` or one of its subclasses if something happens during a database call. Your code should be set up to catch this exception, deal with it, and clean up any database resources that have been allocated. The basic skeleton of any JDBC code I write looks like this:

```
Connection conn = null;

try {
    // create the connection and execute your transaction
}
catch( SQLException e ) {
    // handle the exception
}
```

```
    finally {
        if( conn != null ) {
            try { conn.close(); }
            catch( SQLException e ) { }
        }
    }
```

Each of the major JDBC interfaces you have encountered—Connection, Statement, and ResultSet—has a close( ) method. Practically speaking, however, you need only make sure you close your connection instances because closing a connection closes all associated statements. The closing of a statement, in turn, closes all associated result sets. By closing the connection in the finally clause, you guarantee that the connection will be closed even when an error occurs.

Prepared SQL

JDBC Statement instances illustrate basic database programming well, but you rarely want to use them in practice. Unfortunately, Statement sends your SQL to the database each time you execute it. It provides the database with very little opportunity to optimize repeated SQL calls.

Consider the following SQL:

```
UPDATE account SET balance = 5.00 WHERE id = 2
```

If you use a Statement to support updating many accounts with a similar SQL call, the database has to process the SQL and determine how it will execute the query every single time you send it to the database. You can avoid this overhead, however, through prepared SQL.

Databases support two kinds of prepared SQL: prepared statements and stored procedures. Prepared SQL provides an advantage over the simple SQL statements you have covered so far; a database can get the SQL ahead of time and create a query plan while you are doing other application logic. Your SQL should therefore execute faster. Furthermore, you have a generic reference to the statement for later reuse instead of repeatedly re-creating similar SQL statements.

The optimization factor comes from the database knowing what you are about to do. When you create a Java instance of a prepared statement or stored procedure, you notify the database of what SQL you intend to be calling without providing any specific values. For example, the SQL to update account balances looks like this as a prepared statement:

```
UPDATE account SET balance = ? WHERE id = ?
```

Instead of sending this SQL as an argument to executeUpdate( ), you pass it to the connection when you create the statement. You then assign values to the two placeholders and finish by calling executeUpdate( ). If you want to make further calls to update other accounts, you can reassign the statement new values and call executeUpdate( ) again.

What Kind of Statement to Use

This tutorial introduces three kinds of JDBC statements. Each kind of statement—even java.sql.Statement—provides performance benefits under certain situations. Unfortunately, you can rarely be certain which kind of statement will definitely provide you with the best performance for a given SQL call without knowing details about the underlying database. I recommend the use of java.sql.PreparedStatement except in a few situations in which stored procedures are demanded. In other words, you should always avoid java.sql.Statement. It almost never is the best choice for optimal performance. Even in the few situations in which it provides the optimal performance, it is uglier code, more error-prone, and more difficult to maintain. I recommend the use of stored procedures only for complex SQL calls that are known to be bottlenecks as prepared statements.

Prepared statements

The PreparedStatement interface extends the Statement interface we used earlier in the chapter. It enables a SQL statement to contain parameters like a function call. You can execute a single statement repeatedly with different values. The act of assigning values to parameters is called *binding* parameters. You might want to use a prepared statement when updating a group of objects stored in the same table. For example, if you update many bank accounts as described earlier, you might have a loop like this:

```
Statement stmt = conn.createStatement();

for(int i=0; i<accounts.length; i++) {
    stmt.executeUpdate("UPDATE account " +
                    "SET balance = " +
                    accounts[i].getBalance() + " " +
                    "WHERE id = " + accounts[i].getId());
}
conn.commit();
```

This statement keeps sending slightly different SQL to the database each time it goes through the loop. Instead of calling this statement repeatedly with different inputs, you can instead use a PreparedStatement:

```
PreparedStatement stmt = conn.prepareStatement("UPDATE account " +
                                        "SET balance = ? " +
                                        "WHERE id = ?");

for(int i=0; i<accounts.length; i++) {
    stmt.setFloat(1, accounts[i].getBalance());
    stmt.setInt(2, accounts[i].getId());
    stmt.executeUpdate();
    stmt.clearParameters();
}
conn.commit();
```

With a prepared statement, you send the actual SQL to the database when you get the PreparedStatement object through the prepareStatement( ) method in java.sql. Connection. Keep in mind that you have not yet actually executed any SQL. You execute that prepared SQL statement multiple times inside the for( ) loop, but you build the query plan only a single time.

Before each execution of the prepared statement, you tell JDBC which values to use as input for that execution of the statement. In order to bind the input parameters, PreparedStatement provides setter methods—like setFloat( ) and setInt( )—that mirror the getter methods you saw in ResultSet. Just as the getter methods read results according to the order in which you constructed your SQL, the setter methods bind parameters from left to right in the order you placed them in the prepared statement. In the previous example, I bound parameter 1 as a float to the account balance that I retrieved from the account object. The first ? was thus associated with parameter 1.

Stored procedures

While prepared statements enable you to access similar database queries through a single PreparedStatement object, stored procedures attempt to take the "black box" concept for database access one step further. A stored procedure is built inside the database before you run your application. You access that stored procedure by name at runtime. In other words, a stored procedure is almost like a method you call in the database. Stored procedures have the following advantages:

- Because the procedure is precompiled in the database for most database engines, it executes much faster than dynamic SQL. Even if your database does not compile the stored procedure before it runs, it will be precompiled for subsequent runs just like prepared statements.

- Syntax errors in the stored procedure can be caught at compile time rather than runtime.

- Java developers need to know only the name of the procedure and its inputs and outputs. The way in which the procedure is implemented is totally irrelevant.

The downside to stored procedures, however, is that every database has its own stored procedure language. If you use stored procedures heavily, you can go to great lengths to make sure your Java application is database-independent yet still be tied to a specific database because of the stored procedures. Worse, different databases do not even share basic semantics that would facilitate porting between database engines. For example, you can retrieve results from a Sybase stored procedure using a plain ResultSet. With Oracle, however, retrieving results from a stored procedure is much more complex.

Using stored procedures, we can revise the balance updating code to the following:

```
CallableStatement stmt = conn.prepareCall("{call sp_balance(?,?)}");

for(int i=0; i<accounts.length; i++) {
    stmt.setInt(1, accounts[i].getId( ));
    stmt.setFloat(2, accounts[i].getBalance( ));
    stmt.executeUpdate( );;
}
conn.commit( );
```

This example illustrates how close stored procedures are to prepared statements from a JDBC perspective. The difference is that you are referencing the stored procedure by name rather than spelling out the SQL you are calling. The result is simply increased performance at the expense of portability.

Some stored procedures may have output parameters. For those stored procedures, you need to register the output parameter before you execute the SQL:

```
CallableStatement stmt =
    conn.prepareCall("{call sp_interest(?, ?)}");

stmt.registerOutParameter(2, java.sql.Types.FLOAT);
for(int i=0; i<accounts.length; i++) {
    stmt.setInt(1, accounts[i].getId( ));
    stmt.executeUpdate( );
    accounts[i].setBalancce(stmt.getFloat(2));
}
conn.commit( );
```

The prepareCall( ) method creates a stored procedure object that will make a call to a specific stored procedure. This syntax sets up the order you will use in binding parameters. By calling registerOutParameter( ), you tell the CallableStatement instance to expect the second parameter as output of type float. Once this procedure is set up, you can bind the ID using setInt( ) and then get the output using getFloat( ).

Advanced JDBC

You can develop entire applications using only the JDBC I have presented so far in this chapter. What you have seen, however, is not the end of database programming. JDBC provides many more interfaces to support a variety of less common, yet very important database programming needs.

Batch Processing

Complex systems often require both online and batch processing. Each kind of processing has very different requirements. Because online processing involves a user waiting on application processing, the timing and performance of each statement execution in a process is important. Batch processing, on the other hand, occurs when a bunch of distinct transactions need to occur independent from user interaction. A bank's ATM machine is an example of a system of online processes. The monthly process that calculates and adds interest to your savings account is an example of a batch process.

JDBC enables you to assign a series of SQL statements to a JDBC Statement (or one of its subclasses) to be submitted together for execution by the database. Using the techniques you have learned so far in this book, account interest calculation processing occurs roughly in the following fashion:

1. Prepare statement.
2. Bind parameters.
3. Execute.
4. Repeat steps 2 and 3 for each account.

This style of processing requires a lot of back and forth between the Java application and the database. JDBC batch processing provides a simpler, more efficient approach to this kind of processing:

1. Prepare statement.
2. Bind parameters.
3. Add to batch.
4. Repeat steps 2 and 3 until interest has been assigned for each account.
5. Execute.

Under batch processing, there is no back and forth to the database for each account. Instead, all Java-level processing—the binding of parameters—occurs before you send the statements to the database. Communication with the database occurs in one huge burst; the huge bottleneck of stop-and-go communication with the database is gone.

Statement and its children all support batch processing through an addBatch( ) method. For Statement, addBatch( ) accepts a String that is the SQL to be executed as part of the batch. The following code shows how to use a Statement object to batch process interest calculation:

```
Statement stmt = conn.createStatement( );
int[ ] rows;

for(int i=0; i<accts.length; i++) {
    accts[i].calculateInterest( );
    stmt.addBatch("UPDATE account SET balance = " +
                accts[i].getBalance( ) +
                " WHERE id = " + accts[i].getId( ));
}
rows = stmt.executeBatch( );
```

The addBatch( ) method is basically nothing more than a tool for assigning a bunch of SQL statements to a single JDBC Statement. Because it makes no sense to manage results in batch processing, the statements you pass to addBatch( ) should be some form of an update: a CREATE, INSERT, DELETE, or UPDATE statement. Once you are done assigning statements, your application calls executeBatch( ). This method returns an array of rows affected by each statement in the batch. For example, the first element contains the number of rows affected by the first statement. Upon completion, the list of SQL calls associated with the Statement instance is cleared.

Using prepared statements and callable statements works very much like regular statements, except you are assigning batches of parameters instead of batches of individual statements. Interest calculation with a prepared statement looks like this:

```
PreparedStatement stmt = conn.prepareStatement("UPDATE account " +
                                               "SET balance = ? " +
                                               "WHERE id = ?");
int[ ] rows;

for(int i=0; i<accts.length; i++) {
    accts[i].calculateInterest( );
    stmt.setDouble(1, accts[i].getBalance( ));
    stmt.setInt(2, accts[i].getId( ));
    stmt.addBatch( );
}
rows = stmt.executeBatch( );
```

Metadata

The term metadata sounds officious, but it is really nothing more than extra data about some object that would otherwise waste resources if it were actually kept in the object. For example, simple applications do not need the name of the columns associated with a ResultSet—the programmer probably knew that when the code was written. Embedding this extra information in the ResultSet class is thus not considered by JDBC's designers to be part of the core ResultSet functionality. Data such as column names, however, is very important to some data programmers—especially to those writing dynamic database access. The JDBC designers provide access to this extra information—the metadata—via the ResultSetMetaData interface. For example, this class can tell you:

- The number of columns in a result set
- Whether NULL is a valid value for a column
- The label to use for a column header
- The name for a column
- The source table for a column
- The data type of a column

Example 11-6 shows some of the source code from a command-line tool that accepts arbitrary user input and sends it to a database for execution.

Example 11-6. An application for executing dynamic SQL

```java
import java.sql.*;

public class Exec {
    static public void main(String[] args) {
        Connection conn = null;
        String sql = "";
        for(int i=0; i<args.length; i++) {
            sql = sql + args[i];
            if( i < args.length  - 1 ) {
                sql = sql + " ";
            }
        }
        System.out.println("Executing: " + sql);
        try {
            Class.forName("org.gjt.mm.mysql.Driver")
                .newInstance();
            String url = "jdbc:mysql://localhost/Web";
            Statement stmt;

            conn = DriverManager.getConnection(url, "dvl", "dvl");
            stmt = conn.createStatement();
            if( stmt.execute(sql) ) {
                ResultSet rs = stmt.getResultSet();
                ResultSetMetaData meta = rs.getMetaData();
                int cols = meta.getColumnCount();
                int row = 0;

                while( rs.next() ) {
                    row++;
                    System.out.println("Row: " + row);
                    for(int i=0; i<cols; i++) {
                        System.out.print(meta.getColumnLabel(i+1) + ": " +
                                        rs.getObject(i+1) + ", ");
                    }
                    System.out.println("");
                }
            }
            else {
                System.out.println(stmt.getUpdateCount() +
                    " rows affected.");
            }
            stmt.close();
        }
        catch( Exception e ) {
            e.printStackTrace();
        }
        finally {
            if( conn != null ) {
                try { conn.close(); }
                catch( SQLException e ) { }
            }
        }
    }
}
```

This code introduces a few new features. The first is the introduction of the execute( ) method. As you might guess from this code, execute( ) enables you to send arbitrary SQL to the database when you may not know whether it is an update or a query. It returns true if the SQL you sent it returned results.

When the SQL sent to execute( ) does return results, you can retrieve them through a call to getResultSet( ). On the other hand, you can get the number of rows touched by an update through getUpdateCount( ).

The point of this example, however, is to illustrate the use of ResultSetMetaData. When this application executes SQL that returns results, it needs to find out about those results. It does so by getting the metadata through a call to getMetaData( ). The metadata tells the application how many columns are in the result set so the application can loop through all of the columns and get the column values.

JDBC supports other kinds of metadata. You will most often be interested in DatabaseMetaData—one of the most massive interfaces in the entire J2EE platform. DatabaseMetaData provides information about your database connection and the database to which it is connected. Finally, you can retrieve information on statement parameters through the new ParameterMetaData interface.

Hidden Features

Some of JDBC's best features are things you never see as a programmer—your JDBC driver handles all the details. You turn them on through configuration parameters in your data source.

Connection pooling

The most important hidden feature is JDBC connection pooling. Up to this point, you have created a connection, done your database business, and closed the connection. This process clearly works fine for the examples I have presented to this point in the book. Unfortunately, it does not work in real world server applications. It does not work because the act of creating a database connection is a very expensive operation for most database engines. If you have a server application such as a Java servlet or middle-tier application server, that application is likely going back and forth between the database many times per minute. Suddenly, the "open connection, talk to the database, close the connection" model of JDBC programming becomes a huge bottleneck.

Through specialized data sources, JDBC supports the concept of *connection pooling*. Connection pooling is a mechanism through which open database connections are held in a cache for use and reuse by different parts of an application. In a Java servlet, for example, each user initiates the execution of the servlet's doGet( ) method, which grabs a Connection instance from the connection pool. When it is done serving that user, it returns the Connection instance to the pool. The Connection is never closed until the web server shuts down.

Unlike the parts of the JDBC API you have encountered so far, driver vendors do not necessarily implement connection pooling. As I noted earlier, connection pooling requires the use of specialized data sources. It can therefore be a function of your application server, your driver, or even your own custom data source. Consequently, you can take advantage of connection pooling even if your JDBC driver has no support for it.

Because connection pooling occurs in the data source, JDBC code using connection pools looks just like the JDBC code we have covered to this point. Your data source that supports connection pools provides you with a special, logical connection implementation that returns the physical connection to the pool when you call close( ). Figure 11-3 shows an activity diagram illustrating JDBC connection pooling.

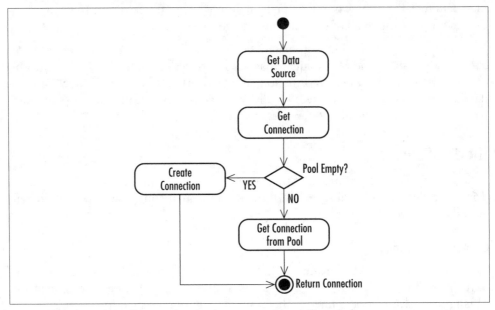

Figure 11-3. An activity diagram showing how connection pooling works

The same as with all other JDBC code, your application grabs a Connection from a DataSource using the getConnection( ) method. Internally, the DataSource talks to a ConnectionPoolDataSource that holds pooled database connections. This Connection-PoolDataSource enables connection pooling. When you close the connection in your application, it returns to the connection pool. Any subsequent attempts to close that connection by your application will cause an error.

Prepared statement pooling

Prepared statement pooling is to prepared statements as connection pooling is to connections. In other words, prepared statement pooling enables you to keep a prepared statement open so you can avoid the potential overhead of re-creating the same prepared statement multiple times.

Prepared statement pooling rides on top of connection pooling and looks exactly like all other JDBC code from an application perspective. The only difference is that some data sources that support connection pooling keep any prepared statements associated with their connections open for later reuse. As with connection pooling, when you close a pooled prepared statement, the close( ) method returns the prepared statement to the pool.

Connection pooling is naturally a trade-off between storing a number of connections in memory and the cost of making connections. You nearly always want to opt to take the memory hit. Prepared statement pooling, on the other hand, does not involve such an obvious trade-off. If you pool all of your prepared statements, you will eat up memory and database resources. You should therefore plan your prepared statement pooling to pool only those statements for which pooling will provide an obvious advantage.

Distributed transactions

All database access so far in this chapter has involved transactions against a single database. In this environment, your DBMS manages the details of each transaction. This support is good enough for most database applications. As companies move increasingly toward an enterprise model of systems development, however, the need for supporting transactions across multiple databases grows. Where single data source transactions are the rule today, they will likely prove the exception in large-scale programming in the future.

Distributed transactions are transactions that span two or more data sources. For example, you may have an Informix database containing your corporate digital media assets and an Oracle database holding product data. When you delete a product from Oracle, you probably want to delete the commercials and pictures for that product from Informix. Without support for distributed transactions, you run the risk of one transaction succeeding and the other failing—your data thus ends up in an inconsistent state.

You could avoid the issue by picking one database to hold everything. If you choose a nice supercomputer with terabytes of storage space and RAM, such a solution might work. A more practical alternative, however, is to choose database engines that are well suited for the type of data being stored and split the data across multiple databases.

As with prepared statement pooling, distributed transactions ride on top of JDBC connection pooling. From the application's point of view, programming with distributed transactions looks *nearly* like single data source transactions. Behind the scenes, your one data source actually hides many data sources. When you get a connection from it, you are actually getting a connection that manages *two-phase commits* through a midtier transaction monitor.

I say that your application code is *nearly* the same as code against a single data source because there are some small differences. In short, your code should not call commit( ), rollback( ), or setAutoCommit(true). Any attempt to do so will result in an SQLException. You do not have to add any special code.

The application server's transaction monitor handles the details of your distributed transaction. The two-phase commit that it manages is a standard protocol for handling a commit across two data stores. Under a simplistic description, the following events take place in a two-phase commit:

1. The transaction monitor (TM) asks data source A if it can commit the pending transaction.
2. If data source A cannot commit, the transaction rolls back and ends.
3. The TM asks data source B if it can commit.
4. If data source B cannot commit, the transaction rolls back and ends.
5. The TM logs the transaction to a distributed transaction log.
6. The TM tells data source A to commit.
7. The TM tells data source B to commit.

The only reason either of the actual commits can fail is due to a server crash or some other terrible event. Fortunately, the transaction log prevents those events from placing the system in an inconsistent state. The transaction monitor maintains a consistent state by having the individual data sources re-execute their portion of the transaction when they come back up.

CHAPTER 12

JDO

> We say that error is appearance. This is false. On the contrary,
> appearance is always true if we confine ourselves to it. Appearance is
> being.
> —Jean-Paul Sartre
> *Truth and Existence*

Java Data Objects (JDO) is one of the first APIs to run through the Java Community Process (JCP). JDO enables application developers to build applications without worrying about persistence issues. In other words, it does for your application the same thing EJB container-managed persistence does for EJB applications. Where EJB seeks to deliver all the features of enterprise systems development—such as a distributed component model and full and distributed transaction management—JDO seeks to provide developers with a more streamlined set of features.

JDO seeks to give applications with persistence needs the following capabilities:

- Simplicity
- Database independence
- Performance

In other words, JDO is a database-independent persistence API that has a simple programming model designed to support the performance needs of common applications. Though EJB is database-independent, it does not have a simple programming model and performs poorly for small- to medium-scale applications.

Architecture

JDO is based on the concept of persistence transparency. In other words, you write regular Java classes without worrying about conformance to any particular contract. An application uses persistent business components in a JDO environment supplied by a JDO implementation. Figure 12-1 illustrates this high-level architecture.

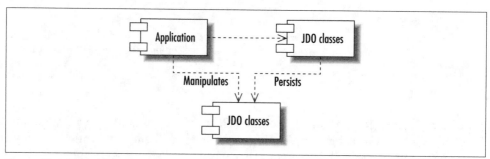

Figure 12-1. The JDO architecture

Business Objects

In JDO parlance, business objects are referred to as JDO instances. Because of JDO's transparency, JDO instances can be regular user-defined Java classes or collections, JavaBeans, or even Enterprise JavaBeans. When you introduce such a class into a JDO environment, it becomes a *persistence-capable* class. Example 12-1 shows a simple, persistence-capable Book class.

Example 12-1. A persistence-capable book class

```
package com.imaginary.ora;

public class Book {
    String author;
    String isbn;
    String title;

    public Book( ) {
        super( );
    }

    public Book(String auth, String num, String ttl) {
        super( );
        author = auth;
```

Example 12-1. A persistence-capable book class (continued)

```
        isbn = num;
        title = ttl;
    }

    public String getAuthor( ) {
        return author;
    }

    public String getIsbn( ) {
        return isbn;
    }

    public String getTitle( ) {
        return title;
    }

    public void setAuthor(String auth) {
        author = auth;
    }

    public void setIsbn(String num) {
        isbn = num;
    }

    public void setTitle(String ttl) {
        title = ttl;
    }
}
```

You should not strain yourself looking for anything unfamiliar. This is the exact same Book class you would write in a nonpersistent application. The only aspect that relates to JDO is that you must have the default constructor. Without it, some *enhancers* may fail during the enhancing process. I will cover the enhancing process later in the chapter.

Applications

Your application uses persistent business objects and is responsible for interacting with JDO to make those objects persistent. Example 12-2 creates a book in the data store using JDO.

Example 12-2. Persisting new books using JDO

```
package com.imaginary.ora;

import java.util.Properties;

import javax.jdo.*;

public class Librarian {
```

Example 12-2. Persisting new books using JDO (continued)

```
static public void main(String[ ] args) {
    PersistenceManagerFactory factory;
    Properties props = new Properties( );
    PersistenceManager mgr;
    Transaction trans;

    // load JDO properties
    factory = JDOHelper.getPersistenceManagerFactory(props);
    mgr = factory.getPersistenceManager( );
    trans = mgr.currentTransaction( );
    try {
        Book book = new Book("Daniel C. Dennett",  "0-262-54053-3",
                             "The Intentional Stance");

        trans.begin( );
        mgr.makePersistent(book);
        trans.commit( );
    }
    catch( Exception e ) {
        e.printStackTrace( );
    }
    finally {
        if( trans.isActive( ) ) {
            trans.rollback( );
        }
        mgr.close( );
    }

    }
  }
}
```

This sample method is the agent that makes your plain Book class a persistent JDO instance. It finds a persistence manager, creates a transaction, associates your new Book instance with the transaction, and finally commits the transaction. In the event of an exception, the code rolls back the transaction. The only hocus-pocus I left out is something you should be familiar with as a J2EE developer. Namely, I left out setting up the properties that help the application interact with the JDO implementation it is using.

You have seen this use of properties in JDBC with the calls to DriverManager and you have seen this in JNDI with initial context properties. What is interesting about JDO properties is that many of them exist to tell the persistence manager what properties to pass to the JDBC driver that the JDO implementation is using behind the scenes. Naturally, these properties are highly dependent on your runtime environment. In addition to telling JDO how to find a JDBC driver, they tell JDO what implementation class to use for a PersistenceManagerFactory class.

Implementations

A JDO implementation is to JDO as a JDBC driver is to JDBC. In other words, it is the set of concrete classes that implements the interfaces of the JDO specification. The JDO implementation performs the operations that make your business objects persist against a data store.

As with JDBC drivers, some JDO implementations cost money while others are free. Sun provides a reference implementation on the JDO web site at *http://java.sun.com/ products/jdo*. Which implementation you use depends on the runtime environment in which you intend to deploy.

The entry point into a JDO implementation is the PersistenceManagerFactory. Example 12-2 showed the Librarian application using the PersistenceManagerFactory to get a PersistenceManager class. This task is in fact the PersistenceManagerFactory's raison d'être. You get access to a PersistenceManagerFactory by calling getPersistenceManagerFactory( ) in the JDO JDOHelper class.

Just about all other interaction between an application and a JDO implementation occurs through the PersistenceManager you got from the factory. Example 12-2 used that PersistenceManager to manage a transaction in which a new Book was added to the library.

Data Stores

A data store is where you store your data. JDO does not require the data store to be a relational database. While it most commonly is a relational database, it can be an object database, a CRM system, a filesystem, or something completely different.

Enhancement

The JDO specification requires every persistent business object to implement the PersistenceCapable interface. Though this seems to contradict what I have been saying about transparency, it does not. JDO leverages a concept called *enhancement* to enable your business objects to implement PersistenceCapable after the fact.

Before deployment of a JDO application, you use a tool on your compiled Java classes to change their bytecode. Your JDO vendor generally supplies the enhancement tool. No matter what enhancement tool you use, the JDO specification requires that all vendors be able to support the reference JDO contract for enhancement. In other words, you can enhance with Vendor A's tools and deploy in an environment using a JDO implementation from Vendor B.

In truth, bytecode enhancement is not a required aspect of JDO. Your vendor, for example, can provide tools to modify the source code. What is essential to JDO is:

- You are not required to code your business objects to any particular specification dictated by JDO.*

- Any bytecode that exists after enhancement can run against any JDO implementation.

Class Metadata

For enhancement to work, you need to tell your enhancement tool about the business object to be made persistent. You accomplish this task through the creation of an XML file that describes the business object class. Example 12-3 is the metadata description for the Book class.

Example 12-3. The Book metadata

```xml
<?xml version="1.0" ?>
<!DOCTYPE jdo SYSTEM "jdo.dtd">

<jdo>
  <package name="com.imaginary.ora">
    <class name="Book">
      <field name="author"/>
      <field name="isbn"/>
      <field name="title"/>
    </class>
  </package>
</jdo>
```

This file enables you to identify all persistent business objects and their persistent fields. This example shows only the most basic metadata description. We can make it more complex by pulling in some design elements from previous chapters.

```xml
<class name="Book">
  <field name="bookID" primary-key="true"/>
  <field name="author"/>
  <field name="isbn"/>
  <field name="title"/>
</class>
```

This code adds a persistent field for bookID—a field that happens to be a unique value across all Book instances. We can also add an Author class that has a collection of books:

```xml
<class name="Author">
  <field name="authorID" primary-key="true"/>
  <field name="books">
    <collection element-type="com.imaginary.ora.Book"/>
  </field>
```

---

* If you intend to use JDO to support a bean-managed EJB, you need to conform to the EJB specification.

```
    <field name="firstName"/>
    <field name="lastName"/>
  </class>
```

This sample code shows how you can specify a persistent field that is a collection. In this case, it happens to be a collection of other persistent objects.

Running the Enhancer

Once you have written metadata files to describe each persistent object, you run the enhancer on it. The exact syntax of the enhancer depends greatly on what JDO implementation you are using. To run the reference implementation's enhancer, you execute the following command line:

```
Prompt$ java -classpath jdo.jar;jdori.jar;xerces.jar options com.sun.jdori.enhancer.
Main classes and metadata
```

The Database

At some point, you need to create the tables in your database to support your persistent objects. In general, the JDO vendor you are using will provide tools that reuse the metadata for your objects to build relational tables. The JDO specification, however, says nothing about how a relational structure should be created.

Queries

Before you do anything else to your data store of books, you need a way to get them out of the data store. JDO provides a unique combination of a query API combined with a simplistic query language to enable access to objects in your data store.

The JDO Extent

JDO makes heavy use of a concept called an *extent*. An extent is like a virtual collection of persistent objects. By *virtual*, I mean that all the objects represented by the extent are probably not loaded into memory. A regular Java collection, on the other hand, has all elements of the collection in memory. The abstraction of the extent is critical to JDO programming since it performs important optimization tasks like lazy-loading while hiding these complexities from your application.

The simplest use of an extent is as a representation for all instances of a particular persistent class. The following code provides your application with all books in the data store:

```
Extent ext = mgr.getExtent(Book.class, true);
Iterator books = ext.iterator();
```

```
    while( books.hasNext( ) ) {
        Book b = (Book)books.next( );

        System.out.println("Got: " + b.getTitle( ));
    }
    ext.closeAll( );
```

Just as the application worked through the PersistenceManager to create new books, it also works through the PersistenceManager to get an extent representing existing books. The second parameter—a boolean value—indicates whether subclasses should be included in the extent. In this example, we indicated that we want subclasses even though we know Book has no subclasses. The application takes an Iterator from the extent and goes through each one, printing its title.

The JDO Query

It is rare that you will want the whole list of objects of a certain class. For most applications, you will want to filter that list based on some set of criteria. The JDO query API provides a key object to enable complex queries, the Query. The following code provides all books by Anne Rice:

```
    Extent ext = mgr.getExtent(Book.class, true);
    Query query = mgr.newQuery(ext, "author==name");
    Collection results;

    query.declareParameters("String name");
    results = (Collection)query.execute("Anne Rice");
```

Using your PersistenceManager, you create a query based on an Extent representing all books and a filter for elements in that Extent. In this case, the filter is based on the author field. It tells the query to look for all books for which the author equals name. The name token is just a placeholder. In the call to declareParameters( ), we tell the query that name is a parameter to be passed in and that it will be a String. Finally, we get all matching books by calling execute( ) in the query with a specific author name—in this case, Anne Rice.

You can specify up to three parameters to any query execution using the preceding syntax. They will be matched to your parameter declarations in declareParameters( ) based on order. If you need more than three parameters, you can use the executeWithArray( ) method instead of execute( ):

```
    Extent ext = mgr.getExtent(Person.class, true);
    Query query = mgr.newQuery(ext,
      "lastName==last & city==cty &state==st  & birthCity == bc");
    Object[] params = { "Allen", "Boston", "MA", "Miami" };
    Collection results;

    query.declareParameters("String last, String cty, " +
      "String st, String bc");
    results = (Collection)query.executeWithArray(params);
```

This uninteresting query returns all people in your data store with the last name Allen who live in Boston but were born in Miami.

Whatever syntax you use, the parameter passed should be an object type—the JDO implementation will unwrap into primitives when appropriate. The best way to execute a multiparameter statement, however, is through the executeWithMap( ) method:

```
Extent ext = mgr.getExtent(Person.class, true);
Query query = mgr.newQuery(ext,
    "lastName==last & city==cty &state==st  & birthCity == bc");
Collection results;
HashMap params;

query.declareParameters("String last, String cty, " +
    "String st, String bc");
params = new HashMap( );
params.put("last", "Allen");
params.put("cty", "Boston");
params.put("st", "MA");
pparams.put("bc", "Miami");
results = (Collection)query.executeWithMap(params);
```

When you use a map, you make your Java code independent of the order specified in your query. You can therefore make changes to the order of the parameters in the query without having to make any changes to the Java code. If you had used an array, you would have to make sure the parameters were placed into the array in the proper order.

Complex Queries

JDO supports many different ways for performing queries depending on your application needs. In an application context, for example, it is common to ask which objects in a subset of objects meet certain criteria. To facilitate these kinds of queries, JDO enables you to operate on collections as well as extents. The following query provides all of the books by a particular author published in 1991:

```
Query query = mgr.newQuery(Book.class, author.getBooks( ),
                            "year==yr");
Collection results;

query.declareParameters("int yr");
results = (Collection)query.execute(new Integer(1991));
```

The code is nearly identical to everything you have seen so far. The key difference is the use of a collection in constructing the query instead of an extent. In this case, author.getBooks( ) is a call to get all associated books from an instance of the Author class representing a specific author. Those books form the set of objects on which the query operates.

In addition to parameters, JDO also enables you to declare variables to be used in filtering. This feature is useful when you want to operate on individual elements in a collection field. If, for example, we wanted all authors who had written for a particular genre, we might execute against the database using the following SQL join:

```
SELECT Author.authorID
FROM Author, Book
WHERE Author.authorID = Book.bookID
AND Book.genre = "some genre";
```

JDO does things differently. As before, you start with the Author extent. This time, however, you create a variable that will represent each of an author's books and compare that book's genre to the target genre:

```
Extent ext = mgr.getExtent(Author.class, true);
Query query = mgr.newQuery(ext,
   "books.contains(book) & book.genre ==genre");
Collection results;

query.declareParameters("String genre");
query.declareVariables("com.imaginary.ora.Book book");
results = (Collection)query.execute("HORROR");
```

This critical aspect of variable usage is the contains( ) call. In truth, it is a rather unintuitive syntactic construct. It is saying that for each book found in the author's list of books (books), that book will be assigned to the book variable and used in the comparison book.genre == genre.

> Unlike parameters, multiple variable declarations are separated by semicolons (;).

The JDO specification requires that your contains( ) clause be on the lefthand side of any & expression. Furthermore, each part of a | expression must have a contains( ) clause.

Finally, you can order your results using the setOrdering( ) method in query:

```
query.setOrdering("lastName descending, firstName descending");
```

As you would probably expect, this call tells the query to sort on lastName followed by firstName. You can sort on fields of any primitive type except boolean. In addition, you can sort on fields of a wrapper type (except Boolean), BigDecimal, BigInteger, String, and Date.

The Filter Language

I have danced around the issue of describing the filtering syntax until now. In general, it is fairly straightforward. It looks and acts a lot like Java. In fact, the only oddity so far has been the use of a single & for "and". As a whole, the filter language follows Java syntaxes with some largely natural exceptions. The exceptions include:

- The filter syntax provides the ability to compare and operate on primitives and wrappers together.

- Objects provide access to only a few methods such as `String.startsWith()`, `String.endsWith()`, `Collection.contains()`, and `Collection.isEmpty()`.

- Operations on `NULL` values do not throw a `NullPointerException`. Instead, they evaluate to `false`.

- You use variable declarations to navigate through collections within the filter.

- You cannot make assignments in your filters.

- `&` is a logical "and"; `&&` is a conditional "and".

Changes

You can now create new persistent objects and read them from the underlying data store. The next task is to modify your persistent objects. JDO does not require any special work for changes to an object—the changes are automatically reflected in the data store. Deletion, however, requires some work.

Just as the `PersistenceManager` enables you to create persistent objects through `makePersistent()`, it enables you to delete them through `deletePersistent()`:

```
mgr.deletePersietent(book);
```

The book is now gone from the data store!

From a technical perspective, deletion is this simple. In reality, JDO does you no favors when it comes to managing object relationships. The preceding call would, in fact, delete the book from the data store. But it would also leave its `Author` object with a `NULL` value in its list of books. You are responsible for maintaining the integrity of the object relationships:

```
Collections books = author.getBooks();
Book book;

// loop through the list, find the one you do not want
books.remove(book);
author.setBooks(books);
mgr.deletePersistent(book);
```

The integrity of your object relationships and the underlying data store integrity are now protected.

Transactions

Early in the chapter, I introduced some basic transactional semantics in the form of a JDO transaction object that enables you to begin, commit, and roll back a transaction. In reality, JDO does not require you to operate in a transactional context. If your environment supports transactions, however, it is a good idea to leverage this functionality since transactions are ultimately the key factor in long-term data integrity.

The Transaction Class

Each PersistenceManager provides exactly one Transaction to manage transactions. In other words, for operations against a given PersistenceManager, you can execute at most one transaction at a time.

JDO supports two transaction types:

- Data store transaction management
- Optimistic transaction management

Data store transaction management is where JDO lets the underlying data store manage your transactions. From the time you begin the transaction until the time you commit or roll back, JDO has an open transaction—and all overhead such as locks associated with it—in the data store. The data store performs and commits or roll backs.

Under optimistic transaction management, a JDO implementation manages transactional integrity locally until a commit or rollback is issued. For a commit, the implementation verifies the data integrity, opens a transaction with the data store, and sends all changes at once.

Telling a transaction to use optimistic or data store transaction management is a single method call:

```
trans.setOptimistic(true);
```

Passing in true turns on optimistic transaction management, whereas passing in false turns on data store transaction management. Some JDO implementations will not support optimistic transaction management. In those cases, this method will throw a JDOUnsupportedOptionException.

Managed Versus Nonmanaged Environments

JDO applications can run either in *managed* or *nonmanaged* environments. So far in this chapter, the examples have assumed a nonmanaged environment. Managed or nonmanaged simply refers to whether the JDO environment leverages some kind of external transaction management system to manage its transactions. The most common managed environment you will encounter is using JDO in a J2EE application server to provide bean-managed persistence to Enterprise JavaBeans.

In a managed environment, your application cannot make calls to commit and roll back transactions. Any attempt to do so will result in a JDOUserException. Beginning, committing, and rolling back transactions are the job of the application server.

Inheritance

In object-relational systems, inheritance can be a tricky beast. The problem with inheritance is the lack of support for inheritance in relational databases. In other words, you need to persist a concept from your application that a relational system has no way of modeling. Fortunately, JDO handles this beast for you. Figure 12-2 shows a Person class with many Role instances. Role, however, is an abstract class. Its subclasses include Admin, Employee, Manager, and Contractor.

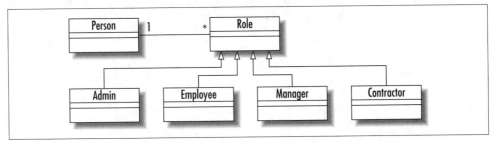

Figure 12-2. An abstract Role with many implementation classes

We can build this class model using the normal Java approach. The next step is to build a metadata descriptor for the Person class as shown in Example 12-4.

Example 12-4. A metadata descriptor with abstract persistent fields

```
<?xml version="1.0" ?>
<!DOCTYPE jdo SYSTEM "jdo.dtd">

<jdo>
  <package name="com.imaginary.ora">
    <class name="Person">
      <field name="personID" primary-key="true"/>
      <field name="lastName"/>
      <field name="firstName"/>
      <field name="title"/>
      <field name="roles">
        <collection element-type="com.imaginary.ora.Role"/>
      </field>
    </class>

    <class name="Role">
      <field name="code"/>
      <field name="name"/>
    </class>

    <class name="Employee"
    persistence-capable-superclass="com.imaginary.ora.Role">
    </class>

    ...
```

Example 12-4. A metadata descriptor with abstract persistent fields (continued)

```
   </package>
</jdo>
```

This code tells the JDO implementation that `Employee` is a persistent object and that it derives some or all of its persistence from the `Role` class.

Earlier in the chapter, I mentioned how the second argument to `getExtent()` in `PersistenceManager` is a boolean indicating whether subclasses may be counted in the extent. If you tell it not to count subclasses, it will return only exact instances of the class in question. This feature enables you to limit queries to a specific class or to the class and its subclasses.

Index

Symbols

! (negation, JNDI search filter), 164
& (conjunction, JNDI search filter), 164
& (logical and, JDO filters), 251
&& (conditional and, JDO filters), 251
* (multiplication, SQL), 205
* (wildcard, JNDI search filter), 164
+ (addition, SQL), 205
- (subtraction, SQL), 205
/ (division, SQL), 205
< (less than, SQL), 205
<%...%> (Java code in JSP), 168
<%=...%> (values to print in JSP), 168
<%@...%> (directives in JSP), 168
<= (less than or equal to, SQL), 205
<= (less than, JNDI search filter), 164
<> (not equal, SQL), 205
= (equal, SQL), 205
= (equality, JNDI search filter), 164
=* (presence, JNDI search filter), 164
> (greater than, SQL), 205
>= (greater than or equal to, SQL), 205
>= (greater than, JNDI search filter), 164
\ (escape, JNDI search filter), 164
| (disjunction, JNDI search filter), 164
~ (complement, SQL), 205
~= (approximate equality, JNDI search
      filter), 164

Numbers

1NF (see first normal form)
2NF (see second normal form)
3NF (see third normal form)
4NF (see fourth normal form)
5NF (see fifth normal form)

A

absolute() method (JDBC), 225
abstract schema name, 110
abstraction, 49
accessor methods (see getter methods; setter
      methods)
ACID properties, 54
Active Directory Service (see ADS)
addBatch() method (JDBC), 234
addition (+), SQL, 205
ADS (Active Directory Service), 157
aliasing, in SQL, 202
Also Sprach Zarathustra (Nietzsche), 97
AND operator, SQL, 205
anomalies, database, 40, 41
application assembler, EJB, 182
application (business) logic
      client/server architecture and, 8
      design patterns supporting, 14
      distributed architectures and, 11
      separation of, 75
application exceptions, 128
applications
      database, architectures for, 3–18
      developers for separate layers of, 76
      Guest Book example (see Guest Book
            application)
      JDO, 131, 243

Comment class, 81, 85
CommentDAO class, 81, 89
commit() method, Database session, 149
commit() method (JDBC), 62, 228
Common Object Request Broker
        Architecture (see CORBA)
comparison operators, in SQL, 205
complement (~), SQL, 205
complex value objects, 120
component models, 15, 18–20, 180
    (see also EJB; JavaBeans)
composite entities (see join tables)
composite pattern, 15
concurrency, 58–62
    optimistic, 63–66
    pessimistic, 64
conditional and (&&), JDO filters, 251
conjunction (&), JNDI search filter, 164
CONNECT statement (SQL), 193
Connection interface (JDBC), 62, 217,
        218–222, 237
connection pooling, 149, 237–238
ConnectionPoolDataSource class
        (JDBC), 238
consistency of transaction, 54
constants, defining literal values in, 88
constraints, 25–30, 31
contact information, O'Reilly & Associates,
        Inc., xiii
container provider, EJB, 182
container-managed persistence model (see
        CMP model)
container-managed relationships (see CMR)
<container-transaction> tag, 106
contains() method (JDO), 250
content generation layer, distributed
        architectures, 11
content management layer, distributed
        architectures, 11
control logic
    as part of application logic, 76
    for Guest Book application, 83–85
conventions used in this book, xiii
CORBA (Common Object Request Broker
        Architecture), 173
CREATE DATABASE statement (SQL), 192
CREATE INDEX statement (SQL), 198
create() method, Comment class, 87
create() method, Database session, 148
CREATE statement (SQL), 192

CREATE TABLE statement (SQL), 194
createDatastore() method, 149
createStatement() method (JDBC), 224
The Critique of Pure Modernity (Kolb), 129
cross join, in SQL, 211
cross-reference tables (see join tables)

D

Darwin's Dangerous Idea (Dennett), 3
data access logic, 76
data access object pattern, 17
data access objects, 117–119
    for Guest Book application, 89–96
    mementos used with, 77
data architecture (see relational data
        architecture)
data, dividing among disks, 6
data integrity, transactions used to
        ensure, 53
data models, 24
    (see also relational model)
data storage layer, distributed
        architectures, 11
data storage logic, 76
data stores, JDO, 245
data types (attribute domain), 26, 29
data types (SQL), 195–198
database, 23
    anomalies of, 40, 41
    binary data in, 126
    connecting to, with JDBC, 218–223
    connection pooling, 149, 237–238
    creating with SQL, 192
    deleting in SQL, 193
    JDO, 247
    locking by, 61
    metadata about, 237
    object-oriented (see OODBMS;
        ORDBMS)
    persistence using, 49–52
      (see also persistence)
    querying, in SQL, 201–204, 224,
        230–233
    transaction log, 67
database application architectures, 3
    network, 4–6
    principles of, 7
    software, 4, 12–18
    system, 4, 6–12

entities, 24
entity beans, 115, 182
    as JDO PersistenceCapable class, 137
    handling persistence for (see CMP; data
        access objects)
    sharing data with client (see value objects)
entity relationship diagram (see ERD)
EntityBean class, 185
equal (=), SQL, 205
equality (=), JNDI search filter, 164
ERD (entity relationship diagram), 34, 37
error handling (see exception handling)
escape (\), JNDI search filter, 164
event management, 53
    (see also transactions)
exception handling
    EJB BMP, 127
    JDBC, 226, 229
    RMI, 178
execute() method (JDBC), 237
execute() method (JDO), 248
executeBatch() method (JDBC), 235
executeQuery() method (JDBC), 224
executeUpdate() method (JDBC), 230
executeWithArray() method (JDO), 248
executeWithMap() method (JDO), 136, 249
EXPLAIN command (SQL), 27
Extent class (JDO), 248
extents, JDO, 247

F

factory pattern, 16
fat client, 8
fat server, 8
field mapping (see object-relational mapping)
fields, table (see columns)
fifth normal form (5NF), 45
filter language, JDO, 250
findByPrimaryKey() method, 184
finder methods
    BMP, 121
    EJB 1.x CMP, 104, 121
    EJB 2.x CMP, 109
first normal form (1NF), 38
FK, indicating foreign key, 34
FLOAT datatype (SQL), 196
flush() method, 149
fonts used in this book, xiii

foreign key, 30–33, 34
fourth normal form (4NF), 37, 42, 43
full join, in SQL, 211
functional dependencies, 39
functions, in SQL, 208–209

G

Gamma, Erich (*Design Patterns*), 75
getApproved() method, Comment class, 87
getComment() method, Comment class, 87
getConnection() method (JDBC), 221
getDatabase() method, 148
getExtent() method (JDO), 254
getMetaData() method (JDBC), 237
getOQLQuery() method, 150
getPending() method, Comment class, 87
getPersistenceManagerFactory() method
    (JDO), 245
getReference() method (JNDI), 161
getResultSet() method (JDBC), 237
getter methods
    for CMR fields, 108
    in JavaBeans, 18
    in ResultSet interface, 225
getUpdateCount() method (JDBC), 237
greater than (>=), JNDI search filter, 164
greater than (>), SQL, 205
greater than or equal to (>=), SQL, 205
GROUP BY clause (SQL), 203
Guest Book application
    business logic for, 85–89
    cache for, 87
    control logic for, 83–85
    data access objects for, 89–96
    design of, 80
    mementos, 92
    sequence generation, 92–96
    view logic for, 81–83

H

hardware, 4–6
HashMap class, 79, 85, 120
Heidegger, Martin (philosopher), xv, 113
Helm, Richard (*Design Patterns*), 75
Hibernate
    field mapping in XML, 141, 145–147
    persistence methods, 149
    persistence with, 140–142, 145–147

Monson-Haefel, Richard (*Enterprise JavaBeans*), 97, 113, 187
Mullins, Craig ("Denormalization Guidelines"), 47
multiplication (*), SQL, 205
multivalued attributes, 52
MVC (model-view-controller) pattern, 14
mysql command, 190

N

Name class (JNDI), 160
Naming class (RMI), 175
naming service, 156
    (see also JNDI)
native algorithm (Hibernate), 146
natural join, in SQL, 211
NCHAR datatype (SQL), 197
negation (!), JNDI search filter, 164
network architecture, 4–6
network data model, 24
network segmentation, 4
Never transactional attribute, 105
next() method (JDBC), 225
Nietzsche, Friedrich (philosopher), xiv, 97
NoInitialContextException, 219
nonmanaged environment, JDO, 252
nonrepeatable read, 59
normal forms, 36
normalization, 35–45
    Boyce-Codd normal form (BCNF), 42
    fifth normal form (5NF), 45
    first normal form (1NF), 38
    fourth normal form (4NF), 37, 42, 43
    goals of, 36
    preparing for, 37
    second normal form (2NF), 39
    seventh normal form (DKNF), 37
    third normal form (3NF), 36, 40
    (see also denormalization)
NoSuchElementException, 150
not equal (<>), SQL, 205
NOT NULL constraint (SQL), 195
NOT operator, SQL, 205
NotSupported transactional attribute, 105
NULL, 33
    comparisons with, in SQL, 206
    Java treatment of, 224
    NOT NULL constraint, in SQL, 195

NullPointerException, 251
NUMBER datatype (SQL), 196
numeric data types, in SQL, 196
NVARCHAR datatype (SQL), 197
NVARCHAR2 datatype (SQL), 197

O

object data model, 24
Object Query Language (see OQL)
object reuse, 8, 76
object serialization, 178
object-oriented database management system (see OODBMS)
object-oriented principles, 49
object-relational database management systems (see ORDBMS)
object-relational mapping, 49–52
    Castor, 141, 143–145
    EJB CMP, 101
    Hibernate, 141, 145–147
objects
    attributes of, multivalued, 52
    caching, 78
    home for (EJB), 166
    lazy-loading attributes of, 98
    mapping to relational database, 49–52
    remote, accessing (see RMI)
    sharing state between (see memento design pattern)
    soft references to, 79
    strong references to, 79
ODBC (Open Database Connectivity), 214, 217
one-to-many relationships, 31, 34
one-to-one relationships, 30, 34
OODBMS (object-oriented database management system), 190
Open Database Connectivity (see ODBC)
open source software, 140
    (see also Castor; Hibernate)
operators, in SQL, 204–207
optimistic concurrency, 63–66
optimistic transaction management, JDO, 135, 252
OQL (Object Query Language), 150
OQLQuery class, 150
OR operator, SQL, 205

ORDBMS (object-relational database management system), 190
ORDER BY clause (SQL), 203
O'Reilly & Associates, Inc., contact information for, xiii

P

P2P (peer-to-peer) architecture, 9
patterns, software design (see design patterns)
peer-to-peer architecture (see P2P architecture)
performance
    bandwidth, 5
    denormalization affecting, 47–49
    disk access speed, 5
    locking affecting, 62
    RAM, 5
    transactions affecting, 55, 56
persistence, 49–52
    design patterns, 17, 75–79
    JavaBeans not supporting, 19
    models, 20
        BMP, 21, 116–123
        Castor, 140–145, 147, 150
        choosing, 129, 138–140
        EJB 1.x CMP, 21, 98, 99–106
        EJB 2.x CMP, 21, 106–111
        Hibernate, 140–142, 145–147, 149, 150
        history of, xi
        JDO, 21, 130, 131–136
        JDO with EJB BMP, 136
        standards and, 139–140
        transparency of, 131
    RMI not supporting, 181
persistence delegate pattern (see data access object pattern)
persistence-capable class, JDO, 242
PersistenceCapable interface (JDO), 137, 245
PersistenceException, 92
PersistenceManager class (JDO), 245
PersistenceManagerFactory class (JDO), 136, 245
pessimistic concurrency, 64
phantom read, 59
philosophers quoted in this book, xiv
physical data model, 35

PK, indicating primary key, 34
polymorphism, 49
prepareCall() method (JDBC), 233
prepared statements, 230–233
    batch processing, 235
    pooling, 238
PreparedStatement interface (JDBC), 231, 235, 238
prepareStatement() method (JDBC), 232
presence (=*), JNDI search filter, 164
previous() method (JDBC), 225
primary key, 25, 26–29
    candidate keys for, 42
    data types for, 29
    foreign keys and, 30–33
    indicating in ERD, 34
    SQL, 198, 200
    unique identifiers for (see sequence generation)
    (see also unique index)
<primitive-array> tag, 147
properties file, for JDBC database connection, 222
provider, EJB, 182
psql command, 190
publications
    about denormalization, 47
    about design patterns, 75
    about EJB, 97, 113, 187
    about JDBC, 3
    about philosophy, xiv
    web site listing, xiv

Q

queries (see EJBQL; OQL; searches; SQL)
Query class (JDO), 248
<query> tag, 110
QueryResults class, 150

R

RAID of IDE disks, 6
RAM
    for database engine, 5
    requirements for batch transactions, 67
RAND() function (SQL), 208
read committed transactions, isolation level, 59
read uncommitted transactions, isolation level, 59

X

XHTML, generating dynamically (see JSP)

XML
  Castor field mapping, 141, 143–145
  EJB CMP field mapping, 101
  generating dynamically (see JSP)
  Hibernate field mapping, 141, 145–147
  JDO metadata descriptions, 246
  JNDI data source configuration, 219
  JSP class mappings in, 170

X/OPEN SQL, CLI (Call Level
        Interface), 214

About the Author

George Reese has taken an unusual path into business software development. After earning a B.A. in philosophy from Bates College in Lewiston, Maine, George went off to Hollywood where he worked on television shows such as *The People's Court* and ESPN's *Up Close*. The L.A. riots convinced him to return to Maine, where he finally became involved with software development and the Internet. George has since specialized in the development of Internet-oriented Java enterprise systems and the strategic role of technology in business processes. He is the author of *Database Programming with JDBC and Java*, 2nd Edition, and co-author of *Managing and Using MySQL*, 2nd Edition. He is also the creator of the world's first JDBC driver, the mSQL-JDBC driver for mSQL. He currently lives in Minneapolis, Minnesota with his wife Monique, daughter Kyra, and three cats, Misty, Gypsy, and Tia. He makes a living as the Technology Strategy Director for digital@jwt in Minneapolis while working on his M.B.A. at the Kellogg School of Management at Northwestern University.

Colophon

Our look is the result of reader comments, our own experimentation, and feedback from distribution channels. Distinctive covers complement our distinctive approach to technical topics, breathing personality and life into potentially dry subjects.

The animal on the cover of *Java Database Best Practices* is a taguan. The taguan (*Petaurista petaurista*) is giant flying squirrel. It lives in dense, tropical rainforests, ranging from the eastern regions of Afghanistan to Java, and from Kashmir, Taiwan, and southern China to Sri Lanka. It is most often found in the Pakistan's temperate forests.

The squirrel conceals its nest in the cavity of a tree, raising 2–3 young at a time. It has a lifespan of approximately 16 years. It is a nocturnal animal, recognizable by its big eyes and reddish color. The taguan consumes a diet of pine cones, fruit, leaves, and nuts.

The taguan is an excellent climber. Additionally, it is referred to as a "flying" squirrel because of the muscular membrane that extends from its wrists to its hind legs, enabling it to glide long distances. It leaps from high tree branches and the tops of trees, controlling the direction of its flight by flexing and relaxing the muscles of the membrane.

Colleen Gorman was the production editor, and Norma Emory was the copyeditor for *Java Database Best Practices*. Linley Dolby and Jane Ellin provided quality control. Angela Howard wrote the index.

Emma Colby designed the cover of this book, based on a series design by Edie Freedman. The cover image is a 19th-century engraving from *Animate Creation*,

Volume II. Emma Colby produced the cover layout with QuarkXPress 4.1 using Adobe's ITC Garamond font.

David Futato designed the interior layout. This book was converted by Joe Wizda to FrameMaker 5.5.6 with a format conversion tool created by Erik Ray, Jason McIntosh, Neil Walls, and Mike Sierra that uses Perl and XML technologies. The text font is Linotype Birka; the heading font is Adobe Myriad Condensed; and the code font is LucasFont's TheSans Mono Condensed. The illustrations that appear in the book were produced by Robert Romano and Jessamyn Read using Macromedia FreeHand 9 and Adobe Photoshop 6. The tip and warning icons were drawn by Christopher Bing. This colophon was written by Colleen Gorman.

Other Titles Available from O'Reilly

Java

Java Performance Tuning, 2nd Edition

By Jack Shirazi
2nd Edition January 2003
588 pages, ISBN 0-596-00377-3

Significantly revised and expanded, this second edition not only covers Java 1.4, but adds new coverage of JDBC, NIO, Servlets, EJB and JavaServer Pages. The book remains a valuable resource for teaching developers how to create a tuning strategy, how to use profiling tools to understand a program's behavior, and how to avoid performance penalties from inefficient code, making them more efficient and effective. The result is code that's robust, maintainable and fast!

Java Security, 2nd Edition

By Scott Oaks
2nd Edition May 2001
618 pages, ISBN 0-596-00157-6

The second edition focuses on the platform features of Java that provide security—the class loader, bytecode verifier, and security manager—and recent additions to Java that enhance this security model: digital signatures, security providers, and the access controller. The book covers in depth the security model of Java 2, version 1.3, including the two new security APIs: JAAS and JSSE.

Java Database Best Practices

By George Reese
1st Edition June 2003 (est.)
304 pages (est.), ISBN 0-596-00522-9

Java Database Best Practices rescues developers from having to slog through books on each of the various APIs before they figure out which method to use! This guide introduces each of the dominant APIs, explores the methodology and design components that use those APIs, and then offers practices most appropriate for different types and makes of databases, and different types of applications.

Java RMI

By William Grosso
1st Edition November 2001
576 pages, ISBN 1-56592-452-5

Enterprise Java developers, especially those working with Enterprise JavaBeans, and Jini, need to understand RMI technology in order to write today's complex, distributed applications. O'Reilly's *Java RMI* thoroughly explores and explains this powerful but often overlooked technology. Included is a wealth of real-world examples that developers can implement and customize.

Java Data Objects

By David Jordan & Craig Russell
1st Edition April 2003 (est.)
384 pages (est.), ISBN 0-596-00276-9

This book, written by the JDO Specification Lead and one of the key contributors to the JDO Specification, is the definitive work on the JDO API. It gives you a thorough introduction to JDO, starting with a simple application that demonstrates many of JDO's capabilities. It shows you how to make classes persistent, how JDO maps persistent classes to the database, how to configure JDO at runtime, how to perform transactions, and how to make queries.

Java Swing, 2nd Edition

By Marc Loy, Robert Eckstein, David Wood, James Elliott & Brian Cole
2nd Edition November 2002
1278 pages, ISBN 0-596-00408-7

This second edition of *Java Swing* thoroughly covers all the features available in Java 2 SDK 1.3 and 1.4. More than simply a reference, this new edition takes a practical approach. It is a book by developers for developers, with hundreds of useful examples, from beginning level to advanced, covering every component available in Swing. Whether you're a seasoned Java developer or just trying to find out what Java can do, you'll find *Java Swing*, 2nd edition an indispensable guide.

O'REILLY®

How to stay in touch with O'Reilly

1. Visit our award-winning web site

http://www.oreilly.com/

★ "Top 100 Sites on the Web"—PC Magazine
★ CIO Magazine's Web Business 50 Awards

Our web site contains a library of comprehensive product information (including book excerpts and tables of contents), downloadable software, background articles, interviews with technology leaders, links to relevant sites, book cover art, and more. File us in your bookmarks or favorites!

2. Join our email mailing lists

Sign up to get email announcements of new books and conferences, special offers, and O'Reilly Network technology newsletters at:

http://elists.oreilly.com

It's easy to customize your free elists subscription so you'll get exactly the O'Reilly news you want.

3. Get examples from our books

To find example files for a book, go to:

http://www.oreilly.com/catalog

select the book, and follow the "Examples" link.

4. Work with us

Check out our web site for current employment opportunities:

http://jobs.oreilly.com/

5. Register your book

Register your book at:

http://register.oreilly.com

6. Contact us

O'Reilly & Associates, Inc.
1005 Gravenstein Hwy North
Sebastopol, CA 95472 USA
TEL: 707-827-7000 or 800-998-9938
        (6am to 5pm PST)
FAX: 707-829-0104

order@oreilly.com
For answers to problems regarding your order or our products. To place a book order online visit:

http://www.oreilly.com/order_new/

catalog@oreilly.com
To request a copy of our latest catalog.

booktech@oreilly.com
For book content technical questions or corrections.

corporate@oreilly.com
For educational, library, government, and corporate sales.

proposals@oreilly.com
To submit new book proposals to our editors and product managers.

international@oreilly.com
For information about our international distributors or translation queries. For a list of our distributors outside of North America check out:

http://international.oreilly.com/distributors.html

adoption@oreilly.com
For information about academic use of O'Reilly books, visit:

http://academic.oreilly.com

O'REILLY®